CHICKEN HILL CHRONICLE

Chicken Hill Chronicle

Memoir of a Jewish Family

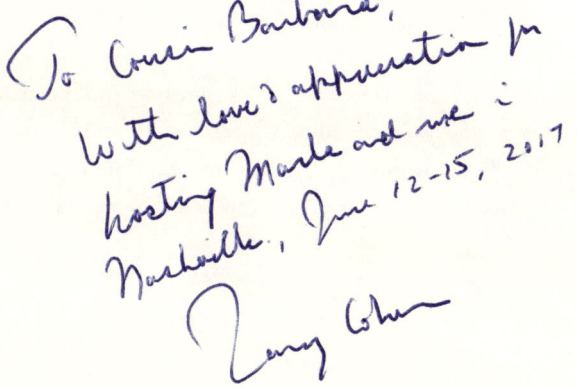

Norman Cohen
and
Lawrence Cohen

Copyright © 2011 by Norman Cohen and Lawrence Cohen.

Library of Congress Control Number:		2011902910
ISBN:	Hardcover	978-1-4568-7436-0
	Softcover	978-1-4568-7435-3
	Ebook	978-1-4568-7437-7

All rights reserved. No part of this book may be reproduced or transmitted in any form or by any means, electronic or mechanical, including photocopying, recording, or by any information storage and retrieval system, without permission in writing from the copyright owner.

This book was printed in the United States of America.

To order additional copies of this book, contact:
Xlibris Corporation
1-888-795-4274
www.Xlibris.com
Orders@Xlibris.com

Contents

Acknowledgements vii
A Note on the Use of Yiddish Words and Expressions ix
Preface xi
Prologue 1

Part I
Die goldene medina

One   Lantzmen 11
Two   Rose 20
Three   Mishpoohah 43
Four   Der Shul 64
Five   Der pedler 79

Part II
Dos Amerikanisch

Six   Dos bruderen 103
Seven   Yetta 123
Eight   Der zigar maker 138
Nine   Der kremer 163
Ten   Pottstown 185

Part III
Norman

Eleven   Yingl 193
Twelve   Bocher 216
Thirteen Sunerling 242
Fourteen The Depression 257
Fifteen   The Army 282
Sixteen   Redemption 307

Epilogue 311

Acknowledgements

To bring this book to life, I wish to acknowledge drawing extraordinary insight and inspiration from the following primary source materials:

"Autobiography of Rabbi Samuel H. Markowitz," *American Jewish Archives* Vol. XXIV November 1972, Cincinnati, Ohio.

"The Families of Menachim Mendel Weisz and Mindel Schwartz (Feuerman) Weiss, The Schwartz-Weiss Clan," Guidebook published for June 1980 gathering of the "clan," Harold J. Berger, editor

A History of Pottstown Pennsylvania 1752-1952 Edited & written by Paul Chancellor, The Historical Society of Pottstown, Pennsylvania 1953.

Pottstown Sesqui-Centennial 1965 150th Anniversary of Formation of Borough A.G. Strothers, editor, the Pottstown Sesqui-Centennial Executive Committee 1965.

Acknowledgements

I am especially and gratefully indebted to the following institutions and individuals, among many others, which permitted access to their archives and original materials or who inspired me to march forward with this challenging endeavor:

Pottstown Public Library, Pottstown, Pennsylvania

Pottstown High School, Pottstown, Pennsylvania

Pottstown Historical Society, Pottstown, Pennsylvania

Russell Cohen, Easton, Pennsylvania

Sylvia Cohen, Philadelphia Pennsylvania

Thomas R. Hutson, Red Cloud, Nebraska

Kira Gale, Omaha, Nebraska

Faye Phillips, West Chester, Pennsylvania

My HHH book group, you know who you are

A Note on the Use of Yiddish Words and Expressions

To retain an immigrant flavor to the narrative, Yiddish words and expressions are seeded throughout the story. Excellent sources exist for translation of Yiddish expressions into English. To convey adequately Yiddish's kaleidoscopic imagery in another language, however, may be impossible. By its widespread internalization of Yiddish, contemporary English has been made far richer. Various lists of Yiddish expressions reflect slight differences in spelling and interpretation. However, for the most part I utilized Michael D. Fein's colorful "List of Yiddish Words and Expressions" as the primary linguistic tool.

Map of Pottstown 1900

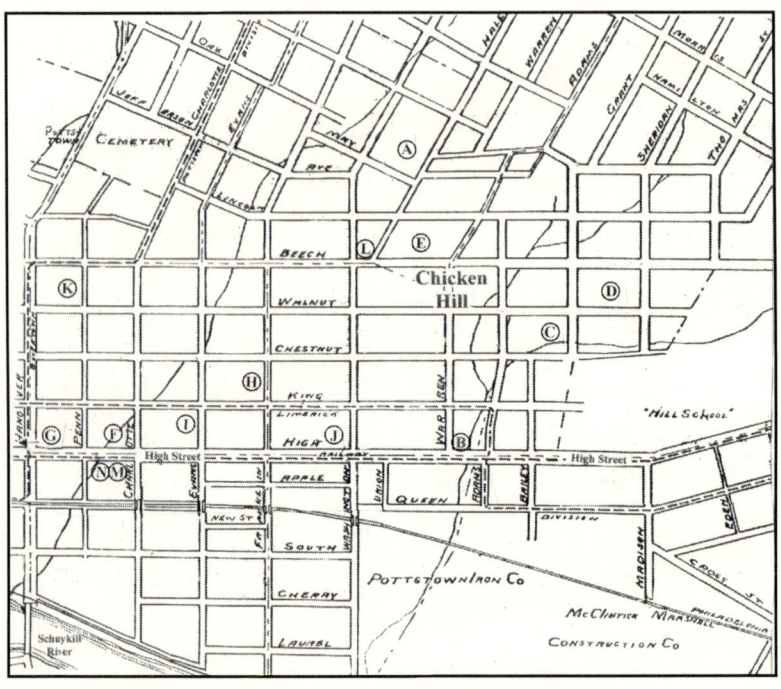

A	Hale Street Synagogue, Chicken Hill 1890's-1925
B	Congregation Mercy & Truth 1925-1963
C	Markowitz Residence Grant Street 1900s
D	Markowitz Residence 719 Walnut St. 1910-1940s
E	Jefferson Elementary School Beech & Adams Streets
F	Royal Shoe Store High & Charlotte Sts. 1917-1920
G	Royal Shoe Store 147 High Street 1920-1940
H	Cohen Residence 77 N. Franklin Street 1926-38
I	YMCA Evans & King Streets
J	Hebrew School 451 High Street
K	Pottstown Junior High & High Schools Penn Street
L	Cohen Residence 521 Beech Street 1939-53
M	Royal Corrective Shoe Store 268 High St. 1938-52
N	Royal Shoe Store 248 High Street 1952-2000

Preface

As Norman Cohen approached his eighty-second birthday, family members perceived little change in his personality or demeanor. Dad was a man of moderate congeniality to most, intense loyalty to a very few. Boy, could he hold a grudge, however. He could be cranky and unreasonable and rarely, if ever, displayed more tender emotion. He was, at times, difficult and demanding. He was often stern and angry but always exceedingly fair to his four children. He worked hard to achieve what he could. He insisted all his children receive the best education possible. It was a mantra chiseled in stone, an "Eleventh Commandment from Mount Sinai." *Thou shall go to college.* Dissatisfied with the caliber of high school education in Pottstown, he sent his children to private school. All matriculated college. Three went to graduate school.

Dad never attended college. He was a "shoe man." Excluding his years in the service during World War II, he had always sold shoes. Or so we assumed. The Royal Shoe Store was a good business. His father Abe started it during World War I, the Great War. Dad took it over from his father in the 1950s. For decades,

Preface

Royal Shoes possessed a prime location on the busiest section of High Street's business district, in Pottstown, Pennsylvania. The store's clientele was not limited to townies. Customers came from all over Montgomery, Berks, and Chester Counties.

Often on Friday nights and Saturdays customers waited patiently for service. The busiest season was just before Labor Day. The end of summer, mothers brought their usually unenthusiastic children to Royal Shoes to be outfitted for school. In the years when sneakers were worn only during gym class, the store kept careful customer records of each pair of children's Stride Rite shoes sold. The Royal Shoe Store possessed a well-deserved reputation for a wide selection in all sizes. Teenage girls insisted on Bass *Weejuns* penny loafers. While not adverse to loafers, older boys often gravitated to buckles.

December meant Christmas and the sale of handbags, slippers, and other gift items. With the first heavy snowfall, winter boots flew off the shelves. Pre-adolescent girls wore black patent leather Mary Jane's for Easter. In April and May, the mothers returned to debate whether to wear their summer pumps in bone or white. Dad described the women's oxfords manufactured by the Miller Shoe Company, Cincinnati, Ohio, as the store's "bread and butter." Sure enough, a legion of older women concerned more with comfort than with pizzazz were loyal Miller customers. Bunions, corns, hammertoes, heel spurs—you name it, the Royal Shoe Store outfitted shoes for it. The men's business really took off when Dad introduced the iconic Thom McAn line.

We spent weekends and summers tending customers, cleaning displays, and moving shoes from one corner of the store to another. While friends scrambled to find summer jobs flipping burgers or running paper routes, our summer plans were preordained. We might attend summer camp for a month. One summer, I took a typing class at Owen J. Roberts High School.

But the shoe store always beckoned. On Friday evenings before the rush, Dad and I dined at the Crystal Restaurant. Fellow High Street businessmen met us there. We returned to the store until the 9 p.m. closing. We learned the business, as much as teenagers could. Yet, Dad never pressured us to follow in his footwear footsteps. Instead, it seemed he preferred we not go into the business. That was certainly okay by me. I had little desire to remain forever in Pottstown.

* * *

Labor Day meant family picnics and barbeques—the larger family of aunts, uncles, and cousins. Gatherings occurred at nearby Green Lane Park or at a suburban back yard overshadowed by a split-level house. By the 1980s, most of the children had left home. The parents had aged. Family gatherings became less frequent. When the parents did meet, the talk centered less on children and more on the previous generation, their own parents—our grandparents—and the myriad of cousins, aunts and uncles, friends, acquaintances, etc., who resided in Pottstown six, seven, and even eight decades earlier.

Such a family gathering occurred during our father's eighty-second year. At this event, however, something snapped like a dry stick which irreversibly altered his life. The moment was innocuous enough. He and his sisters were speaking about their father Abe. In casual conversation, someone made a comment. The words seemed innocent. "Daddy was a good businessman. There had always been food on the table, even during the darkest days of the Depression."

That simple chain of words sparked a profound change in Dad. His eyes, the facial feature that most resembled his mother's, narrowed to just slits. His jaws tightened. His blood pressure, always too high, really hit top end. His face reddened like a tomato. His dry, crinkled hands began to clench. The scar across the palm of his left hand, consigned there over fifty years earlier when Dad served in the army, seemed to come alive.

"How could you say that?" he retorted. The words could barely get out of his mouth. "Daddy was a lousy businessman! He didn't know the first thing about running a store," he shouted. "I was there! I saw everything!"

The room was silenced. Were they referring to the same person? From where did this emotional outburst erupt? What was the big deal?

The simple remark—that their father was a good businessman—released something imprisoned deeply within Dad's psyche. A wound was ripped open, a wound evidently there a long time. Our grandparents passed away a quarter century earlier. What secret, what experience pained Dad so? We were confused. For our familiarity with our father—his stories about *his* grandfather's peddling business, his army service at military camps from New York to Oklahoma, his love of horses, his uncles—Grandmom's brothers—we knew precious little about him.

Over the next months, images from his past took shape. Memories long repressed cascaded from Dad's mind. They were released in a spring flood of disconnected visions and angry rants. Like a jigsaw puzzle that with patience and time inexorably comes to completion, Dad maniacally lashed together chapters from his life. The emerging story distressed him profoundly. He sank deep into depression. Many nights he lay awake. He cried incessantly. In all our decades with him, none of us remembered witnessing a tear or suppressed sob, even when he buried his parents. Drawing upon unfathomable emotional despair, he displayed sharp fury. He directed most of his rage at Grandmom. In his outpouring of grief, he repeated haunting questions no one understood.

"Why did you take such advantage of me?" he whimpered. "Why did you treat me so badly? I did everything you wanted. Why didn't you let me go to college?"

What was Dad talking about?

To his credit reflecting compulsiveness about health—for example, Dad was a fiend about eliminating sodium from his diet—he agreed to meet with a psychiatrist. For an octogenarian who disdained personal interest in psychiatry and cared even less about psychiatrists, this was a remarkable concession. After just one session during which time he unburdened himself of his pain, he thanked the doctor and pronounced himself no longer in need of a follow-up appointment!

Dad opened a door in his mind that had been padlocked a long time. But to where did it lead? And would he permit us to enter?

* * *

For years Dad and I shared a close interest in family history. While he drove the Buick Estate station wagon, with the 455 cubic inch V8 engine, on country lanes that laced rural Chester County, I listened to stories regaled by my great-uncles, my grandmother's brothers. When they came to town for a visit, they insisted on going 'peddling.' I sat in the front seat between Dad and Grandpop. Uncle Sam, Uncle Francis whom we children called Uncle Baloney, and Uncle Mike were in back. The three brothers could never stop cackling. They teased each other incessantly. When one of them referred to the Harmonyville blacksmith, they went into hysterics. "You are a God damn liar!" one would say in a booming voice in imitation of their father Adolph. And when they snickered about the behaviors of other family members, living and deceased, I could not stop laughing.

Dad enjoyed the banter, but I do not remember him emitting more than a chuckle while his uncles had the floor.

My curiosity in our family past began in earnest the summer after my junior year of high school. Dad and I traveled to New England with Grandpop to visit college campuses. We also visited shoe factories. We passed through Providence, Rhode Island; Boston and Worcester, Massachusetts; Hartford and New Haven, Connecticut. New England still possessed a shoe manufacturing industry. Dad knew all the companies. We toured the Stride Rite factory floor in Roxbury and met the head of the company. Dad and Grandpop kept referring to the Green Shoe Manufacturing Company, its original name. We visited the new Alden of New England factory in Middleborough. At Thom McAn headquarters in Worcester, a nattily dressed salesman with a garishly wide tie introduced us around the plant as "Mr. Cohen, Mr. Cohen, and Mr. Cohen." In West Hartford and Bridgeport, we visited cousins whom I had not met before. It was the first, and last time the three of us traveled together. Grandpop died the following March.

Two decades later, Dad and I collaborated on more sophisticated genealogical research. After his retirement from the shoe store, Dad possessed plenty of time to conduct research. To bring order to ancestral complexity, he utilized an early generation of genealogy software on his Radio Shack Tandy computer. He contracted with a genealogy expert in Poland to check leads. He duplicated a unique family tree that he distributed to family members. He obtained translations of old documents. I videotaped his reminiscences. We discussed the topic often. Genealogy gave Dad a hobby in retirement and brought us together.

Now we faced a more urgent matter. As Dad confronted his demons, we decided to collaborate again. This time, we would fashion a personal history project, an autobiography. Instead of repressing memories, Dad would release everything he could remember. He agreed to write about himself and the people in his life. I would edit. From his personal computer, chapters emerged in no order or context. Dad's style was barebones, almost terse as if a fee was charged on every word, every paragraph. I reworked his prose, reordered his sentence and paragraph structure, and asked incessant questions.

Dad's story gathered momentum. He mentally transported himself to the 1920s and 1930s. His words described an unhappy youth in a poor Pottstown neighborhood, Chicken Hill. But he did not stop with his own life. He unfolded various family yarns of immigrant foibles, unethical and unscrupulous business behavior, identity crises, missed opportunities, friendships and feuds. His writing brought the past to life with incredible vivacity. He recounted stories told to him by his grandfather. Few details escaped him. Dad replayed a movie in his head—and it wasn't a silent movie!

We worked intensively on the project even as Dad's health was failing. Perhaps the effort to relate his story kept him alive a bit longer. I do not know. When he passed away in November 1999, the tightly knit single-spaced manuscript crammed with detail covered over seventy years. Dad shoehorned into it everything he could remember. He could not add any more. He had extricated everything he could salvage from his mind, soul, and heart. That's when his heart finally gave out.

This narrative is built on Dad's cathartic release. His wonderful stories, fresh and vivid, deserved repeating. Herewith is that effort.

Memories differ. *Chicken Hill Chronicle* is based on the memories of one individual. Events therein are not presented as absolute fact. It is drawn from a personal memoir, not a history. Errors and ambiguities contained within it are ours alone, Dad's and mine. Although portions of the chronicle have been embellished slightly to assure a narrative flow, the story is not fictional. Its characters existed. Out of respect, their names are not veiled by pseudonyms. Although the story is done imperfectly, all the persons represented throughout this chronicle possess a remarkable legacy. To every single one of them, I dedicate this book.

Lawrence Cohen

February 2011

Prologue

At the commencement of junior year, fifteen-year old Norman Cohen began to give considerable thought to college. It was September 1929. The young Norman, the eldest of four children, was the dutiful son of a hapless shoe store merchant and a domineering mother. Despite a compulsive shyness, Norman performed well in his classes, worked long hours in the shoe store, and assiduously, if not naïvely, kept out of trouble.

Norman wanted to study engineering. Given his math abilities, it was a logical selection. Despite being the youngest student in his Pottstown High School class, Norman excelled in algebra and geometry. A teacher he respected added a bonus. "Most college engineering programs do not require a foreign language," he explained. "An engineer needs to read blueprints," he said, "not French." Norman promptly dropped Miss Moses' sixth period French class.

Norman sent away for college catalogues. All it took was a penny postcard. His father Abe frequently sent him to Bentz's Drug Store to pick up twenty-five at a time. A few taken here and there would not be missed. Norman soon received catalogues from all the local Pennsylvania colleges: Ursinus, Albright, West Chester, Gettysburg, even Bucknell in Lewisburg where three of his uncles matriculated. He studied the catalogues carefully. Despite thorough examination, the teenager failed to detect much academic difference among them.

As Norman began his senior year, circumstances had changed. The country's economic fortunes had nosedived into what would soon be called the Great Depression. Already by mid-1930, Pottstown felt its horrific grip. Unemployment in the town's many factories quadrupled. As factory workers lost their jobs, Abe's shoe business softened as well. Fewer customers entered the Royal Shoe Store. Those who did had less money in their pockets and purses. When not in school or studying at home, Norman labored in the store. He observed the decline in business. Still, the Cohen family enjoyed the *semblance* of normal life. That was far better than many other families in town could claim.

College was Norman's obsession that autumn. Despite the community's evolving economic hardships, and the decline in sales at his father's store, Norman thought of little else. He became compulsive about entering the right engineering program. All his young life, he decided, he had put his family first. "Now it's my turn," he felt. His grades were excellent. By working long hours all summer at Fogelman's shoe store in nearby Reading, he saved enough money to pay for the first semester. Since business was slow, his father's shoe store did not need him.

Early that October, Mr. Emery, the mechanical drawing instructor, approached Norman, his only academically inclined student. "What are you planning to do after graduation?" Emery inquired. Norman explained he intended to go to engineering school. He listed the colleges from which he had received catalogues. "Don't bother with them," Emery said. "Apply to

Rensselaer Polytechnic Institute in Troy, New York. You are the perfect candidate."

When Norman received the Rensselaer Polytechnic Institute catalogue, all the others went into the trash. He prepared just one application and transmitted it with his transcripts to RPI.

"Are you sure you should apply to only one school?" his best friend Al Leblang asked.

Norman demurred. "Why should I hand over a one dollar application fee to another college? RPI is where I want to go." Al rolled his eyes. He knew he would not be attending college the following fall.

But his buddy's comment planted the seed of doubt. Norman's anxiety worsened when he read about other excellent engineering schools such as Drexel, Lehigh, Carnegie-Mellon, and the Massachusetts Institute of Technology. The school librarian rattled off the names like reciting the batting order of the champion Philadelphia A's. Most of these institutions were closer to home. Norman also learned another disconcerting fact. In an era of strict Jew quotas, he had unknowingly applied to the one engineering program least likely to accept a candidate whose last name was Cohen!

Tense weeks passed. Late one afternoon Norman arrived home from a long day at school. The moment he reached the porch of the house, he sensed something was wrong. As he stepped inside the door, a chill that had nothing to do with the winter weather struck him. In the dim light of the living room stood his mother. An opened letter was in her hand. The letter was from Rensselaer Polytechnic Institute. It was addressed to Norman B. Cohen, Esq. 73 Franklin Street, Pottstown, Pa. The RPI emblem was emblazoned on the envelope underneath the school's return address. Along the top edge the letter had been neatly and evenly scissor cut as if by scalpel. This was not his mother's usual method of opening letters, Norman knew. Dad used a letter opener at the store, but his mother never did. She usually tore one end of an envelope flap and impatiently enlarged the hole with her index finger.

With an icy sternness, Yetta handed the letter to Norman. She gazed at her son as he unfolded the paper.

Norman read the letter. In fine prose the Dean of Admissions of Rensselaer Polytechnic Institute congratulated Norman B. Cohen for his academic scholarship and achievement at Pottstown High School. The Dean announced that after careful review the RPI board of admissions had approved the candidacy of Mr. Norman Cohen into the school's first year engineering program. To reserve a space in the incoming class, the letter explained, the enrollment fee should be submitted within two weeks of receipt. Registration information was also enclosed.

Norman's mother took back the opened letter from the hand of her eldest child. Her fingers seemed glued to the paper. Her expression remained stern, cold, and intensely serious. No words had yet been exchanged between the two. Then, after an endless silence, his mother found her voice. The words jumped from her mouth, as if caged one moment, released the next.

"Norman, you know we cannot afford to send you to college."

Her words ripped into her disappointed son. Although neither a grin nor smile crossed her visage, Norman sensed that his mother was pleased. Her voice resonated smugness, a trait he knew she possessed in abundance. It was as if she had been waiting forever to say the words just spoken. There was no sadness or empathy. It was an emotion Norman could not identify immediately. Then it struck him like a brick. His mother, he surmised, seemed relieved.

The young man stood immobile, his mind stripped. He was unable even to question, let alone raise an objection. How could he? Mother's word was law. Arguing with her would be fruitless. Besides, Dad would not challenge her decision even if he disagreed with it. After all, there was a depression going on. Many families had it worse.

Norman meekly accepted the harsh verdict. He turned to go upstairs. He mechanically climbed the stairs. He did not cry. He could produce no tears. He was beyond crying.

Following high school graduation, Norman labored in a variety of dead end jobs in shoe stores throughout eastern Pennsylvania. He scraped by on baloney sandwiches and nickel Cokes. Movies were an unaffordable luxury. From top floor rooms in boarding houses and low rent apartments, he scanned back alleys in Lebanon, Wilkes-Barre, Scranton, Hazelton, and other Pennsylvania factory towns. He observed the ubiquitous soup lines and emerging shantytowns known as Hoovervilles. He met other young men, boys really, who were down on their luck. Many were in far worse shape than he. He learned to repress the pain of suppressed aspirations. But he never succeeded in eliminating the numbing disappointment from his scarred memory.

* * *

In 1936, six years after Norman was told he could not go to college, the next oldest Cohen child reached her senior year. Lillian also desired to go to college. Academically, she was worthy. She was well on her way to becoming Pottstown High class valedictorian. Yet business in the shoe store was still poor. The store survived more on the basis of its almost non-existent payroll than on sales. At home there was always food on the table. But the family had little money for much else. Under President Roosevelt's New Deal, the Great Depression softened slightly.

Prologue

However, it hardly mattered. Half of Pottstown's factories remained closed. The others had slashed their workforce. Salvation Army soup kitchens continued to serve the hungry. Homeless families slept in empty railcars and rough, windowless shacks made of cardboard and scrap lumber. Arguably, Pottstown was in worse shape than it had been in 1930.

With Norman's sisters Lillian and Sylvia, their mother took a different approach. Over the years, both during the plush Twenties and the harsh Thirties, Yetta Cohen secretly stashed college funds for her daughters. Careful frugality and a hawk's eye over the bank account assured enough money for at least a year's tuition and board, perhaps two. Although a tidy sum, the kitty was not overly endowed. It certainly was not enough for four years. To make up some of the difference, Yetta had a plan. She leaned heavily on Abe to approach the wealthy attorney Joe L. Printz to plead for a partial scholarship. Years earlier, the young Printz pulled an unethical if not illegal property deal which cost the family dearly. Abe remembered the incident. However, he had swallowed his pride then and would do so again.

Abe approached Printz for the money. The attorney acquiesced. He agreed to front the necessary funds. However, as a condition for this financial assistance, Printz requested a small favor. Printz was co-chair of Pottstown's Republican Committee, an assembly of the community's blueblood business, banking, and professional elite. Committee members stood on the opposite side of the social spectrum from Pottstown's working class and myriad ethnic groups. Hardly any of Pottstown's Jews had ever voted for a Republican. One notable exception was Abe's father-in-law. But Printz's condition stood. To get the scholarship, both Yetta and Abe agreed to change their political affiliation from Democrat to Republican!

One weekend while home from his low wage job in some upstate factory town, Norman learned of his parent's deal with Printz.

Yetta and Abe had made a pact with the devil! He was disgusted. How could their parents so brazenly discard their pride and sell their political registration—and to the most despised person on earth, Joe Printz!

Norman reflected back to previous elections. For years the family had been staunch Socialists. His parents, he knew with certainty, had supported presidential candidates Eugene Debs and Norman Thomas. With Roosevelt, they became liberal New Deal Democrats. Their low opinion of Herbert Hoover was no secret. To sell their votes as if they were immigrants fresh off the boat and bribed with shots of whiskey by Tammany Hall appalled Norman.

Years later, Norman discovered the second part of his mother's plan, her secret hoarding of family funds for his sisters. His mother had told him the family had no money to send him to college. Yet she kept separate bank accounts for their future education. Norman did not understand. He pondered but failed to grasp the implication. When his mother said that 'my daughters will go to college,' Norman assumed her two sons would receive the same opportunity.

Yet, despite the shock of hearing about the selling of his parents' political souls to the fiendish Printz, Norman could not stifle a chuckle. He was absolutely certain his parents continued to vote for the Democratic Party—and President Franklin D. Roosevelt.

PART I

Die goldene medina

One

Lantzmen

A dozen passengers occupied the second class coach of the Philadelphia & Reading Railroad's 3:50 p.m. Mount Carbon and Pottsville express run departing Reading Station. Few well wishers had been on hand to send them off; the handful already fled the station platform. Negro baggage porters, their brief work completed, congregated on the deserted platform to share stories of the day and compare meager tips collected from the departing passengers.

The station clock indicated the 3:50 run was departing on time. The year was 1884. The conductor blew a loud whistle, the engine shrieked. The train jerked clumsily then gradually accelerated. The Baldwin locomotive number 417 pulled just three passenger cars and a caboose, a light load. Soon, the train was traversing North Philadelphia. It skirted behind brick warehouses and soot covered factories where laborers scurried about. The train raced past unnoticed. Within ten minutes the train reached Philly's working class neighborhoods. In row houses no wider than a horse cart, women in plain aprons took in their day's laundry from clothes lines strung across constricted backyards. Scruffy children hoed gardens and pulled weeds. After a brief halt in Germantown, the train again picked up speed for Manayunk, its next stop. The express skipped Bridgeport and Norristown. Phoenixville station was next on the schedule.

From the train's left side, through a patchy strip of trees and broken down docks, passengers occasionally spied a river, the Dutch-named Schuylkill. The Schuylkill began in the coal region of upper Schuylkill County. It flowed southeast from the Appalachian Mountains through the fertile Pennsylvania piedmont and emptied 130 miles later into the Delaware River below south Philadelphia. From Philadelphia, the Philadelphia & Reading Railroad traced the Schuylkill upstream to the industrial city of Reading and then to Pottsville, almost to the river's source at Tuscarora Spring.

The mid-afternoon April sun drenched the train's port side. The white glare off the windows pained the eyes of the travelers, bothering those who sought some slumber. Passengers who chose seats on the train's left switched over the aisle to the more tolerable shadowed side. To avoid this inconvenience veteran riders of the P&R late afternoon express already made the proper seat selection.

Alexander Estreicher and Jacob Feldman had taken seats on the right side. Resting on the overhead, their well-worn satchels contained hardly more than a change or two of work clothes, bread, and a bottle of schnapps. Although he was hardly familiar with the route, for Estreicher this train ride was not a complete novelty. Three years earlier, he reached America after fleeing enlistment in the Hungarian army. Even in America he feared the long reach of Hungarian authorities. To the uniformed authorities at the Castle Garden immigration station he gave his last name as Astirich, a revision of his true name Iscovitz. The immigration clerk cared little for unseemly Eastern European, steerage class riffraff beginning to trickle in on trans-Atlantic steamships. He could not understand the disheveled Jew standing in front of his desk. In his logbook, Astirich became Estreicher.

In 1881 Estreicher had journeyed on the same trek from Philadelphia to Pottsville where he obtained work at the Shenandoah Coal Company. For his efforts, he saved a small nest egg of several hundred dollars. Perhaps for Americans such *gelt* was a modest sum. But back home in Galicia, it was a small fortune. Following his tenure as a coal miner, Estreicher returned with dreams of wealth to his village of Rebnitza, only to loose his accumulated earnings in a series of bad investments. Now, he was returning to the Pottsville coalfields. This was his second try at the golden ring. He promised himself not to make the same mistake again. This time when the time is right his family will follow him to *die goldene medina*, the golden country, America.

Feldman's experience in America could not compare with that of his *lantzman* Estreicher. Unlike his colleague, Feldman was a true greenhorn in the New World. On this day beginning before dawn, Feldman took his first steps off Manhattan Island since his recent arrival from Europe and the short ferry ride from Castle Garden. Except for the crowded streets and tenements of New York City, this day was his initial exposure to America. It extended no wider than the view from the Hudson River ferry and the sliver of New Jersey seen from the Pennsylvania Railroad between Hoboken and Philadelphia. With his Yiddish, Feldman could make himself understood with America's many Germans. But he could not yet communicate with anyone else. Between the two, the men possessed a pocketful of Indian head pennies and a few buffalo head nickels. The ferry and train fares from

New York to Pottsville and the second hand suits for the journey had absorbed almost all their carefully hoarded cash.

As the train raced past the marvels of nineteenth century America, Estreicher and Feldman spoke little. Each was lost in thought. They stared out the window. Estreicher thought of his wife and four children back home. With the money earned in the coalfields, he would send for them, God willing, within the year. His mind flashed back to his arrival at Castle Garden the moment when he had given his name as Astreich, but the immigration clerk wrote it as Estreicher. Estreicher chuckled. Even Astreich had not been his actual name. That was the surname he made up when the Hungarian army conscription officer came to the village with his actual name, Iscovitz, on a list. As his mind played back the episode, he unconsciously nodded his head. There was nothing wrong with Estreicher. A name is just a name.

The 3:50 p.m. express passed through Norristown. Estreicher thought about these industrious Americans. In factories large and small, thousands of workmen of countless names and nationalities manufactured limitless products for delivery throughout this vast land. A forest of tall chimneys dotted the Philadelphia suburbs. Identical grey coal smoke columns rose high into the Pennsylvania air. Then, as if bent by an invisible hand, the smoke leveled horizontally eastward before gradually dissipating into vaporous wisps. Not in Austria-Hungary, Estreicher thought, not even in Prussia, had he seen such industrial might.

But beyond the Philly suburbs the two men observed the real miracle of a marvelous land. The odor of freshly laid manure wafted into the train. It reminded Feldman of spring planting back home. He admired the painted farmhouses. Many had second floors, shingled roofs, broad wrap around porches, and so many windows! Even the modest and humble Pennsylvania homesteads dwarfed those of the wealthiest Szobrance landowners. And all were painted!

Feldman gazed at the massive barns. Each seemed larger than the largest synagogues in Nagymihaly or Ungvahr with enough space to spare to perform a *hakafa*, the parade of the torah scrolls on the festival of Simhat Torah. He marveled at the countless Holstein cows. Since it was late in the day, the cows were heavy with milk-laden udders. A Galician farmer with five milk cows was considered exceptionally fortunate. Here, farms had dozens. And on none could he see ribs! In farmyards, innumerable plump chickens pecked at unseen food. Each was capable, he was certain, of laying unlimited quantities of fist-size eggs.

"This is truly the land of Egypt in its seven fat years!" Feldman remarked to Estreicher. "The God of Joseph has blessed this land."

Draft horses more mammoth that any in Galicia pulled steel plows that carved the rich Pennsylvania soil like a *sochet's* knife slicing through a well-boiled cabbage. Wood fences, rock walls, wells, green pasture stretched to the horizon. Being early spring, farmers were preparing for planting, as they would be doing in every village back home. Yet, Estreicher and Feldman understood instinctively it was very different here. With farms such as these, hunger in their impoverished Galicia settlement would be but a memory.

"*Oy*, if only I could have a farm like that one," Feldman sighed pointing to particularly well maintained property, "I would die a happy man." For once, Estreicher could not think of a Yiddish retort.

Although Estreicher could not read English, he did possess a fractured fluency. His speech combined the coal mining vocabulary of Irish and Polish immigrants with heavily accented

New York City melting pot slang. His linguistic capability was typical of immigrants to the United States in the 1880s. "Just enough to get us into trouble," Feldman teased him. In his pocket, Estreicher fingered the well-worn, folded handbill from his earlier sojourn in the coalfields. Carefully placed below the printed English words "Shenandoah Coal Company" and the address of the Pottsville hiring agent were the Yiddish transliterations he wrote there three years before. In his head, again and again, he hypnotically repeated that last word, Pottsville, POTTS-ville. His mind emphasized that somewhat Germanic first syllable rather than the French-like second. The mesmerizing rhythm of the rails felt comforting. The stress of the journey had been exhausting. Estreicher began to nod off. Feldman himself was sound asleep.

Abruptly, the magic word shot through his head. It jarred him awake. His mind instantly shook off its hazy fog. Walking towards the front of the car, the conductor had just announced their stop! Estreicher's pulse quickened. He looked over at the groggy Feldman. His *lantzman* was aware of the conductor's announcement but did not comprehend its implication.

"This is our destination," Estreicher pronounced with an anxious excitement he could not suppress. "Let's go!"

With both urgency and trepidation, the *lantzmen* pulled their satchels from the overhead. Each moved deliberately, laboriously to the end of the carriage and descended the train. They stepped onto the platform. A bell clanged rhythmically from the steam engine. Steam hissed from the brakes.

They had finally arrived.

For more than a minute, Estreicher and Feldman stood glued to the terminal platform. They waited for their excited pulses to slackened. They inhaled the fumes from the train and absorbed the metallic smells of the polished rails and train undercarriage. Neither spoke. Behind them passengers quickly climbed aboard for the train's onward destinations. Estreicher's mind emptied itself of the journey. Such travails—the muddy roads of Bohemia, the cruel Prussian officials, the nauseating Atlantic passage in steerage, the tension of the arrival at Castle Garden, the hardback benches of today's two trains—it was as if God had been testing him. The journey had been almost too much to bear. And now, he kept saying to himself, it was over. He exhaled deeply as if he had been holding his breadth for the entire journey from Galicia.

The conductor blew his whistle. He waved ahead to the engineer and remounted the train. With a whistled shriek, the P&R 3:50 slowly accelerated. It picked up speed and continued westward towards the setting sun. Estreicher and Feldman watched it depart. Although the station and its surroundings were not familiar, Estreicher gave no thought to the discontinuity. After all, they had made it! He would soon get his bearings. Within the hour, the two men would reach the office of the hiring agent. By the following day they would be earning a king's wage.

Beneath a sign hanging from the terminal awning, the two men re-gripped their satchels. Neither man took notice of the sign with the name of the town. The *lantzmen* entered the almost vacant terminal building. They walked into the waiting room.

From the cantilevered ceiling, gaslight fixtures hung halfway to the floor. They were now turned on as dusk approached. Their eerie glow gave the waiting area a supple feel so different from the glare of the day's bright sunshine. Benches which moments earlier held waiting passengers were empty. A lone clerk stood behind a gated window. He was clean-shaven and wore a starched blue uniform. Silver buttons reflected the soft light from the gas lamps. Sown on each collar were shield-shaped P&R patches. On the clerk's round cap, a medallion gleamed with the letters

P&RRR. With head down, the clerk focused on tallying the day's receipts.

After an extended moment, a hesitation, the clerk sensed the presence of customers. He raised his head. He called out to the two solitary figures. "Hey, we're closed. The last train for Reading just left. You fellas need help?" Feldman prodded Estreicher forward.

Estreicher cautiously approached the window. After an initial pleasantry he timidly parsed his words. "Which way Shana Dowa Coal?"

"Huh?" replied the confused clerk. "Didn't ketch it. Could *ya* repeat that?"

"Coal mine, Shana Dowa Coal," Estreicher said.

"A coal mine? Hereabouts?" The clerk's quizzical expression seemed to fill the void of the empty waiting room. "I *dunno* no coal mine."

A shiver raced down Estreicher's spine. He could barely make out the English and the clerk's accent was torture. He realized that his question had been answered by a question. That was not a good sign.

A sharp pain shot through his brain and a bead of sweat appeared on his forehead. His confidence, methodically formed with months of planning about this moment, vanished in a heartbeat. For a moment, Estreicher froze in place. He stared vacantly at the clerk, unable to move a muscle, his jaw cemented open.

"The handbill, show him the handbill," Feldman urged, in *Yiddish*. Estreicher collected his composure, his eyes refocused. He pulled from the satchel the carefully preserved folded paper.

He handed it to the clerk who read it. His eyes almost jumped out of their sockets. The clerk looked back at the two men.

"This here paper says Pottsville, the Shenandoah Coal Company." The clerk snorted, rubbed his chin, and looked down again at the handbill. "You certainly ain't in the right pew. And I can say you ain't even in the right church!" Estreicher could barely interpret the clerk's sharp words, but he deciphered immediately a potential crisis with the clerk's elevated voice.

A sly grin broke out on the clerk's face. "PottsVILLE," he spat out with an emphasis on the 'VILLE, "is a ways up the line, above Reading! That's where the last westbound, the express, was a goin'. This here's PottsTOWN!"

The town's name ricocheted off the bare walls of the empty terminal. It was immediately followed by guffaws then laughter so uncontrollable tears began welling up in the clerk's eyes.

Two

Rose

"Raisal, Raisal," Adolph yelled to his wife from across the field. "It's a letter, a letter from your brother Mendel. From America!" Raisal raised her head from the garden where she had been weeding. Her infant son lay on the ground next to her. Three small barefoot children emerged from the one room cottage.

"A letter? From Mendel?" Her husband was returning from Ungvahr, the district capital half a day's walk from their hamlet of Rebnitza.

"Yes, yes," Adolph called out, walking faster as he closed the distance with his wife, "and it contains a *shiffskart*, a passage, for me!" Raisal's face went vacant. She heard the words, but they did not register in her dazed mind. She repeated what Adolph had just said.

"A *shiffskart*? For you?"

"Yes, yes," Adolph repeated, "take a look."

Raisal pulled herself up from the rows of freshly planted cabbage. She wiped her dirt encrusted, swollen hands on her dirty apron. Her skirt stained by the topsoil from their small garden still showed the imprint of the soft earth. Foot coverings, for they could hardly be called shoes, could not prevent a mud-caked tinge on the soles of her feet. Raisal's unkempt dark hair was wrapped with a kerchief. Her eyes blinked rapidly as they caught the late morning sun when she looked up. Adolph handed her the packet letter from Mendel. The envelope was stiff. She carefully fingered it, as if she were touching the silk of a *tallis* or the soft velvet of a torah cover.

The envelope was addressed "Adolph Markovits Letzte Post, Unghvar Österreich-Ungarn." Neither their hamlet of Rebnitza nor any nearby village had a post office. The address was written in a script she could not decipher, not that Raisal could read. From her father, Raisal had learned some Hebrew *alef-bais*, indispensable for prayers. Formal schooling was never an option for her family or in her native village. Other than a *chedar* for the boys, there was no school.

Raisal ran her forefinger across the American return address. Adolph explained it was the number 25, followed the words 'New York.' The postmark indicated the year 1887, although to Adolph and Raisal, the actual year was 5647; the month was Nisan, not the Christian April. *Pesah*, Passover, was just a couple of weeks away. Although the words meant nothing to her, Raisal discerned the vaguely familiar style of her brother's handwriting. In his own Hebrew lessons, her brother always pressed heavily to form the Hebrew letters. Their father, she remembered, pointed this out to Mendel, urging him to bear down more lightly on the precious pencil in order to save lead.

Raisal examined the three American stamps on the letter's upper right corner. Profiled on the stamps were bareheaded men. She assumed they were leaders of America. Their faces were plain, their clothing unembellished. How unlike were these Americans from the bedecked Emperor Franz-Joseph who adorned Austrian-Hungarian postage. On the few letters Adolph and she had received from distant family, the Emperor's portrait seemed bland, even ghostlike. His face was surrounded by garish swirls, crowns, ribbons, and double-headed eagles. Raisal knew nothing about the Emperor; his reality was as detached from hers as their tiny *shtetl* was from the moon! But on these stamps were American faces. They displayed nothing aristocratic or monarchial. On the contrary, the men on the stamps reminded Raisal of something else. She saw in them her baby brother, grown up of course, a real *mensch*, and living in New York! He had been absent from the *shtetl* almost two years.

"Oh Mendel, Mendel," she sighed. Her eyes watered at the fleeting memory of her younger sibling who had gone off to America the summer before last. "*Vos vet zein, vet zein*, what will be, will be," he told her as he departed Rebnitza. If the smiling Mendel meant to reassure his sister that his mission to *die golden medina* would turn out for the best, the lighthearted quip had frightened her even more.

Raisal's mind sped ahead. With the arrival of Mendel's letter, she knew a life changing decision had to be made. On the day he departed for America, Mendel promised to send for his brother-in-law. She remembered his light-hearted words well. "Keep your *lepisch man*, your clumsy husband in good health, my Raisal. He'll need a strong back and real *sechel*, brains, when he gets to New York!"

The time when Mendel's promise would be fulfilled then seemed so distant, a faint possibility like snowfall in the middle of summer. Yes, God might order the rain turned to snow. He might also turn their milk cow into a horse and make her husband a wealthy man. But why would God go to the trouble? They were poor Jews living in a poor village. Why would beneficence fall on them like manna on the Children of Israel?

Until this moment Raisal imagined Mendel's promise was akin to the hope expressed by every Jew at the Passover *Seder* when would be proclaimed 'Next Year in Jerusalem!' To be aspired, of course, but who ever, in truth, expected one day to wake up in the Holy Land? Like most dreams, it seemed so vivid, so real while asleep. But at the moment one awakes, who can remember what took place in the dream?

Both Adolph and Raisal were in their mid twenties and, *kain ein horeh*, in good health. Life in Rebnitza was arduous. Their parents already had aged rapidly in the *shtetl*. Raisal thought of her late father-in-law, may his memory be blessed, whom she never met. He died well short of his fortieth birthday. She thought of her own grandparents who also were taken by God before Raisal was born. Any person in Rebnitza or in the surrounding villages who survived into their fifth decade or, *seit gezunt*, their sixties was truly blessed by God with the gift of life.

During *Neilah*, the most solemn last hour on Yom Kippur, the most holy day of the Jewish calendar, God determines who shall live and who shall die. Now Raisal confronted her own personal *Neilah*. She considered her six years of marriage, the four childbirths, the one miscarriage, the deaths of grandparents and uncles, illness, hunger, joy, and sorrow. Raisal reflected on their lives and the future of their four tiny children, of Markovics/Schvartz family to come. If her husband left for America, the separation could be for years.

Raisal would have help, of course. Many *mishpoohah*, extended kin, lived in this corner of Galicia. Her parents Chaim and Rivka Schvartz and her younger sisters Fannie, Freydel, and little Mollie lived in the next village over, in Gaydos. Adolph had repaired the raw, weather-beaten timber boards of their modest single room hut. The straw thatch roof was in fair shape. It certainly could survive one more winter, maybe two. The vegetable and potato garden was seeded. With spring rains and longer days tiny shoots were already emerging. Behind the cottage, the small patch of winter wheat seemed in fine shape. For heat in the winter, she and the children could gather turf, peat, and dead wood from nearby forest. As long as the chickens provided eggs and her garden flourished, she had items that could be exchanged for butter, candles, and other necessities.

But how, she wondered, would they get by if the summer rains failed, if the crops did not grow? A strong winter wind might damage or even destroy the modest cottage. What if the animals got sick or the Angel of Death, *chas v'cholileh*, came for her children or for her?

If she insisted he stay with her and the children in Rebnitza, Raisal knew her husband might grumble but would not depart. The decision was hers. The family could remain in the cottage, repair the thatch every spring, tend their tiny garden, and gather wood for making soup and winter heat. Their chickens and the cow that more often than not, provided barely enough milk for the hungry children could sustain them. Adolph could hire himself out as a laborer. He could earn a few *groshen* loading or unloading wagons, carrying rocks, or pulling tree stumps. He could receive a little extra food teaching *chedar*, religious studies, to the children of parents just as poor as they. With his baritone voice and perfect pitch, he could serve as *chazen*, the cantor, during the High Holidays. Thank God her husband possessed a strong voice that could fill every synagogue crevice to the farthest rafters. There may not be enough food on the table and seldom Shabbat and holiday wine, but at least the family celebrated these events together. Her parents, sisters, and cousins resided nearby. Moreover, her widowed mother-in-law

Lena also depended on Adolph, the oldest of her 12 children. If Adolph were gone, what would happen to her and Adolph's younger brothers and sisters?

Raisal continued to reflect. Perhaps God's blessing might actually be falling on their heads? She felt both suffocated and helpless in Rebnitza. Any day, a fancy uniformed officer with swanky feathered hat, Hussar sword, and white gloves might appear with a troop of Hungarian soldiers and order her husband into the Emperor Franz-Joseph's military. There he could disappear forever. Stories of such forced conscription of Jews in Polish Russia just over the Carpathian Mountains from Hungarian Galicia, was constant fodder for gossip. "Thank God Rebnitza was not located in Czarist Russia!" she thought. Adolph and Raisal considered themselves loyal citizens under the Austro-Hungarian crown. But at any time anti-Semitic magistrates from the provincial capital at Kaschau, police officials, or tax collectors might descend on Rebnitza. They were a constant threat to all Jews, especially poor and helpless ones. Their cottage and tiny plot of land could be taken for the flimsiest of reasons. How would they live then?

A small streamlet, a trickle really during summer months, separated Rebnitza's Jews from the hamlet's Orthodox Ruthenians, Catholic Hungarians and Slovaks. Villagers referred to it as the "river." The word was apt. Between the Jews and the non-Jews, the cultural and social gap was as wide as the Danube. Rebnitza's Jews and Christians shared no institutions such as schools or communal water. There was not even a common language. Each side ignored the other. Yet if the fragile peace were to be broken, all clearly understood which side of the "river" would have the upper hand.

Raisal grasped the situation perfectly. The decision whether Adolph should or should not go was illusory. Here in Rebnitza, they had no future. Life would just be a continuation of a dreary past, heavy with foreboding and pervasive uncertainty.

Raisal looked intently into her husband's eyes. She grasped his right hand tightly between both of hers. She steeled her courage for what she was about to say. With all her will to prevent her moist eyes from tearing up, she forced a voice to emerge from her heart.

"You must go to *die goldene medina*," she said, softly but purposefully.

* * *

At dawn the following day as the sun began to warm the fields, Adolph set out for his long journey. There was no reason to postpone the inevitable. He had the *shiffskart* in hand. The sooner Adolph earned some money, the quicker, God willing, the family would be reunited, in America. *Pesah* was coming; being apart for the holiday would have been unimaginable before. However, neither she nor her husband could think of *Pesah* now. "When a *zon*, a tooth, goes bad, delay in getting it taken out only intensifies the pain," her father consoled. "The agony of pending separation is even worse. It is best Adolph leaves now. Waiting for his departure will only make the pain of parting worse."

Within his *pintelle*, a small bundle, Adolph had placed all he would need for his journey. It would serve also as his pillow. A patch of grass, a plank, the back of a wagon, even a ship's deck would be his mattress. His widowed mother Lena was there. She bid her eldest son good-bye before returning to her cottage to tend to her garden. Adolph hugged his sobbing children. He urged his eldest boy to care for his siblings. He kissed his wife passionately and held her tightly. He bade farewell to Rebnitza's well wishers. The hamlet's Jewish families, perhaps thirty in all, and *mishpoohah* from surrounding villages, including his father-in-law and mother-in-law, turned out. One of the elders brought forth the hamlet's torah. Adolph kissed it reverently. He then recited a *barucha*, a prayer for traveling:

"May it be your will, Lord our God and God of our fathers, to guide me in peace, to lead me to my desired destination, America, in health and joy and peace, and bring me home in peace. Save me from every enemy and disaster on the way, and from all calamities that threaten the world. Hear my supplication to You our Lord. Praise be to You, Lord our God, who hears the prayers of his children."

"*For gezunterhait, zay gezunt!*" his family and friends shouted, as Adolph paused for one last look back. By the time Adolph's small form disappeared on the post road to Nagymihaly, no amount of willpower could hold back Raisal's torrents of tears. Her body shook uncontrollably. Guilt overtook her consciousness.

"*Gut in himmel,*" Raisal shouted upward. "Is this the right path? Please God look out for my Adolph, and for us."

* * *

Seven weeks later, Adolph Markowitz landed in Boston. Following the precise instructions sent to him in the letter and the last of his money, he made his way to New York City, a tenement building on Manhattan's Lower East Side. There he moved in with another of his wife's brothers, Emmanuel Schwartz who had followed Mendel to America, and Schwartz's wife Hannah.

Emmanuel had reached America almost a full year earlier. To his greenhorn brother-in-law, Emmanuel possessed a beguiling *savoir-faire* about life in this strange metropolis. Schwartz was a short man with a thick torso. His bushy beard hid a contagious smile, while his eyes danced from one side to the other in an almost perpetual sweep of the room. Although Emmanuel's English was still very rudimentary, he possessed a keen eye and an insatiable thirst for accumulating money. The young man already was saving what he could to facilitate the passage to America for other Schwartz family members.

Having learned well the tailoring trade in Galicia, Emmanuel practiced a vocation quite appropriate for New York's Lower East Side. But he discerned that his sister's husband had no such skill and, given his independent character and physical nature, would never achieve it. "No problem," Schwartz assured his brother-in-law. "We'll find you something better!" So for the wage of one dollar for a twelve-hour day, Adolph obtained work in a pipe factory.

It was mean, never ending labor. However, Adolph persevered. Even if he wanted to leave the sweatshop, where would he go? Who had time to line up better employment? Unskilled immigrant laborers were plentiful, but jobs were scarce. The days were endless. Weeks slowly stretched into months. And Adolph's savings remained pitifully small. A weaker man might have given up.

One Shabbat in Schwartz's tiny apartment, Adolph met a *lantzman*, Alexander Estreicher, formerly Iscovitz. Estreicher was in New York to meet his wife and children who just arrived in America. Fifteen years older than Adolph, Estreicher had been well regarded in their Galicia community for his common sense and Talmudic wisdom. Adolph knew Estreicher as a man who weighed his decisions carefully. Yet once a direction was selected, Estreicher tossed doubt aside and doggedly followed his chosen path. Adolph was vaguely aware that Estreicher had found a new life as a shopkeeper in a small provincial town. He listened intently to the more experienced man.

"This pipe factory business is no place for you," Estreicher confided. Adolph knew this to be true. He hated the low wage and the squalid sweatshop surroundings. The rancid air combined coal dust with the odor of sweat and urine. One year in the factory seemed an eternity. He had saved less than he had hoped, barely enough for even one *shiffskart*. Moreover, Adolph despised the factory supervisor who treated his workers worse than animals. However, jobs that provided both self-respect and a real wage were almost impossible to find on the Lower East Side, a place crowded with pushcart vendors and rag peddlers.

"You are *shtark vi a ferd*, strong as a horse! There are plentiful good paying factory jobs in Pottstown for immigrant newcomers like you." Estreicher himself had not worked long in a factory. After a couple months in which he saved fifty dollars, he started a small grocery store in a *shvartza* neighborhood. Earnings were sparse, but it was enough to bring over his wife and four children. Adolph was intrigued.

Estreicher urged his *lantzman* further. "Don't be like one of these New York *scheps*, these sheep! Leave this place. The McClintik-Marshall Company is hiring at good wages!" He added, "I know the boss there and can get you in the door."

Adolph, it was true, possessed superior strength and was a hard worker. Short and stocky but not fat, Adolph's broad shoulders and back had been honed by farm chores and heavy labor back home. He was unafraid of manual labor. Adolph was willing to work anywhere, do anything, to shorten the time when he could be reunited with Raisal and the children. And if going to Pottstown meant getting out of the filthy Lower East Side where the air burned his eyes and clogged his nose, so much the better.

He held out his hand to Estreicher. "I'll come," Adolph agreed.

Estreicher was true to his word. Factory jobs for immigrants in the town's steel fabrication, farm equipment, and boiler factories were relatively plentiful. Not only at McClintik-Marshall, but also at Potts Brothers Iron Company, the Ellis & Lessig Iron Works, Warwick Furnace, Sotter Brothers Incorporated, the Pottstown Iron Works, the March-Brownback Stove Company, the Keystone Agricultural Works, and elsewhere. While the pay at these factories was not as elevated as Estreicher had implied, by avoiding an extravagant lifestyle—no problem for Adolph who boarded with Estreicher—he knew he could save money.

However, to work in one of Pottstown's new factories took a certain type of individual. Adolph was not that kind of person. He disliked taking orders, especially from harsh, ignorant, anti-Semitic factory foremen. He hated the noise of the heavy machinery and found the brutal rigidity of the time clock onerous. In the evenings after a long twelve-hour shift, his head continued to vibrate. An ache grew in his neck and moved down his shoulder. Usually a heavy sleeper, he slept fitfully and arose irritable. Adolph was only a spark away from a full blown, hot-tempered Markowitz explosion.

After just a couple of months, Adolph turned his back on McClintik-Marshall and the other factories that produced the industrial bounty of his new country. He approached Estreicher and asked for a small loan.

"I have an idea," he told Estreicher. "I want to try something else. Its simple, requires little skill, doesn't cost much money, and could, with diligence and a *shtikel* of luck, provide a respectable income."

Estreicher suspected right away what Adolph was going to say next. "*Nu*, you want to be a *pedler*? I can see your mind more clearly than you can."

Adolph nodded. The choice of such a profession was natural and perfectly suited for a *macher* like himself. Estreicher believed the younger man possessed both the hardheadedness and inexhaustible energy that peddling required. The elder man remembered his own experiences a few years earlier when he had struck out on his own with only a few pennies in his pocket. He agreed to front Adolph the necessary start-up cash.

* * *

Adolph Markowitz began his peddling career with one pair of well-worn boots, an old leather pack, and an abundance of moxie. With Estreicher's guidance and seed money, Adolph set out to call on area farms, blacksmiths, coopers, tanners, cabinet makers, wainwrights, weavers, and other artisans in villages within a day's walk of Pottstown. If buying and selling the unwanted items of others was not a formula for making his fortune, at least through hard work Adolph might pay for his family's eventual crossing to America.

"I must save Raisal and bring her here," he confided to Estreicher. His *lantzman* understood completely his compulsion.

To this end, Adolph resolved to live on almost nothing. Using the burly back given him by God and strengthened in Rebnitza's fields, he collected iron scrap from area farmers, artisans, and shopkeepers. He deposited the material at one of Pottstown's iron foundries. In a typical day, Adolph earned about two dollars, on a good day, perhaps three dollars and some change. Estreicher's own house became increasingly crowded with young children so Adolph moved into a boarding house. He shared a room with two other single men who had recently arrived in town and worked towards the same end as he. When on the road Adolph slept in stables and barns, even on the coldest winter nights. The novice peddler demonstrated a single-minded intensity that, many who knew him would readily concede, characterized him throughout his life. The young man hoarded every cent he could.

Eventually, Adolph accumulated almost five hundred dollars. "God willing," he told his mentor Estreicher, "I can send for Raisal and the children by Rosh Hashanah," the Jewish New Year.

Through his brother-in-law Mendel, still resident in New York, Adolph posted occasional letters home. He wrote infrequently, perhaps once every six or eight weeks. More frequent letter writing was useless. Who had time to write letters? Moreover, he knew that unless a *lantzman* or family member visited Unghvar, the letters could remain uncollected and unread for months. While Adolph had much he could say about his experiences in *die goldene medina,* after a long day on the road, and the constant battle to overcome the language barrier, he also had little energy and even less concentration.

Adolph required concentration since writing, even in Yiddish, was an underdeveloped skill. When Adolph did write, his messages were stiff and formal. He possessed neither the writing skills to convey his emotions nor eagerness to exhibit how much the absence of his family hurt him. He addressed the letters to his father-in-law who unlike Raisal could read. He knew that her father would read the letters to Adolph's illiterate wife and many family members would be present. However, the letters Adolph crafted were long and, to the best of his capability, newsy. They accentuated the positive and avoided mention of the tribulations—of which there were many.

* * *

Raisal's apprehensions were not unwarranted. Since the spring day her husband trekked the imperial post road westward, the family's fortunes foundered. Although famine did not strike that year or the next, hunger could not be completely avoided. The aged and soon skeletal milk cow finally was led to the *shochet* whose knife quickly dispatched the beast. The meat was sold rather than consumed; the money helped the family through another winter. A particularly heartless tax collector, as Raisal feared, came through the village and tightened a chokehold on the impoverished Galitsianer Jews. The loneliness she suffered was worse than her worse trepidations. She relished each of Adolph's rare letters, read and reread to her by her father. The words caused her heart to yearn even more for his embrace.

Then in 1888, the second summer following Adolph's departure, the *malah hamawzes*, the Angel of Death, in the form of a diphtheria epidemic swept through the province. Half of Rebnitza's children under five were stricken, including three of Adolph and Raisal's four children. The calamity was over in just two horrific weeks.

In a message to Adolph written by her father, Raisal poured out her heart. "My eyes grew dark, my hands numb," dictated Raisal through Chaim Schartz's tight, carefully embellished Yiddish. "Oh I cried and cried, beseeching God to take my life and spare little Moischek, sweet Gitel, and lovely Sarah." She continued, "But the Lord, *Baruch ha Shem*, did not hear me. I tried—you must believe me—to block the Evil Eye that held our little ones in its malevolent gaze. I prayed until my throat was like ash, my lips raw as dog weed. I had no tears left, my eyes were stones..." Raisal could get no more words out.

Her father finished the letter for her. "Two of the three angels died on the same day, the third on the day before the Ninth of Av of all evil days!" he added. "Even after God, *Baruch haShem*, took our Moischek, Gitele, and Sarale, your blessed Raisale stayed with Harry, and God, *Baruch ha Shem*, heard her sobs, saw her misery. His heart softened and he spared the little *mizinik*, your precious Harrycik." Raisal's composure returned. Her father continued to scribe on her behalf. "I pray for the hour we reunite in this world or the next if God wills it, as long as we are together."

Two months later Adolph read his wife's lamentations. His hands trembled as he followed her words. His eyes watered.

"*Gotteniu*, Oh God! I am such a *shmegegi* a total idiot! My life means nothing if I cannot safeguard my family. I am no husband, no father, if I cannot protect my helpless beloved!" That night, Adolph wept as he had never wept before.

With an even greater determination, Adolph pushed his efforts at peddling. With the death of three children, he sadly now had enough funds for the ship passage to America for Raisal, his mother and his son. It was late spring 1889, two years after he departed Rebnitza. While Adolph had enough funds for three, he had another issue to consider. Adolph calculated he could squeeze a bit more money from peddling to pay for his own passage to Europe to retrieve them. But this would take at least three more months of arduous labor, delay the family's reunification, and leave no money for setting up a residence on their return from Europe. In addition, it would mean postponing the return to America until the following spring since a winter crossing of the Atlantic was too onerous even to consider. On the other hand, he dearly wished to see friends and family members. He yearned to tell them wondrous stories about America, the prosperous farms, the incredible public institutions, transportation networks that spider-webbed the country and, most importantly, the freedoms America offered—from voracious tax collectors, anti-Semitic magistrates, army dragoons, fanatical priests and heartless landlords.

In the end, Adolph decided to remain in Pottstown and prepare for the family's arrival. He determined he would squeeze every ounce of value from the iron scrap he carried to the foundries. He would save every penny, spend almost nothing except for food. When his dear Raisal, his mother, and son reached Pottstown, a house would await them.

Adolph sent the money for the *shiffskarts* to Mendel in New York whom he knew would arrange things. He remained in Pottstown. Each day, Adolph rose before dawn and drove himself late into the dusk, every day, even on Shabbat while his *lantzmen* gathered at one of the apartments to pray. Saturdays, Adolph recognized, were best for collecting from farms, an important source of scrap. On the road under his load of scrap, Adolph prayed for God's *selihot*, forgiveness of his transgression of the Shabbat. The faces of Raisale and the children, the mental picture from that ever sadder spring day of his departure, occupied his every thought. In his nightmares while lying on beds of straw on barn floors, Gitele, Sarah, and Moishek called out to him, even as the Shadow of Death passed across the threshold of their humble cottage. Their ghostly fingers tapped his brow and he screamed out their names, disturbing on occasion a few barn animals. He awakened many nights in a cold, damp sweat.

As the long, humid days of August drained his energy and self-confidence, Adolph continued to choke on his self-doubt. Should he have gone back to Rebnitza to collect the family? Could Raisal manage the arduous trip without him? The decision was already made, he repeated to himself, in time with the pace of his hiking the back roads around Pottstown. The more he walked, though, the more he wondered. "Did I fail them?"

"For what purpose!" he finally said out loud with no witnesses except for robins, squirrels, and an occasional rabbit. He knew the *schlep* to Europe and back would be a distraction. "The time for brooding is over. Instead, I must focus on preparations to receive the family. I must be ready for their arrival, secure a proper place to live, a permanent roof over their heads." The family also required a garden and a few chickens. For financial stability as a peddler Adolph knew his back was insufficient. To compete with Pottstown's other peddlers he needed a horse and wagon. Each item cost money he did not yet possess. Meanwhile, he prayed each day for his family's safe crossing.

In late November 1889, Raisal, Harry, and Adolph's mother Lena made the Atlantic passage on the Steamship Laurestina of the Hamburg-Amerikanische Packetfarhrt line. The three-week crossing was no smoother or less harrowing than the identical voyage taken by innumerable steerage class immigrants on countless other ships. In late autumn the North Atlantic can be ferociously rough and coat-ripping cold. Raisal later depicted the ship and the interminable journey to her husband.

"Oh, the nauseating odor of the overcrowded steerage compartments, the overflowing toilets, the unwashed and chronically ill passengers," she recollected. Restless children fought for floor space and demanded incessant maternal attention. Harry fidgeted and whimpered constantly. Spilt cooking oil from small kerosene stoves made the steerage deck sticky. We were always afraid of fire. When we were allowed to go above to the main deck, the freezing salt air and suffocating coal dust made me gasp for breath. But it was welcome relief to the thick air below. How can I forget the pitching of that ship which turned my stomach inside out? The creaking of the ship's riveted plate walls frightened me. The cries and wails of the sick and, in some cases, dying still haunt me!"

Early one brisk morning, the Laurestina made New York Harbor. From the ship's main deck, Raisal was unprepared for the sight of the "Lady with the Lamp." Dedicated only three years earlier, the Statue of Liberty was still a novelty for the increasing hoards of immigrants. Word of its existence had not reached Rebnitza. Since Adolph entered America though Boston, he never mentioned it in his letters. During the voyage Raisal gave little credence to the *bubbe maisses*, grandmother's tales, of the other mothers who whispered of its existence. The sight from the Laurestina's port side caused her heart to stop in mid-beat. A gasp escaped from her chapped lips. Nearby, some passengers from Russia began to dance the lively *kazatskeh*. Others placed small children on their shoulders to offer a better view over the crowded railing. On seeing the site, one bearded old man prayed aloud the Hebrew prayer for arriving at this miraculous day.

"Praised are you, Lord our God, King of the universe who granted me a miracle in this place!"

Raisal openly sobbed.

Hours later, Adolph collected his haggard but overjoyed wife, mother, and child from the immigration building on Castle Garden Island. The four embraced. He took in hand their frugal possessions wrapped in a patterned *shmatta*. They ferried to Battery Park and walked together to Emmanuel Schwartz's Spartan walk-up apartment off Delancey Street. Following a brief two-day reunion with Raisal's two brothers and sister-in-law, Adolph took his family on the same route he had traveled on his own inaugural journey to Pottstown. Traveling across the marvels of their new country, little Harry gazed, Lena prayed, and Raisal mostly slept.

"I believe you will like the house I found," Adolph said as the family descended from the train. Hand in hand they walked up High Street. Adolph had rented a narrow row house on Warren Street between Chestnut and Walnut Streets. This was Chicken Hill, a neighborhood of row homes and seedy taverns, corner grocery shops and small stables, rutted streets and muddy alleys. Many of Pottstown's immigrant newcomers and much of its working class resided there. From High Street, the town's main east-west thoroughfare, Chicken Hill stretched north across King, Chestnut, Walnut, Beech and Lincoln Streets to the top of a hill, the site of a former chicken farm broken up into lots. Running north and south, Franklin, Washington, Warren, Adams, and Grant Streets completed Chicken Hill's matrix. From Beech Street, striking diagonally northeast towards Chicken Hill's summit ran Hale Street.

Raisal agreed that Pottstown was a wondrous albeit overwhelming place. Their new neighborhood was a far cry from their Galician village. Minus the tenement buildings, the constant noise and the thick choking coal dust, low rent Chicken Hill emulated, in microcosm, New York's Lower East Side. While generally poor, few of Chicken Hill's inhabitants were truly impoverished. All dreamt of upward mobility. Low wage jobs were easily available. On its linguistically cacophonic streets resided Italians, Germans, Poles, Slovaks, black families up from the South, and Irish down from the coalfields. Catholics, Lutherans, Baptists, Russian and Greek Orthodox lived in the neighborhood, but no Episcopalians or Anglicans. They resided in Pottstown's more "posh" neighborhoods. A handful of Chicken Hill inhabitants were neither immigrants nor children of immigrants. Some were disabled Civil War veterans or social outcasts unable to keep steady jobs. Not a few were deeply attached to, if not addicted to whiskey.

Chicken Hill's dirt streets witnessed a beehive of activity during daylight hours—gas streetlights and Thomas Edison's new fangled electric lighting appeared only a decade later, around 1900. Even when school was in session, few neighborhood children attended it beyond the fourth grade. When not performing chores or other labors, local boys played stickball in the streets or nearby fields. Produce vendors flogged vegetables and fruit freshly pick that very morning. Milk and meat wagons and not a few honey wagons collecting manure for fertilizer crisscrossed the neighborhood in search of customers.

Like most houses on Chicken Hill, the Markowitz residence lacked indoor plumbing. Water was carried from a pump twenty yards from the house. A large cooking stove stood in what served as the kitchen, dining room, and for the most part, living room. It also provided heat for the house. Up a narrow stairway were two sleeping rooms. In his peddling efforts, Adolph obtained four broken but repairable chairs, a severely scratched table, and a second hand bed with a feather mattress. When Raisal entered the house, this was the sum total of their furniture. Accommodations were modest. But compared to their cottage in Rebnitza, Raisal felt the new home palatial. Raisal smiled. She told her husband she was satisfied with the house.

That first night after putting their son to sleep wrapped in an old army blanket, Adolph tenderly held his wife in his arms. The room was cold; it was early December after all and morning frost already crusted the small front porch. Neither Adolph nor Raisal, however, felt the chill. Lying together on a real bed for the first time in over two and a half years, they spoke of their travails since parting, and of their children living and dead.

"I missed you so terribly," he whispered. "Many nights after I got your *geferlech* terrible letter, I felt so helpless. I went almost *meshugga* crazy with frustration that I could not be there. The *gebrenteh tsores*, the utter misery that you went through! I am sorry it took so long to bring you here."

Raisal examined her husband carefully. Physically, Adolph had not much changed. If anything his shoulder muscles were tougher, his back stiffer that before. The creases in his forehead she did not remember. But inside, she sensed he possessed a new hardness and self-confidence. During thirty months in America, he had matured. Her husband was no longer a product of a Galician village. He seemed more cosmopolitan, more assertive.

With a light finger touch Raisal etched the lines on his forehead. She was sure, they had not existed in Rebnitza. His skin, particularly on his back and shoulders, seemed more leathery than she remembered. No doubt, she thought, the result of carrying heavy loads.

"God made us pay a heavy price," Raisal agreed. "There was nothing," she reassured him, "that you could have done to save Moischek and Gitel and Sarah. I pray that in our new life He will provide us his *rachmones*, his compassion. May he grant us *simantov*, the good fortune of our now being together in *die goldena medina*."

Raisal stared into her husband's eyes. "You will earn money, we'll have more children, this American house will be crowded with little *yiddisher mensches*, Jewish boys who will make you proud. And we will also have grandchildren in our old age. You'll see. Our family will grow and prosper."

Adolph took Raisal, kissed her from the top of her head to her feet. She welcomed his caresses and reciprocated in kind. They made love for the first time in the New World, hastened but not rushed. They would have the rest of their natural lives for more leisurely matrimonial behavior.

Into this house, their first child in America, Yetta Rivka, was born September 8, 1890. Five brothers: Sam, Mike, Ben, Robert, and Francis, followed, and a sister Kate. Until the youngest Francis was born in 1907, all were delivered at home with the assistance of a mid-wife, Mrs. Forkush. Francis was delivered in a hospital with an actual doctor in attendance. His birth was even registered with the State in Harrisburg! He was also the sole child to enjoy a baby carriage, a later source of constant ribbing by his siblings.

And what of Harry who alone of four children born in Rebnitza survived the diphtheria epidemic and the Atlantic crossing? Like most children of Chicken Hill, Harry spent much of his young life on Pottstown's streets. He attended the community's makeshift *chedar* and learned Hebrew. But Adolph was dissatisfied with the caliber of the *chedar* teacher who was not *really* a teacher. He was determined that *his* son must receive a proper *Yiddishkeit* education and he taught the child himself in the evenings. Like all Jewish males Harry had his Bar Mitzvah at 13. But except for being called to the torah, it was a non-event. In his only concession to the occasion, Adolph shared a bottle of *shnapps* that Shabbat with the other synagogue attendees. Warm and cheerful, Harry was a dutiful son and good older brother to the increasing number of American-born siblings. However, at age 16 while spending the summer working at his uncle's bakery in Pittsburgh, Harry fell ill with appendicitis and died.

With her life reborn in Pottstown Raisal settled into the never-ending routine of homemaker and mother, assisted by her mother-in-law. She never mastered more than rudimentary English. However, she accepted without hesitation her new American identity. For the rest of her life among friends and strangers alike, Raisal employed the Anglicized version of her name, Rose.

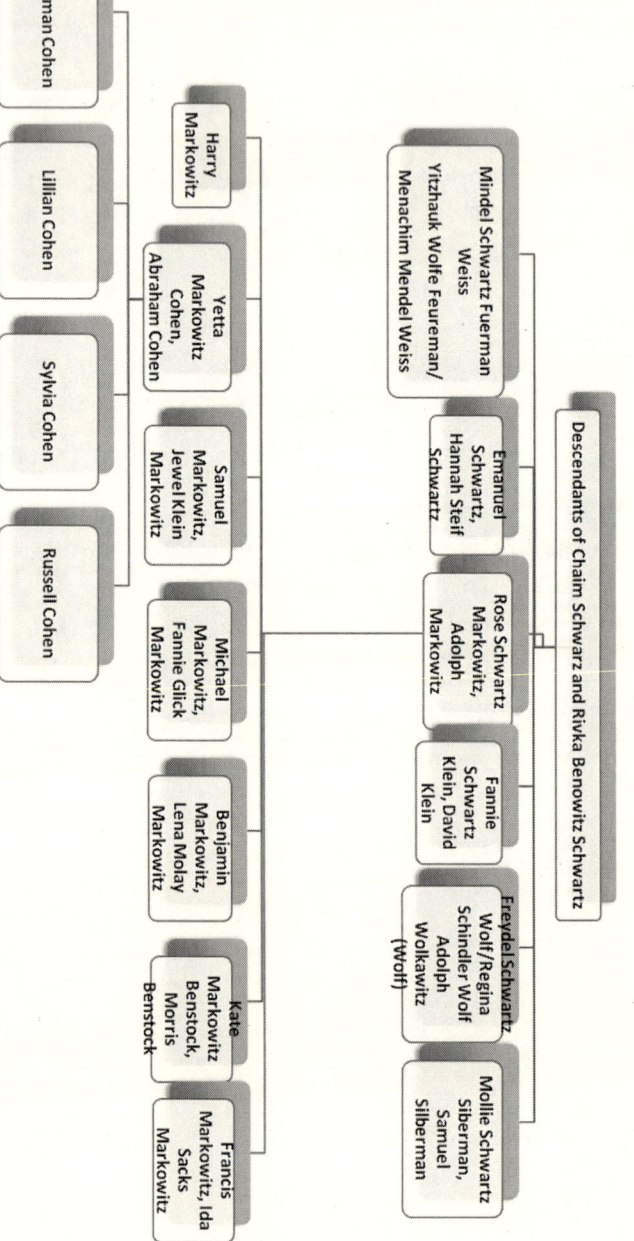

Three

Mishpoohah

With his family settled and Rose pregnant with their first American child, Adolph raised with his wife the most pressing topic on their minds: whom next from their extended family to bring to America. Our duty, Rose concurred, is to "our *mishpoohah*," our kin. For those left behind, life in Rebnitza remained perilous. Of their four children born in the old country, three perished in an epidemic. If they delayed too long, the Angel of Death might again stalk their families.

"We must bring all of them to America, the sooner the better," Adolph urged. Rose agreed wholeheartedly. Both understood the sacrifices to be made, most likely for years.

"*Deigeh nisht*," Rose whispered. "Don't worry! God willing, we will succeed."

Adolph and Rose accumulated passage money to America for Adolph's surviving siblings. It was a Herculean effort that required three years of unremitting labor. Upon arrival in America most of the Markowitz clan stayed briefly with Adolph and Rose in Pottstown. First to receive passage was Adolph's brother Benjamin who slept downstairs on a straw mattress. Being a baker by trade, Benjamin bought a small local bakery. But a year later during the Panic of 1893, the business went bust. He remained in Pottstown only a few more weeks before moving to Braddock, outside Pittsburgh, where a cousin resided. Adolph's brother eventually became one of the wealthiest, most successful Jews in that community. "The only reason of my success," Benjamin later said, "is work." He described how he had worked day and night in the bakery. "During the whole year," he said, "I did not sleep in bed even once, except on Saturdays when we did not bake."

Young single men and women freshly arrived in the New World were nothing if not impatient. Each Markowitz sibling was eager to exploit the chance at a new life in "The Golden Country." A small factory town in rural Pennsylvania that contained pitifully few available Jews of the opposite sex offered little attraction. As each member of the *mishpoohah* departed Pottstown for elsewhere in *die goldene medina*, another took his or her place. With help from Adolph and Rose, they established lives throughout America and even in Canada where Adolph's brother Max and sister Hannah eventually settled.

Adolph and Rose were dedicated to rescuing family members still residing in the old country. Neither reflected on the personal cost. Thousands of families like theirs were doing the same thing. Rose's own brothers were rapidly bringing over the Schwartz *mishpoohah*. They viewed their actions not as a *mitzvah*, a good deed. They found sanctuary in America with the help of others. They were obligated to do the same. Adolph described his actions in simple terms. "Every morning," he said, "I put on *teffilim*, phylacteries, and pray. Each day, I must earn a living. How is helping my 'greenhorn' *mishpoohah* any different?"

Adolph's mother Lena Bleich wholeheartedly supported this mission. After all, these were her children being brought over from Europe. But Lena was not prepared to coddle them once they came to America. Indeed, her mothering days, she affirmed, were over. Instead, Lena desired to pass the rest of her days in Pottstown being a *bubbe*, a grandmother. It was a role she performed quite well.

Lena's soft nature when with her grandchildren contrasted greatly with the rest of her personality. A widow for almost a decade, she was serious, acerbic, and impatient—traits passed by the mother to the son. She possessed an intensely strong will, a quick temper, and a rigidly opinionated mind. Her late husband Rev Haim had been no different. Although only in her fifties, Lena's lined face, arched back, craggy hands and pronounced limp suggested a woman much older. In life she confronted and overcame many challenges. When God presented the bill for allowing her to survive all tribulations, she repaid in full the expense with any youthful cheerfulness she may have once possessed.

Despite a domineering nature honed by nurturing a large brood during many years of widowhood, Lena showed exceptional prudence with daughter-in-law Rose. As the mother-in-law, Lena could have made life hell for her son's wife. Instead, Lena allowed Rose a measure of matriarchal authority in her own home. Rose knew other *mechutainista*, mothers-in-law, back in Rebnitza and even in America who dominated their sons' wives. Too many demonstrated anger with the choice of daughter-in-law and refused to share control of the home. The result often was bitter fruit. Rose wondered about her relations with Lena. Do men actually marry their mothers? It was a yarn she had heard from the *yentas* back in Galicia.

"Ah," Rose sighed, "to be able to consider what the Talmud prescribes regarding relations between a man's wife and his mother!"

Of course, Rose never approached Adolph with such a question. He would assuredly think she was *meshugah* for raising such a preposterous thought. Rose recognized the special nature of Lena's respect and deference for her. Both women sought cooperation over confrontation. Although close proximity for two decades caused stress to build up and flare occasionally, relations between the two were never seriously strained.

* * *

In a letter to Adolph, Rose's savvy brother Emmanuel Schwartz, still resident in his Lower East Side apartment, asked his brother-in law to look for a suitable business in Pottstown. Among the teeming tenements of New York, life for the ambitious Schwartz had become uninspiring. "I am ready to leave this place," he wrote. "Rents are high, wages low, and my *shaineh* pretty wife is pregnant with child."

Enter Jacob Sostman who had established a small kosher butcher business on south Washington Street. Unfortunately for him, Sostman was not cut out to operate a butcher shop in Pottstown. He sought to sell the business and recoup his investment. Adolph sought the help of another *lantzman*, Refoole Moskowitz. A butcher in the old country and thus an expert on the profession, Moskowitz was sent by Adolph to examine the business unobtrusively and make a recommendation. In New York, the portly Moskowitz was courting Rose and Emmanuel's sister Rachael Feydel. He had high hopes of winning her hand. When Rachael went to live temporarily with her sister Rose, Moskowitz followed her to Pottstown. This was a solid personal reason to assist. Moskowitz agreed to check out the Sostman business.

"I recommend you make an offer to Sostman," Moskowitz's message to Schwartz read. "He is ready to sell and sell cheap."

With the inside information in hand, Schwartz arrived in Pottstown. The negotiations with Sostman were short and one-sided. He bought Sostman's butcher business for less than he had been willing to offer.

Schwartz knew nothing about the butcher business. Moskowitz eagerly agreed to tutor the neophyte. Schwartz remained a butcher for just one year, however. Evidently, he was not cut out to be a kosher butcher in Pottstown. In 1891, he removed his butcher's apron for good. Accompanied by his infinitely patient wife and two small children, Schwartz decamped Pottstown for ventures elsewhere. He went first to Keasby, New Jersey, and later Brooklyn, New York.

Still unsatisfied and impatient to make his fortune in America, Schwartz just two years later again brought his long-suffering family back to Pottstown. This time, he decided to enter a more lucrative and less "sullied" enterprise than a "meat shop." He decided to go into wholesale and retail liquor. With savings from his earlier undertakings, Schwartz opened a liquor store at 41 High Street. Across from the Merchant's Hotel, it was an excellent downtown location. Business was good; it certainly provided better income than the meat trade. Schwartz stayed for a few years and accumulated quite a nest egg. But it was not good enough. For the second and final time, he departed Pottstown for New Jersey. There, Schwartz entered into real estate. It was a venture that paid larger dividends than even liquor and matched his people skills with his keen financial know-how. In an enterprise joined later by his sons, Schwartz became a wealthy and by all appearances a satisfied man.

As for Refoole Moskowitz, Rachael's suitor remained in Pottstown still pursuing the young Rachael. However, onto the scene appeared another Ungvahr *lantzmen,* Adam Volkavitz "Wolf". A youngster not yet 20, Volkavitz arrived in Pottstown a few months earlier. In contrast to the bland and uninspiring Moskowitz, Adam Wolf was swarthy, self-assured, and handsome. Upon his arrival in Pottstown Adam Volkavitz applied for a job at McClintik-Marshall. The hiring agent could not understand his thick Yiddish accent. "From now on, you're Wolf" the agent instructed.

The young man did not remain long at McClintik-Marshall despite the steady income. Like others from the villages of Galicia, Wolf found life in the factories too constraining. As with his mentor Adolph Markowitz, he preferred labor in the open air, and himself for a boss. Wolf chose to emulate his friend. One evening he announced to Adolph he would become a *karabeinik,* a country peddler. Adolph presented a gift to his *lantzman.* "Adamcik, this is the leather pack I used for two years. *Kaynahorah,* it will serve you as well as it did me!" Wolf enthusiastically launched his own peddling and junk business.

Wolf was a frequent visitor at the Markowitz house on Grant Street. There, he became acquainted with Rachael. The charismatic Wolf quickly captivated the young Rachael. Within weeks she allowed herself to be courted by Wolf and rejected the older, more boring Moskowitz. With the blessing of her *mishpoohah,* she agreed to marry him. The ceremony took place on October 14, 1890 at the Beech Street home of her brother Emmanuel Schwartz.

Although Schwartz had just exploited Moskowitz's expertise regarding the Sostman butcher business, he perceived no irony that *he* encouraged his sister to marry Wolf instead of Moskowitz. When asked about his role in breaking his sister's engagement to Moskowitz, Schwartz demurred. "My sister is a *kalleh moid,* a girl of marriageable age," Schwartz replied. "She can make up her own mind!" True enough. Although Wolf and Moskowitz were *lantzmen*, back in the old country members of the *Volkavitz* family frequently had married Schwartz *mishpoohah*. It was, Schwartz confided later, a "closer fit."

Out of the marriage between Rachael Schwartz and Adam Wolf came five children. Then in 1898 at the youthful age of twenty-eight Rachael fell off a chair while doing housework. She was mortally injured as a result. The devastated Wolf was cast adrift. He had little option but to distribute his children, ages six years to six months, with *mishpoohah*. Two children were sent to live with Uncle Emmanuel and his wife Hannah, at this time resident in New Jersey. The other three moved across the street to live with their *Tanta* Rose and her family.

Severely strained by the plight of his children, distracted in his efforts to conduct a viable junk business, and distressed by the lack of a companion, Wolf eagerly sought a mate. While visiting cousins in New York, the widower was introduced to twenty year-old Regina Schindler. She was a recent immigrant. He was struck dumb. Schindler captivated him from the first moment.

In a letter to Adolph and Rose, Wolf poured out his feelings. He romantically described "her surpassing glamour and allure." Adolph knew the lonely widower was smitten. Wolf quickly arranged a *shidech*, a betrothal to Regina. They were married in the house of a mutual friend and returned to Pottstown. The year was 1899.

Before their arrival in Pottstown, Wolf had neglected to inform his young bride about one noteworthy issue. The widower never mentioned to her his five young children! An outraged woman would have been a not unexpected result. If Regina was angry with her new husband, and under the circumstances she undoubtedly was, the newlywed did not display any rancor publicly. Regina accepted her stepchildren without issue or repercussion.

Wolf collected his children from their respective foster homes. With the assistance of the Pottstown *mishpoohah*, Regina took on the burden of rearing the motherless children. Adam and Regina Wolf went on to have eight children of their own. All thirteen were raised as one family under one roof. Over time the five children born to Rachael lost all memory of their birth mother. They were never told nor reminded of their maternal parentage, the eldest having repressed all recollection. Evidence of Rachael was erased from the household.

Amazingly, all the cousins, aunts and uncles with whom the Wolf children grew up never mentioned Rachael. All knew. How could they not? Rachael had been a sister and aunt. Yet the entire *mishpoohah* successfully preserved the truth from the Wolf children, or at least never brought the subject up.

After almost 40 years of marriage to Wolf, Regina died in 1938. After the funeral, the family was lined up to enter the cemetery for the internment. Wolf's children, as he, were *cohanim*, descendants of the high priests of ancient times. According to Jewish law, *cohanim* are prohibited from entering a cemetery or having contact with a corpse, except for an immediate family member. At the cemetery gate the children now adults with children of their own lined up by age to enter with their families. As the sad parade was about to enter the cemetery, Adam Wolf halted the procession. He pointed to his five oldest children.

"You and you and you," he instructed, "must remain outside." There was some consternation and discussion back and forth. Only then did the Wolf offspring learn that they came from different maternal parentage.

Many of Pottstown's early Jewish community, including Rose Markowitz, Mendel and Emmanuel Schwartz, and the late Rachael Wolf, were children, grandchildren or cousins of Chaim Schwartz and Rivka Benowitz Schwartz. Chaim and Rivka were the patriarch and matriarch of the Schwartz clan. For a decade, the two witnessed the departure from Galicia of almost every one of their many children. "It broke my heart each time one of my children or sons-in-law set out for America," Chaim later admitted in a rare moment of personal reflection. Yet, in contrast to how ecstatic his own children had felt when the time came for their own emigration from Austria-Hungary, the old man did not experience any personal unburdening or emancipation. His trepidation at leaving his home was agonizingly deep.

Both Chaim and Rivka were born in 1835 in the village of Revicse in the Austrian-Hungarian province of Zemplen, located between the towns of Nagymihaly and Ungvahr. In 1848 when the two were just thirteen years old, the provincial ruler issued a harsh edict. Henceforth, it said, marriages among his Jewish subjects are prohibited. The edict would take effect once provincial messengers had reached all the communities in the province, expected to take no more than a few weeks. Under Jewish law, Chaim and Rivka had just attained the age of adulthood. Their parents swiftly arranged a marriage under rabbinical auspices before the edict could be enforced. The two did not begin to live together as husband and wife until they each reached the age of eighteen.

During her rugged and laborious life in Revicse, Rivka gave birth to eight children. All were girls. This deeply distressed the young couple. The girls who survived infancy were loved, of course. But each represented a potential future liability for Schwartz. Dowry and wedding costs would be most burdensome on the poor family. Once married, none could perpetuate the family name. "Who would inherit the cottage and field?" asked Chaim. And most important to the ultra orthodox Schwartz, no female could say *kaddish* for him after his death.

"Such a string of bad luck!" Chaim confided to his wife. "We will never be able to marry off so many girls!"

There was only one course of action. The perplexed Chaim and Rivka went to their village *rebbe*, the rabbi, for guidance. A weeping Chaim implored the rabbi for help. "*Vai is mir*! What can I do?" he asked. "I am *gebentsht mit kinder*, blessed with children, but all are *bas-yekhide*, girl daughters. I need sons!" Rivka looked on in trepidation. Her lips were tight, her eyes moist. Would the *rebbe* blame her for the frustrating series of female births, she wondered. Had she committed some sin or been *shlecht*, bad in the eyes of God?

The *rebbe* listened carefully to Chaim's entreaty. He paused to reflect on the issue. He did not need elaboration. All children were a blessing from God. However, male children, *bene-yokhid*, were vital to preserve the family name and take care of parents in their old age. He noticed Rivka's anxiety and Chaim's apprehension.

The solution came to him. He fingered his beard and leaned back in his chair. He glanced briefly at the perplexed husband but then glued his eyes to the wife. The *rebbe* weighed his words carefully. "I know that both of you are righteous in the eyes of the Lord. He has seen fit to provide you with only girls; that is true. You, Rivka, are a terrific housekeeper, a *baleboosteh*, and a comfort to Chaim. There is no blame that rests on your shoulders."

The *rebbe* paused before continuing.

"I will write a special prayer of these holy words on a slip of paper. This very day place the paper in the eves above your bed." He wrote the prayer on a paper that had been resting inside a prayer book. "God willing," the *rebbe* said, "the Holy One, *baruch ha shem*, will bless your abode with a son."

"*Gai gezunterhait*," the *rebbe* called out to Chaim as the latter rushed out the door. Rivka was slower and more deliberate as she rose to leave. She glanced back at the *rebbe*.

"Go in good health, daughter," the *rebbe* said softly. "*Tateniu-foter*, God our father, will care for you in your hour of distress."

As instructed by the *rebbe*, Chaim folded the small slip of paper containing the special Hebrew prayer asking God for a male child. He placed the folded prayer above the bed. Nine months later the couple's first son, Emmanuel, was born. The paper with the special prayer must have remained in place on the rafter, intentionally or forgotten. One year later, a second son was born.

Nine Schwartz children, three boys and six girls, reached adulthood. All the daughters were married off. They moved into their own cottages, tilled on small plots of Carpathian soil. Their husbands entered various trades. Years later, the youngest of the children, Samuel, married his niece, the daughter of his older brother Emmanuel. Some of the siblings remained in Revicse; others left the village to live in nearby *shtetls*. After her marriage to Adolph Markowitz, Rose moved to Rebnitza, a few leagues away.

The exodus of Galician Jews to America commenced slowly, like the trickle of rain before a cloudburst. One by one then in multitudes during the 1880s and 1890s, long anchor chains of immigrants stretched across the Atlantic Ocean. By the thousands they emigrated westward. One link pulled the next and the next. Chaim and Rivka's children were a part of this mass migration. Eventually, the entire Schwartz clan, every sibling, departed Galicia. The last immigrant was Mindele, or Mollie, who as a widow arrived in America in 1906 with her five youngest children.

As each member of the Schwartz clan arrived in America, they linked up with *mishpoohah* already established in Pottstown. Most remained a short time in the small industrial community before moving to more promising, exciting destinations.

Chaim and Rivka Schwartz reached America in 1892. Already middle-aged by the time they reached America, Chaim and Rivka found adjustment to their new environment difficult. Chaim especially grew homesick for the Carpathian hills. To start over in a new culture, confront an utterly foreign and unfathomable language, and even adjust to an American home, frustrated the usually self-reliant Chaim. Religious life in the new world seemed artificial and trite. He brooded and fell into a trance of self-pity.

"I am unhappy with this *goldena medina*," he confided in his wife. "I do not feel close to God anymore. My mind drifts from the Talmud. I cannot breathe this air without coughing. Everything is so fast, so much talk of *gesheft* and *gelt*, business and money. It's a land for young people, not *alter kockers* like us."

With no skills that could be readily transplanted to this strange land, no yearning to labor the rest of his life in a factory, and no desire to remain dependent on his children and sons-in-law, Chaim questioned why the couple had come to America. He became despondent. After just sixteen months in Pottstown, the frustrated and bewildered patriarch announced an astonishing decision.

"Your mother and I are going home to Galicia," he told his startled family. The pronouncement was made jointly, but the decision was clearly his. While Chaim spoke, Rivka sat behind her husband. She held her expressionless gaze on the back of his head. The statement caused consternation among the children.

Yet, despite entreaties from the entire *mishpoohah* that to return to Austria-Hungary was *meshugeneh*, absolutely crazy, Chaim's remained unswerving in his decision. "There is no future there," Adolph told his father-in-law. The young Adam Wolf, also a son-in-law, also stepped in at the urging of his wife Rachael.

Emmanuel begged his father to reconsider. But Chaim was nothing if not unswerving. The words of warning from his family were heard but not heeded.

Crazy or not, Chaim and Rivka Schwartz took a boat back to Europe. The ship was almost bereft of passengers. Few people returned to the Old World from America. Those traveling to Europe were overwhelmingly husbands and single young men. The former intended to bring their families quickly back to America. The later wanted brides from their own communities; then they would again return to *die goldene medina*. Less than a month after departing New York harbor, Chaim and his wife reached the border of Austria-Hungary.

The couple settled with a niece and her husband in the village of Tibowa, only a few miles distant from their original humble cottage. With funds provided to him by his family, Chaim purchased a cow, chickens, and a small plot of land. He spent his days studying Talmud, lost in his own philosophical world and only tenuously connected to the everyday reality of their mutual loneliness.

Rivka, on the other hand, missed her children and future grandchildren terribly. To relieve her anguish she could not escape into the meta-physical. When not doing chores or tending the garden, she succumbed to depression. She spent hours sitting and staring at a family photo taken in Pottstown. Rivka had opposed the decision to return to Europe. Missing from their lives was *mishpoohah*. Before departing Pottstown, she told her husband in private she wanted to remain in America with her children and grandchildren. But Chaim was too arrogant and stubborn to retreat from his narrow-minded obsession with and nostalgia for the old country. He told her the decision was final.

With children and increasing hoards of grandchildren residing an ocean away, Rivka knew even before boarding the ship for

Europe they were making a colossal mistake. The return to village life rapidly aged the couple, especially the heartbroken Rivka. She died in 1894, just one year after their resettlement in the Carpathian foothills.

The patriarch was devastated. The sensible decision, certainly, would be for the widower to return to America. But although sinless and righteous in many ways, Chaim suffered from one sin he could not overcome, an outsized pride. He could not admit he had erred in his foolish decision. Nor could he accept that he had caused his dear wife to decline so rapidly. Fourteen long years later, Chaim passed away. Until the last moment on earth allowed to him by God, he suffered from the plague of regret that left a deep festering wound in his soul.

* * *

In the years following the family's arrival, Yiddish was the exclusive language of the Markowitz household. Political discussions, a review of the activities of the day, the latest jokes, gossip from neighbors, family disagreements, conciliatory words, even settlement of vendors' bills all were conducted in colorful Yiddish with a few expressions of English slang or vulgarity thrown in for good measure. Adolph, Rose, Lena, and their *mishpoohah* may have been physically in America. But spiritually and linguistically, the family still resided in their Galician *shtetl*.

Adolph's own language was colorful. Whenever Adolph saw an acquaintance, no matter how far away, he barked in his bellowing voice, "*Hi putz, vee gayts?*" Loosely translated: "Hello prick, how ya doin'?" Anger from Adolph usually generated a "*Kush in toches arein*, Kiss my ass!" A *shlub* was a jerk, the *little pisher*, a nobody. Referring to a third person with no ambition he might say "*Er drayt sich arum vie a fortz in Russell.*" He wanders around like a fart in a barrel. In a measure of disbelief, Adolph exclaimed in

Yiddish, "And if my grandmother had balls, she would be my grandfather!"

Adolph was not the only Markowitz family member to employ vibrant Yiddish expressions. In playful Yiddish retorts, Lena chided her grandchildren "Pimples should grow from your tongue" or "Onions should grow from your bellybutton!" Grandmother Lena was descended from a long line of butchers. She complained bitterly of the *gedempte flaysh*, mystery meat, which often passed for a prime cut of beef obtained at dear price from the *sochet* whom she invariably mistrusted. Rose frequently told her children "*Azoy vert dos kichel tzekrochen.*" That is how the cookie crumbles!

Because of their exposure to English speaking peers, the Markowitz children swiftly introduced English into daily family dialogue. As a result, the older children blended English and Yiddish. The children conversed equally smoothly in either language, too smoothly perhaps since sentences and even word fragments became hopelessly mixed together. "*Vos zogt ir?*" their mother and grandmother constantly asked. "What are you saying?"

Adolph recognized the predicament that language injected into the Markowitz home. Should he insist the children speak Yiddish inside the home and English outside? They obviously would master English. Would they loose Yiddish if they did not speak it? He shared his concerns with *lantzmen*. What ultimately was his family's identity?

After intense soul searching, Adolph determined the children had to master the tongue of their future, not the speech of their parent's past. "From now on, you will speak English in the house," he instructed them. "After all, you are Americans; you were born here."

Neither Lena nor Rose liked his decision. They feared learning even simple English would be worse, and certainly more painful, than anything else they confronted in America. But they appreciated that it was a decision made in the best interest of the family.

Relieved of the obligation of speaking Yiddish at home, the children quickly absorbed English. Soon they used it almost exclusively—at least when their father was around. They understood Yiddish anyway through constant interaction with *mishpoohah*. Adolph himself needed to learn more English in order to conduct business. The children taught him. Still, communication occasionally hit a roadblock. Adolph consented that the children could use Yiddish when at a loss for the correct English word or phrase

Rose never overcame her reticence to move away from the Yiddish of her heritage. For her, the use of English by her children was torture. She understood simple conversation. She quickly learned the English names of objects and places. School, shop, stove, stable—these were familiar everyday words. However, many entire discussions entirely escaped her comprehension. Only slowly and with trepidation, she began using a few words in English taught to her by the older children.

In the tough times between his arrival in America and the adolescence of his older children, Adolph earnestly strived to learn the language of his new country. Initially, he did not make much progress. Pottstown did not offer language classes for immigrants. Even if it had, who had the time, or money, to attend such classes? Through force of will and, of course, through the children who so easily absorbed English in school and on the streets, Adolph forced himself, word by word, sentence by sentence, to master English. Eventually, he spoke Yiddish only to his peers, his mother, and Rose. Surprisingly, Adolph eliminated any foreign accent one would expect from an Eastern European immigrant.

To improve his English reading skills, Adolph determined to read whatever he could get. However, as with everything in the Markowitz household, cost was the critical determinant.

One autumn afternoon a local alderman visited the neighborhood to solicit votes for an upcoming election. The man was sharply dressed with a broad, radiant smile, pink cheeks, and a high collar that seemed to pinch his Adam's apple. The politician addressed Adolph as if the immigrant peddler was his most important constituent. That a man of such exalted rank as alderman would solicit votes door to door stuck Adolph as amazing. Yet here the man was, standing on the front stoop, and speaking to Adolph as if the two were the best of friends. After a few general courteous words, Adolph told the alderman of his eagerness to improve his English. Grabbing Adolph's shoulder with his left hand and clasping his wrist with his right, the alderman beamed.

"Well, my good man, it is the right of any constituent to request from their Congressional representative free copies of the U.S. laws passed for that year. I can pass the request for you if you like." Adolph jumped at the offer. He also decided to vote for the man in the next election.

As a result of the alderman's appearance, each spring for almost four decades Adolph received a thick book of the nation's new laws. He read these books cover to cover while sitting for hours in his rocking chair, stroking his van dyke beard, and cradling a second-hand dictionary underneath the book. He never seemed to tire. Adolph slowly mouthed and enunciated by syllable the more difficult words. "SO-LI-CI-TOR, solicitor." He repeated the word out loud until it was thoroughly chiseled into his head.

Eventually, after years of reading the nation's laws, the immigrant peddler became quite a legal expert. "A judge can be a layman," Adolph told his family one evening at the dinner table, "and can still perform his job. All he needs is common sense." *Lantzmen* occasionally called upon him for advice, although Adolph himself in later years retained his nephew Bennie Wolf as his attorney.

Rose, on the other hand, demonstrated little capacity to master English. She never received formal schooling, possessed only the most rudimentary Hebrew necessary for prayers, and learned neither to read nor write Yiddish. With chores, her husband's requirements, and the demands of the children, how could this housebound homemaker set aside the time to study English?

Her Yiddish, however, was adequate to speak with the red-bearded German dairy farmer who daily brought a large container of milk to the house. Five or six quarts, costing 5 or 6 cents a quart, were required each morning to feed her growing brood. From the German-speaking Mennonite fresh produce farmer, Rose bought *eppil*, apples, *kukarits*, corn, and other vegetables right off the wagon. Meat, of course, came from the Yiddish-speaking Jewish butcher; dry goods and food were purchased at a nearby Jewish-run grocery store. Few neighbors spoke Yiddish but many understood German. Rose made herself intelligible with a mixture of English nouns and Yiddish verbs.

Rose need not worry about her lack of English when the *Mazel Choper*, the luck grabber, came to town on his annual visit from Philadelphia. He had a name, of course, but to the Markowitz family, his nickname stuck like glue. From his well-traveled panel wagon with its pair of snorting bay horses, the *Mazel Choper* brought various house wares—pots and pans, kosher soap, religious items, Shabbat candles—to peddle to the Jews of Pottstown. Rose spent two or three hours culling through the *Mazel Choper*'s collection, interrogating him about each article, appealing to his honor to provide a fair price, and regurgitating her own *tsores*, her woes, since his last visit. The *Mazel Choper* was a good listener. Rose exercised her own highly honed negotiating skill, a trait both inherited and practiced. The *Mazel Choper* smiled and nodded in acknowledgement of her offer. If a counter-offer was necessary, the *Mazel Choper* readily threw in another item, as a *geschank*, a small present.

If Adolph was home, he and the *Mazel Choper* enthusiastically shared gossip of their respective Jewish communities. The two were contemporaries, ambitious men who also possessed exceptional interest in local and national affairs. Adolph was eager to gain insight into rich Jewish families of the "big city" and its synagogues with hundreds of members. The *Mazel Choper* welcomed information about his Pottstown customers. If his visit was late in the day, Adolph offered a shot of *shnapps* or, if a bottle was available, whiskey. The men often talked late into the night.

The *Mazel Choper* was a particular delight for the Markowitz children. The youngsters shouted with glee when the *Mazel Choper* came to the house. "What do you have for us?" they asked. With a twinkle in his eyes, the *Mazel Choper* laughed and told the children to line up. One by one each would reach, with great anticipation, deep down into his jacket pockets to snatch good luck charms. Thus, the source of his nickname!

In the evening after chores were completed and care of the children satisfied, Rose listened avidly as her husband sat in his rocking chair and read aloud to the entire family from the daily Yiddish newspaper the *Tageblatt* which arrived in Pottstown each afternoon. She was particularly interested in the *roman*, the serialized novel that uniquely combined conflict and love. For the busy housewife, the romance fiction provided an escape from the drudgery of raising a family and keeping a home.

Grandmother Lena also listened to her son's readings. Unlike her daughter-in-law, Lena was not enthralled by lovelorn stories of nouveau rich city Jews. Instead, she was captivated with the matchmaker marriage columns, births and deaths, although only a few family names were recognizable to her. Adolph also related the important issues to Jews of that time such as the Dreyfus Affair in France and the emergence of Theodore Herzl and the nascent Zionist movement. When he did speak of these events, everyone, even the children, became more pensive, more attentive.

Adolph was a stickler for education and the respect Adolph and Rose held for America's public school system was immeasurable. That their children could attend the same school and get the same education as non-Jewish children, they believed, was "the true gift of the *die goldene medina*, Golden America!" When praising the American system, Adolph constantly expressed his awe. "No matter how many children a man has," he exclaimed, "the cost of educating them is only the tax on his property!"

Yet, in other ways, Adolph remained steadfastly loyal to certain aspects of the culture of Austria-Hungary. "People in America are too violent," he argued. "They are too willing to start a fight; too eager to use fists." Certainly, they were not at all like the meek, respectful populace of his native Galicia. In addition, America's higher education system, he felt, was inferior to that of Europe. To prove his point, Adolph frequently cited Dr. Elmer Porter, considered Pottstown's best medical doctor. "Porter is a *real* doctor because he attended medical school in England," he repeated whenever the subject of higher education came up in conversation. For a non-Jewish doctor to earn Adolph's supreme compliment was high praise indeed!

Years later, a *lantzman* asked Adolph why his contemporary and peddler rival Mayer Pollock became a wealthy man in the same business as his. Adolph derisively sneered, then became serious. "Mayer kept his sons in the business and I sent mine to college." He need not add that *his* sons had attended college *in America.*

With his intense interest in the law burnished by constant reading of the law books sent from Washington, Adolph overtly hoped that one or perhaps two of his sons would become the lawyer he could never be. The old man would be disappointed. Two sons did begin law study at Bucknell University. Neither, however, completed the program. The true Markowitz lawyer was Adolph himself.

In later years, Adolph grumbled sardonically about the ironic twist of fate. "All I wanted was a son who could debate me on the merits of law, who could argue pro or con the laws I read each evening." He was an immigrant peddler who had been penniless when he reached America. Yet, he had sent three sons to college. The other two boys had not been college material. If they had been, perhaps one of them might have become a lawyer.

With a heavy tinge of Yiddish sarcasm, he poked fun at his sons. Over shots of whiskey with Adam Wolf or his brother-in-law Emmanuel, Adolph put his finger on what really bothered him. "*This* son became a doctor," he bemoaned, "and *that* son became a rabbi. Yet neither of them know anything!"

Four

Der Shul

When the first Eastern European Jews reached Pottstown, the establishment of a *shul*, a synagogue, was their foremost priority. Particularly given the town's exceedingly foreign and intensely non-Jewish surroundings, the first immigrants needed their religion as an anchor in a turbulent sea of uncertainty and anxiety. For the newcomers, preserving Jewish identity in this strange and wholly Christian land was paramount. To keep the tiller straight and the ship on course, the greenhorns gripped firmly to their well established, deeply embedded religious traditions so different from those of the German Jews who earlier had reached America. The impetus to start a synagogue differentiated the newcomers from the handful of Pottstown's German Jewish families. During their own tenure in the small Pennsylvania town the German Jews had not created any lasting Jewish institutions.

Pottstown's first Jews, three "Deitch" families, arrived in 1859 just prior to the Civil War. Clusters of German-speaking farmers and tradesmen resided throughout the southeastern Pennsylvania piedmont. Cultural and linguistic ties with other Germans attracted the German Jews. After all, both Jews and non-Jews shared similar reasons for fleeing Germany in the first place. Over a quarter century, German Jewish families drifted unnoticed into Pottstown. Some settled and established roots, others remained but a short duration then departed for settlements further west in the American interior.

The town's few German Jews were content to remain invisible. As just one diminutive religious sect they sought to live inconspicuously among Christian neighbors within the multiethnic mix of the expanding industrial town. The family heads were small store merchants, tradesmen and laborers in the new factories. They went about their business without flourish and made only the smallest impact on the community writ large. The German Jews recognized their marginal significance to society. They preferred not to bring attention to themselves. Given their small numbers, they also perceived the establishment of a synagogue as impractical.

By the 1880s Hungarian Jews began to arrive in Pottstown. Initially, the town's already established Deitch Jews such as the Shmulovitz and Zimmerman families looked down on the Yiddish-speaking newcomers. The *shtetl* Jews with their old-fashioned traditions and narrow-minded orthodoxy were exactly the type of co-religionists from whom the Germans distanced back in Europe. For a few years, the two small groups warily maintained a tolerant but cautious relationship. The two sides were courteous for sure, helpful and sharing when asked. But they remained far from united in outlook and lacked any sense of loyalty or commitment to the other.

From the outset, the *shtetl* newcomers confronted a considerable challenge to life in *goyish* Pottstown. In their European hamlets, formal institutions such as synagogue congregations were unnecessary. The community's social fabric, already so full of Jewish ritual and life, was all encompassing. A *rebbe* and a small building that doubled as a *shul* and *talmud torah* for the children were sufficient. Impressive synagogues were for wealthy city Jews. Differentiating a Jew from a Hungarian Catholic, an Orthodox Ruthenian, or a Slovak was as easy as differentiating a horse from a cow. Jews lived on one side of the hamlet, non-Jews on the other. Among the groups little communication and marginal interaction existed.

However, in small town America, the non-Jewish atmosphere was suffocating. Absolute physical separation could not exist between Jews and non-Jews. Most small communities such as Pottstown contained no "Jewish" neighborhood. No *rebbe* served as a community's spiritual guide. America was a Christian land. Pottstown was a Christian town. Few of Pottstown's inhabitants had ever met a Jew.

For Pottstown's microscopic Eastern European Jewish population, their small numbers begat an urgent issue. Religious obligation required a *minyan* of ten men in order to conduct religious services. Pottstown's Jews lacked the requisite quorum to meet this requirement. Especially, the High Holidays of Rosh Hashanah and Yom Kippur called for proper religious practice. To make a *minyan* for the duration of the ten-day holiday period, Pottstown's seven *shtetl* Jews hired three Jewish men from Philadelphia to travel to Pottstown.

By the late 1880s, animosity between the *Deitch* Jews and *shtetl* newcomers from Hungary abated. German fears that the flood of newcomers would escalate anti-Jewish prejudice proved unfounded. And the recent arrivals recognized that despite their lack of ritual and religious orthodoxy, at heart the Germans were still Jews. The two sides agreed to establish a *chevra*, a burial society. They named it *"Chevra Chesed shel Emes."* In life self-sufficiency was fine. In death however, Jews had to band together! The Chevra purchased a narrow acre of land west of town. Half the plots were reserved for the German Jews, half for the Hungarians.

With most ill will overcome, Pottstown's three German and seven Hungarian families decided to create another permanent Jewish institution, a *shul*. On March 11, 1889, the group received from the Montgomery County Court of Common Pleas a charter for Congregation *"Hahawas Achem"* (Love of Brethren).

Pottstown's Jewish population soon quadrupled. By 1892 about forty Jewish families resided in Pottstown. The majority was from the same obscure corner of Emperor Franz Joseph's Hungarian domains as the Schwartz-Markowitz clan. The Hungarians were a close-knit group. They were *lantzmen* for the most part whose families, including the Markowitzs, had known each other for generations in the Galician *shtetls*. Family ties were deeply intertwined.

Since the *shtetl* Jews desired to maintain a strong Jewish identity and follow strict religious observance, a clash with the outnumbered, more secularized German Jews was inevitable. Among other differences, the German and Hungarian Jews could not agree on religious issues. How could there be peace when the Germans bought their meat from a *traif*, non-kosher butcher shop and rode the train to Philadelphia during the High Holidays?

In early 1892 the Hungarians decided to disband the young *Hahawas Achim* Congregation. A new congregation that did not include the Germans was formed. The name chosen was *"Chesed Shel Emes"* taken from the name of the *chevra*. Not knowing the actual English meaning of the Hebrew expression, the immigrants used its literal English translation, Congregation "Mercy and Truth." A year later, the young congregation erected a *shul* on Hale Street near Pottstown's highest point, on Chicken Hill. To avoid any association with the Germans, a second cemetery was purchased for 50 dollars. It was situated on low, marshy ground. At 75 dollars, a more attractive lot across Hanover Street, later the site of a small church was deemed too expensive. Over the next century Pottstown's Jewish community would expend much wealth and effort to fix the poor drainage associated with the "less expensive" property.

* * *

While the view from the summit of Chicken Hill was magnificent, the newly built *Chesed shel Emes* synagogue was sternly modest and strictly utilitarian. Small windows just above eye level lined the sides of the two-story, barn-shaped structure. No spire or steeple topped the red brick edifice, these being architectural attributes of Christian churches. The plastered interior walls held no decorations. A few plaques memorializing deceased family members already were bolted on one side of the entry.

A six-branch menorah topped with a Star of David was placed next to the bare wood torah ark that stood prominently against the *shul's mizrach vant* or eastern wall, towards Jerusalem. After *minyan* and Shabbat services, member *tallesim*, the fabric or silk prayer shawls with *tzitzis* dangling from the ends, were also placed inside the ark which the *shamus*, the *shul's* caretaker, padlocked. Of the religious objects in the *shul*, these *tallesim* and the torah were the most irreplaceable. The *pushkeh* box for collecting *tzedakeh* money on weekdays also was secured there. For use on "special" occasions, i.e. whenever the men got together, a couple bottles of *shnapps* or Shabbat wine were hidden in the ark's back corner.

One modest torah, covered with an embroidered blue velvet mantle and silver breastplate rested peacefully inside the ark. A *yad* or torah pointer hung on from one of the torah rollers. The torah had been brought from Europe by one of the Hungarian immigrants whose family was descended from a long line of torah scribes. Although the scroll was ancient, the rollers and handles were new.

The small torah almost brought tragedy to Pottstown's small Jewish community. One morning as the men watched the *sefer torah*, the holy scrolls, being placed within the ark for the first time, one of the two rollers broke and part of the scroll fell to the floor. A volcanic cry erupted. "Terrible, terrible, *shandeh un a charpeh,* the shame and disgrace!" The men shouted instructions at each other. "*Finster yor,* FINSTER YOR," a horrible year, yelled one. The scroll was swiftly rerolled, but the damage was done. Witnesses would have to fast for the Talmud-mandated forty days as *tikun*, atonement to lessen their accountability for the failure to care for the torah.

Then the men noticed that the wooden rollers and handles were riddled with wormholes. During the long, damp voyage from Europe, the wood had been infested. Perhaps carelessness was not the cause of the calamity. Someone suggested sending an overnight letter to a respected rabbi in Philadelphia. "Let's get learned advice from a real *rev*!" The group rushed down to Pottstown's post office to post a letter before the afternoon mail train departed for Philadelphia.

Within two days a letter in Yiddish arrived from the big city rabbi. It sought to reassure the men. "Don't worry. You do not have to fast," the rabbi wrote. He understood this was the first time since leaving Europe the tenderly cared for torah had been unwrapped from its protective quilt. The infection of wormwood, he explained, was a final curse from pogrom—ridden Europe, a devilish attempt to destroy the lives of the recent arrivals in their new homeland. "It is not your fault," the rabbi reassured the immigrants. "Replace the rotten *shtetl* rollers with good American wood. The torah will be a blessing for you and your children!"

An elevated *bimah* for reading the torah and for the *hazzan*, the cantor, to conduct prayers stood in the center of the sanctuary floor. Well-worn, heavily scratched wooden benches were obtained from a local church that had procured new seating. The benches faced forward or towards the *bimah*. Along the rear wall of the *shul*, wooden cubbyholes held member *Siddurim*—prayer books, *tefillim*—phylacteries, and other ritual objects required for a proper service.

Behind the rear of the building above the main entrance, wooden stairs ascended the *shul*'s outside wall to a small landing. A door led to the women's balcony. Pottstown's Jews could not even imagine non-segregation of men and women at *shul*. Women sat in the balcony, men below. The balcony held three rows of the worn benches stretched across the rear quarter of the *shul*.

Jewish life centered in the *shul*. Congregants attended Shabbat and holiday services dressed in their best clothing. Men usually were attired in second hand frock suits—who could afford a new suit?—adorned with vests, stiff collars, and black Windsor or bow ties. Headgear, of course, was obligatory. Some congregants wore older style pancake-brimmed Pennsylvania Dutch hats, the type used by most of the farmers in Chester and Berks Counties. Other worshippers wore wool felt bowlers or high black derby hats with a matching ribbon around the base of the crown. Most married men had beards. Some like Adolph kept beards well trimmed in the style of the times. Others let their beards grow bushy as they had back in Galicia. Work clothes within the *shul* confines were absolutely *verboten*. The men placed muddy boots or shoes just inside the door. Many prayed in slippers left in the *shul* or in stocking feet.

Rhythmically like metronomes, the pious men *daven*ed. Forward and back, forward and back, the worshippers devoutly followed the liturgy. Some bent their torsos at the waist or tilted their full body precariously to one side. Some wailed aloud while others murmured in concentration as they followed the prayers in their *siddurim*, their prayer books. Occasionally, the acting *hazen* called out a page number or the torah portion chapter and verse. But the men needed no assistance or direction. Most knew the prayers by heart. Not a few could cite chapter and verse from the *Tanach*, the Holy Scriptures, so rigorous had been their *chedar* training back in the old country.

During services women were few in attendance. Mothers with young children rarely attended prayers. How could they? Yet children of both sexes, girls below the age of puberty, were permitted below in the sanctuary. They wandered around the praying men. Except for the most persnickety worshippers, the men smiled back pleasantly at the little ones. Upstairs in the balcony, women attended services in their best clothing. Usually, they wore work or camp dresses or broad skirts typical of their conservative culture. Felt or straw bonnets were the most common headgear, along with shawls in cooler weather. In winter the balcony was icebox cold. Warmth from the synagogue's lone potbelly stove below rarely radiated enough heat to reach it. During the more frigid times, the women rarely removed coats and gloves. In summer, the balcony was often furnace hot. Breezes entering the ground floor windows usually failed to reach very far upwards.

A female minority sufficiently versed in Hebrew *daven*ed along with the men. However, the majority of women possessed little more than a rudimentary knowledge of the Hebrew prayers. Possessing at best only a perfunctory familiarity with the liturgy, most just listened. In contrast to the male-only ground floor, the women's balcony was thus detached from the world of prayer. Instead, it served a different function. Many of the housewives had little opportunity to socialize outside the home. The balcony was their one opportunity to socialize, compare notes on childrearing, or learn the latest gossip. And what an opportunity to catch up with local news and gossip! While the men *daven*ed, the women *kibbitz*ed. When the balcony buzz became too distracting for the more finicky of the men below, a sharp "*shtimm zich*, shut up," or the occasional Hebrew "*sheket!*" shot upwards. But somberness from the castigated balcony occupants rarely lasted more than a couple of minutes. It was a losing battle for tranquility, and the men downstairs knew it.

September meant the arrival of the Hebrew month of Tishri and the Jewish High Holidays. During Yom Kippur, the most solemn day of the year, just about every Jewish male in the community and a few out-of-towners squeezed into the *shul*. The balcony too would overflow with every seat occupied. On this day the women made every effort not to disturb the cacophony going on below. A scolding from the *chazzan* or torah *shamus* on THIS day would be a terrible embarrassment. To keep from nodding off during the long fast day, the men passed smelling salts and snuffboxes back and forth. Periodically, the men and women went outside to get some fresh air before returning to prayer.

On this holy day, one might also see the highly venerated and esteemed Alexander Estreicher, a *levi*, the assistants to the priests in ancient times, washing the feet and hands of the much younger Adam Wolf. Wolf was a *cohen*, a descendent of the temple high priests. Each Yom Kippur he made his *deichen* or priestly blessing over the congregation. The sight of Estreicher washing Wolf's feet never failed to awe worshippers. Estreicher was the community's patriarch. Not only was he first to arrive in Pottstown. In Galicia he had been the *melamed*, the religious schoolteacher in the *chedar* for many in the community, including his *lantzman* Adolph Markowitz.

In these early years, the congregation was neither sufficiently large nor wealthy to employ a full time rabbi, *chazzan*, or religious teacher for the growing number of children. Until the arrival of Rabbi Solomon Bless in 1917, the *shochet*, the ritual slaughterer, served the community as cantor and torah reader during Shabbat and holidays. He also was the *melamed*, providing Hebrew instruction to the young boys, the authority on most ritual matters and procedures, and, most critically, the slaughterer of cattle and fowl. Tenure was generally for no more than two years. During this time grousing from the same certain congregants about his performance inevitably escalated. Compensation for teaching was negotiated between the *shochet* and parents who with few financial resources to put forward might offer an "in-kind" payment. In a Jewish community as small as Pottstown's, income from these services was invariably meager. If the *shochet* had a family, to make ends meet he supplemented his income with other occupations such as selling whiskey, wine, or coal.

Adolph never considered any of these *shochetim* qualified to teach HIS children *Ivreh*, Hebrew. To remedy the situation, he undertook to teach them himself, even the girls. Naturally, the boys were prepared for their Bar Mitzvahs which took place on a Shabbat soon after their thirteenth birthdays. The two girls were taught to *daven* properly but in a simple fashion compared to the boys. Bat Mitzvahs for girls! It was a preposterous notion. The female counterpart ceremony to the Bar Mitzvah had not yet come into fashion, even in America's new Reform Congregations.

Adolph's mother Lena Bleich held a very negative attitude towards the local *shochetim*. Descended from a long line of esteemed butchers, she knew the correct cuts of meat! The kosher butchers of Pottstown, Lena felt, conducted their businesses improperly and with little understanding of what they were doing. She absolutely refused to eat any meat prepared by

Emmanuel Schwartz, the brother of her daughter-in-law. How could she? In her view Schwartz was selling *traif* products. Not only were his cuts of meat *traif*, he delivered his allegedly kosher food in the same meat wagon as non-kosher products for his non-Jewish customers! From her arrival in Pottstown until her death 25 years later, Lena foreswore meat and ate a strictly vegetarian diet.

The *shul* served also as meetinghouse for the *chevra*. In addition to its role as a burial society, the *chevra* also functioned as a "men's club" and management for the nascent congregation. It met on a biweekly basis. Since every *chevra* meeting was considered a "special" occasion, a bottle or two of *shnapps* almost always made an appearance.

Chevra gatherings were loud, boisterous affairs. They were made more so by the liquor and the colorful Yiddish which, on many occasions, referred to certain body parts or unnatural acts. Synagogue finances frequently generated caustic debate, especially when issues of synagogue debt or membership arrears were tabled. The first year's accounting showed congregation income of $7.43 but expenses of $12.11. Ritual issues also sparked acerbic exchanges. In the absence of a rabbi, everyone was a religious authority.

Sometimes the arguments became quite heated. One involved Gill Geltziler and Mayer Pollock. The two started shouting at each other over some obscure and unimportant issue. Harsh words were exchanged. Then a fight broke out. Attempts to quell the feud evidently failed since the two persisted to struggle outside the synagogue and later continued to scrap on High Street. On another occasion, Louis Gussman called Sam (Shia) Fuerman a *ferd* (horse), Yiddish slang for a fool. The *Chevra* presiding officer told Gussman, "You can't call another *Chevra* member a *ferd*. If you do, I'll fine you twenty-five cents!" Gussman walked up to the president, laid a silver dollar down on the table, faced Fuerman and shaking his index finger at him shouted four times, *"de bis a ferd, de bis a ferd, de bis a ferd, de bis a FERD!"*

Behavior during Shabbat and the holidays was more restrained and somber. Since they were *cohanim*, either Adam Wolf or Louis Singer almost always had the privilege during services of being called up to the Torah for the first *aliyah* (honor). Once, years later, when he was saying the blessing over the torah, Wolf made a very noteworthy Hebrew mistake. Adolph's son-in-law turned to his father-in-law.

"Why don't you say something?"

Adolph looked at his son-in-law with surprise. "It's not right to shame a person!"

There may have been another reason why Adolph refused to be critical of Wolf. Wolf always supported Adolph during *chevra* meetings. He often seconded Adolph's motions.

With his strong, powerful voice, Adolph always served as the annual *chevra* auctioneer for selling the "aliyah" honors prior to the High Holidays. It was an important income generator for the congregation. A successful auction meant members would not pay additional dues later in the year.

"FINIF SHILLING FER MOFTIR ICH HUB—ZEEX SHILLING," Adolph called out, seeking the highest bidder. For visitors a shilling was equivalent to a dollar, but congregation members received a 50% discount.

Mayer Pollock, the wealthiest member of the congregation, always bought the opening of the ark for the long Nehilah prayer at the close of Yom Kippur. Opening the ark for the last prayer of Yom Kippur was indeed a great honor. It was worth a noteworthy price, the highest of the auction. Pollock always sat in front at *chevra* meetings. For the Nehilah honor, he never realized he was bidding against false offers. Adolph made sure Pollock always overpaid. Everyone knew it. However, no one ever said a word to Pollock.

Years later Adolph was asked what would have happened if Pollock ever stopped bidding. A wry smile briefly crossed his face.

"I would swear" he replied, "that I thought I had seen somebody in back raise a hand but was mistaken."

Essential for Jewish life in the community was the synagogue's *mikveh* or ritual bath. Women used the *mikveh* prior to marriage as well as after each monthly cycle. Some of the more religious men used the *mikveh* prior to Shabbat and Jewish festivals. *Mikveh* water had to be pure. There were few sources of pure water on the heights of Chicken Hill. Unfortunately for the congregation, the woman who owned the farmhouse across the street from the *shul* would not allow the synagogue to obtain water from her well, even for a fee. Not to be so easily defeated, resourceful *shul* members surreptitiously tunneled under the street and tapped into her well. Another time, a few kids put a bullfrog in the *mikveh*. Expecting a shout or cry from an adult or two, the children reacted with disappointment not to hear any reaction. Possibly the frog escaped.

By the early 1920s, Pottstown's Jewish community severely outgrew the Chicken Hill *shul*. A much larger structure was required. The congregation procured a lot at High and Warren Streets, a prime location. It sought to raise funds to erect a new synagogue. The task of leading the fundraising effort was assigned to a finance committee consisting of three men: Adolph Printz, Sam Lipkin, and Ben Berger. From the beginning, Adolph Markowitz had his suspicions. The first two, he felt, were men of questionable character, and Berger, the treasurer, could be easily manipulated. Congregants were asked to solicit funds from business people with whom they dealt. One response from Julius Rosenwald, President of Sears, Roebuck, came with the advice "Do not spend more for a building than you have."

At the end of the drive, Adolph asked to see the books before he handed in his building pledge. He was told the books were lost. Not surprisingly, Adolph refused to pay his pledge. "If you don't pay your pledge you'll be dropped from the congregation membership rolls," Printz warned. Of course, if anyone ordered Adolph to do anything, the opposite outcome was a sure bet. Not a dime was handed over. Adolph, a founder of the *Chesed Shel Emes* congregation, was dropped from the roles.

The spat with *shul* leadership followed Adolph to his grave. At the time of Adolph's death in 1940, Joe Prince, Adolph Printz's son, was synagogue president. He solemnly informed the Markowitz sons that burial of their father would not be permitted in the congregation's Hanover Street cemetery until his dues structure was brought up to date. Although it was Adolph's wish to be buried in the smaller Jewish burial site on State Street where affiliation with the *shul* was not necessary for internment, the family wanted Adolph to rest in the *Chesed shel Emes* cemetery next to his wife Rose who predeceased him. So the family paid the back dues. Later, Adolph's sons discovered that they had been hoodwinked. Their father already possessed a recorded deed for a plot in the Hanover Street cemetery. Permission from the synagogue president or anyone else for his burial there had not been necessary.

The new synagogue was built at a cost of $80,000. With its dedication on June 20, 1926, Pottstown's Jewish community finally owned an edifice comparable to any of the major churches in town. And on High Street no less! The impressive temple served not only as a coming of age for the community but demonstrated in a manner that could not be misinterpreted the economic success of the *shtetl* immigrants and their triumphant integration into American society.

Physically, there was no comparison to the small Hale Street *shul*. The exterior walls of the new structure were handsome yellow brick. Ornate Spanish tile capped the roof. Facing Warren Street a wide ramp of twelve steps led to three oversized arched doorways. Two broad towers framed the wide entry. A balcony reminiscent of famous Eastern European opera houses looked west towards Pottstown's commercial center. Inside, significant alterations gave the sanctuary a modern appearance more typical of large, big city Conservative movement congregations. In the main sanctuary the *bimah* and ark were placed on a carpeted stage. Six twenty-foot tall stained glass windows lined each side of the main sanctuary. Classrooms, a social hall, and office space were located on a lower floor.

What happened to the Chicken Hill *shul*? It was sold; later it became a black Masonic Lodge. Ironically, the structure still stands more than 120 years later, while the synagogue at Warren and High Streets, the pride of Pottstown's Jewish community, lasted less than thirty years before it succumbed to the wrecking ball. A branch office of Philadelphia National Bank was built on the site.

Five

Der pedler

The Markowitz family outgrew the Warren Street house and moved to a larger row home on Grant Street. Grandmother Lena inhabited a one-room shanty located on the alley behind the house. It was no fancy brick carriage house! The two windows were ill-fitted in rough, unpainted frames. The roof consisted of old wooden shakes. But Lena insisted on having her own space. Besides, the structure was a Hohenzollern palace compared to lodging in Galicia.

Behind the house inside the enclosed yard was the "shop." There, Adolph stored his more valuable scrap metal such as copper and brass. In an open shed next to the shop he kept less precious items such as rags and paper. Just beyond the shop beside the alley, a small stable contained stalls for two horses or one horse and a wagon. The stable stood at a precarious angle, the result of shoddy construction.

Der pedler

In 1900 four Jewish families, the Markowitz clan, Joe Lerner, Hoena Klein, and the widow Mrs. Labor, resided on Chicken Hill, although Alexander Estreicher on Walnut between Washington and Adams Streets lived fairly close. The rest of the Jewish community still preferred to reside south of High Street.

Whether one horse or pair of horses occupied the stable behind the house indicated the measure of the Markowitz family's wealth and served as a gauge of its economic prospects. When Adolph the "rag and junk peddler" possessed one horse, the Markowitz family considered itself poor albeit financially stable. The mare's brawn pulled the peddler's cart and put food on the table. Certainly, he household's circumstances were no worse than the majority of families living on Chicken Hill at the dawn of the twentieth century. On those occasions when Adolph could afford two horses, well, that meant affluence!

"Why are Mother and Daddy crying?" four year old Sam asked his older brother Harry who was unable to answer. Their father was sitting at the kitchen table, his head in his hands. Purple veins lined the side of his neck. The creases on his forehead sank deep into his sun-tanned skin. Rose was shouting at him.

"You, the *gantseh k'nacker*, the big shot, just had to show off." Rose taunted her husband. "You had to race down a hill. Now look at what you've done! How could you have been so careless with the horse?"

Adolph could not answer. Whether the horse's severe stumble had been his fault or an act of God, the result was the same. The trusty chestnut mare had to be put down. Moreover, Adolph did not have the ten dollars to purchase another. While some of Adolph's friends described him, even to his face, as *gezunt vi a ferd*, strong as a horse, the Yiddish was not intended to be quite so literal.

Her accusation bit savagely into his heart. Rose was right. He had been reckless. Adolph pondered his next move. He would have to borrow ten dollars, perhaps from Estreicher or from his brother-in-law Emmanuel. And he had to act quickly. Even a few days off the narrow lanes and dirt roads of Chester and Berks Counties could mean lost customers, missed opportunities, and possibly no milk on the table for the children. There were now four with another on the way.

In order not to compete directly with each other, Pottstown's Jewish peddlers demarcated precise territories. None of his *lantzmen*, he was sure, would dare exploit his bad *mazel*. The same was not true for the non-Jewish competition. While immigrant Jews had taken over much of the old peddling routes, a few old-timers—so-called Yankee peddlers—and a handful of non-Jewish immigrants still made the rounds in rural districts around Pottstown. When word got out that Markowitz was incapacitated, someone would fill the breech.

Still, the setback was not a fatal one. After ten years in Pottstown, Adolph had established himself as a dependable peddler. Scrap buyers trusted him, extending credit when needed. Among his Jewish peers, he enjoyed a reputation for evenhandedness combined with first-rate business acumen.

This did not imply that all his peers relished his personality. From his cronies Adolph acquired the nickname "Perky" because of his persistence in returning to a point of criticism or compliment. Even when he proved a point contrary to popular opinion, Adolph still had to get in the last word. Although well respected for his common sense, Adolph, deservedly, earned scorn for his persnickety behavior and outspokenness. Moreover, as farmers in Chester County and foundry managers in Pottstown learned to their annoyance, his stern, hard exterior was often difficult to penetrate. On occasion Adolph's stubbornness served as

Der pedler

a hindrance to reaching a mutually welcome and profitable agreement.

On the other hand Adolph's compulsion with learning English had a positive impact on business. He thirsted to excel in English. Since his arrival in Pottstown, Adolph easily outdistanced his immigrant cohorts in the idiomatic use of the language. By asking numerous questions, rephrasing them when necessary, Adolph surmounted a major hurdle to learning a foreign language, a reluctance to jump in the water and swim. Speaking with farmers, small shopkeepers, and tradesmen forced Adolph to correct his grammatical mistakes and build vocabulary. Eliminating the language barrier with customers reduced misunderstanding. The peddler learned quickly that if he spoke like a greenhorn, he would be treated like one. Farmers may not have liked Adolph personally, many may have harbored anti-Jewish sentiment, but at least peddler and customer understood each other

Reading during the evenings helped. Adolph's second-hand English dictionary received a constant workout. Most important for comprehension, Adolph listened carefully and intently, especially to conversations to which he was not privy. None of this might have mattered if Adolph not possessed a natural affinity for languages, facilitated perhaps by familiarity with the various languages spoken in Galicia.

"RAGS, RAGS for sale! BONES, BONES, sell me bones! SCRAP IRON, SCRAP IRON, good price to sell!" A strong voice, one with a musical cadence, was a terrific asset in the peddling profession. Adolph possessed such a voice. The clop, clop of the trotting horse kept beat. Its tail swished back and forth in time. Pans and metal utensils hung from the sides of the wagon and clanged together in off-key accompaniment. As Adolph's weight shifted slightly with each bounce, the creaky springs below the wagon seat made accordion sounds. Occasionally, a snort from the horse, an 'enough with the operatic performance, let's get this peddling over with so I can get back to my stable and eat my oats' snort, broke the mesmerizing spell.

"PAPER, BUNDLES OF PAPER, I BUY PAPER."

Over cups of fresh morning milk and just baked bread, a bearded Mennonite dairy farmer and Adolph engage in conversation rich in German and German-sprinkled Yiddish. A few English words are thrown in the mix. The two sit on the front porch of the farmhouse. They look out across the barnyard towards the dirt road Adolph just traversed. The wife offers Adolph more milk. The two men share local gossip. Rains in recent weeks should make for a good corn crop. However, milk prices in town are down slightly from last year. The farmer fears prices may fall further since local farmers are planning for larger herds. A county magistrate is accused of taking bribes. The two men commiserate about crooked politicians and deeply rutted country roads. The local blacksmith was kicked last week and broke his collarbone. He'll be incapacitated for two months. The farmer down the road is planning a barn-raising event.

Finally, the farmer and Adolph talk business.

Over druben barn artz a vagon ful a oll hufeisen. You vant, I git. Ve make gut geschaft, peddler, gut deal. Zehn cents fur phund, okay?"

The men walk to the barn and look at the scrap. After friendly dickering, a deal is set with a handshake. Eight cents a pound is the agreed price. It is less than the farmer's opening offer and a penny more than Adolph hoped to pay. Still, it is a fair bargain for both sides.

As Adolph loads the wagon with the scrap, the farmer turns to pat the horse's hindquarters. "Better git your work in early, peddler" the farmer says. "It's going to storm something awful by suppertime." Only a few wispy cirrus clouds on the distant horizon marred a perfectly blue sky. But Adolph knows to trust the farmer's instincts. Perhaps the barn animals are restless or sparrows by the bird feeder have taken flight. As a boy in Galicia, his father complained to him about having aching joints just before the weather turned sour. It is a piece of advice Adolph takes seriously. A heavy wagon in a rainstorm while deep on Chester County's dirt trails was no picnic.

On occasion, Adolph found himself innocently using vocabulary, usually picked up in his evening reading, even the native-born farmers, Americans their entire lives, had not mastered. In these rare victorious instances, he lightened his step back to town or gave the horse an extra swish of the whip to accelerate the trot home. He rushed to inform Rose of his achievement.

"*Gantseh megilleh*! Big deal! So you know more than those *schnooks*," Rose teased. Adolph's mother Lena joined in on the act, "*Nu*? Those *schlemiel* farmers? Why would they speak better English than you?" But of course, both women were exceedingly proud of these precious accomplishments brought on by Adolph's compulsion to master their new environment.

A reputation for honesty and dependability among peddler colleagues and *lantzmen* and the reality of everyday commercial transactions with the *goyim* were two sides of very different coins. Religious observance, Jewish law and strict moral values dictated life within the small Jewish community and at home. Pious behavior with fellow Jews though had not the slightest relationship with daily conduct with the outside world. Hypocrisy in business was practiced without the slightest hesitancy. Nor was it viewed disapprovingly. In doing business with outsiders, invariably always non-Jewish, no restrictions pertained on dishonesty or even theft. Why should there be?

Christian America, and especially rural Christian America circa 1900, viewed itself socially and intellectually superior from the Jews. This was intensely true following the wave of Yiddish-speaking immigrants. Stereotyped from the pulpit to the living room, Jews were perceived as being just a step above blacks. Jewish peddlers, in particular, were regarded as shrewd Shylocks, out to extract their pound of flesh from innocent Christian Antonios. Adolph and his cohorts possessed an almost genetic pre-disposition against this historic prejudice. All agreed ill treatment by the Christian race had been many times worse in the old country. Still, "if this is how they behave towards us," Adolph noted to Adam Wolf, "why not take what we can in order to make a profit?"

Like most of his generation, Adolph was exceedingly frugal. This frugality combined with his well-honed Galician toughness made him a keen peddler. Adolph reversed Ben Franklin's adage. To him every penny earned was a penny saved. This obsessive and compulsive nature served him well. After all, he succeeded in bringing the *mishpoohah* to America. Adolph held firmly to the "rags to riches" fables of Horatio Alger dime novels. Gripping the ladder to economic progress, he climbed with confidence and on his own terms.

* * *

Adolph's journey into peddling resulted from vast economic changes taking place during the nineteenth century. In both America and Europe, an entrepreneurial revolution was taking place. Dramatic technological advances in transportation, communication, and manufacturing combined with new market institutions such as banks and large-scale production facilities spurred this shift. Mass assembly industrialization significantly lowered costs of production. Products of an increasingly higher quality and standard became more affordable to the public.

Throughout America, subsistence farming, tiny workshops run by skilled craftsmen, and horse travel were giving way to new systems, new techniques. Commodities and manufactured goods produced in one location now could move great distances to meet customer demand elsewhere. Roads, canals, and railroads laced together the country's widely separated parts. Telegraph and later the telephone facilitated almost instantaneous communication. Barter gave way to monetized exchange as buyer-seller transactions increasingly utilized cash and credit. Americans increasingly possessed an unparalleled ability to select consumer products based on more than simply local availability.

Because sellers and buyers no longer need live in the same small community or region, the "market revolution" required a new innovation, the middleman. Peddlers were the infantry in this revolution. They purchased goods, new or used and often on credit, transported and delivered the same to far-flung consumers. Usually, the connection serviced was urban-rural, rural-urban. To be tied into the new American economy a small farmer living at the end of a long country road almost anywhere in rural America could utilize a peddler middleman and not leave his homestead. By 1900 another innovation, mail order catalogues such as the annual Sears Roebuck Company catalogue, gained widespread acceptance. Through the improved U.S. Post Office Service, mail order provided the American people direct access to the industrial bounty of America's manufacturers. Although peddlers lost some business to catalogues, they continued to perform a valuable service by purchasing and reselling recyclable items that people no longer needed such as scrap metal, old clothing, paper, and even animal bones.

Young men formed the backbone of the immigrant peddler story. Peddling was a difficult occupation. It required long hours on the road on foot, horseback, or on uncomfortable hard wagon seats. Peddlers had to demonstrate superior negotiating ability, often with only the barest English language capability. It was an occupation that required a strong will, a tough body, common sense, patience, and a large chunk of *chutzpah*. But, it was also a vocation that required little start up capital and no training or education.

Selling or buying secondhand clothing, notions, utensils, and other cheap products did not come naturally to all who attempted it. Some peddlers failed miserably. Many never overcame their penurious existence. Not a few returned disappointed to Europe. To those with the right combination of moxie and perseverance, peddling was a stepping-stone to greater wealth. It could be an apprenticeship perhaps to starting a dry goods or clothing store. Former Jewish peddlers founded many of America's most famous department stores—household names to generations of Americans. Or, like Adolph's enterprising colleague Mayer Pollock, a small peddler could remain in the scrap business, accumulate capital, develop contacts and connections, and eventually create a major company employing hundreds.

* * *

Not unlike military conscription instituted during the Great War, Adolph made sure HIS sons did not avoid HIS draft, that is, the draft of assisting their father in the peddling business! From a young age, the Markowitz boys assisted their father. They worked throughout the year, during the school term and summer vacations. When school was out, one, two, or sometimes three of the boys joined their father on his peddling rounds. When the boys reached thirteen or fourteen, they peddled on their own. Even when home on college break, Adolph's sons continued to help their father from the buckboard of a peddling wagon.

"You think this food comes for free?" Adolph told his sons. "You think God serves you the way he served manna to *Moisheh Rabbenu* and the children of Israel? Of course you will work the wagon."

Der pedler

Summer meant long daylight, warm evenings, and the possibility of spending the night eight or ten miles from home in a farmer's barn, stable, or tool shed. Except for the depths of winter, the boys arose as early as 3:00 a.m. to feed, curry, and harness the horse, or when times were good, pair of horses. A scale was placed in the wagon along with a pillow for the "old man" to sit on. The wagon was set up with bags for merchandise such as rags, rubber, bones, and iron—all the various articles available from the farms, blacksmiths, harness shops, coopers, and other tradesmen in the villages surrounding Pottstown. Rags were plentiful during the spring when housecleaning was in full swing. Late in the year prior to Thanksgiving farmers slaughtered their livestock and prepared the meat for the winter. Hence bones were aplenty and all the Pottstown peddlers would be out early and home late. At times, paper, tinfoil, and metal, including brass and copper were collected, and bags had to be available for these items as well.

Getting up so early was necessary also to prepare the fire in the stove for the "old man's breakfast" at 6:30 a.m., or perhaps a shade earlier. This meant the boys ate their own breakfasts from 5:30 a.m. To walk fifteen minutes up Beech Street and reach school by 8:00 or 8:15 a.m., little time was available for additional sleep. The trek was always made on foot. Earlier, a bicycle had been stolen and another remained chained to a tree beside the house. School did not end until 4:00 p.m. On occasion in afternoon class, Sam, Ben, or another of the boys nodded off, head resting across their arms on the desk. A son of Adolph might awaken only after the final bell had sounded. Then, girls giggled and boys poked the napping Markowitz kid awake. The snickering continued as their fellow students walked formally down and up each aisle to exit the classroom.

No two of Adolph's sons were alike. Even from a young age, Sam was more intellectual and prone to introversion. Benny possessed both a warm personality and inherent ability. Mike was a tightwad and maintained a craving for gambling. Robbie was personable and sensitive but somewhat misguided and full of himself. Francis, the youngest, was lazy and kept falling into bad company as an adolescent.

Sometimes, it seemed unclear whether the "old man" really understood the character of his children. One summer afternoon, Mike and Ben escorted their father on the peddling wagon. A farmer asked Adolph if the boys were smart. Adolph turned and looked at his two sons.

"He's the smart one," Adolph noted, pointing to Mike, "but the other, Ben, he's not too smart." Ben eventually became a highly successful medical doctor, while Mike spent his life in the shoe business.

The dichotomy between family morality and business ethics with the outside world knew no limits. One late August day with shadows lengthening and most farmers already back at their farmhouses, Adolph halted the wagon at an attractive cornfield. School was still a week away and three of the boys sat with him. Close to harvest time, the stalks were golden and heavy with ears of field corn. He directed the two youngest boys, "go to both ends of the cornfield and keep a lookout for anyone coming." While the boys scouted, Adolph sent the third over the fence to gather up and hand him the succulent ears of corn. He hid the corn under the seat. The boys knew better than to question their father's motives. Decades later when called to task by his grown sons for such behavior, Adolph offered only lame excuses.

"There is nothing wrong," Adolph affirmed with a sly wispy smile, "with helping oneself to the bounty of the Lord!"

"You ignore the obvious," Sam replied. "Taking corn from a farmer's cornfield is, in fact, helping oneself to the bounty of the farmer!"

Adolph drew up to his son. He was not about to let any child of his have the last word! "Whether the Lord's or the farmer's few ears of corn, 'I would like to go to the fields and glean among the ears of grain . . .'"

Sam quickly caught the quote from the Scriptures. "But Dad, Ruth the Moabite also told Naomi, '. . . behind someone who may show me kindness.' I do not remember following anyone and I doubt the name of the farmer from whose cornfield you gleaned was Boaz of the family of Elimelech!"

In one instance, Adolph bought a roll of wire at a very good price from a middleman with whom he occasionally traded. From another peddler, he learned that in all likelihood the wire he purchased had been stolen. "If you are caught in possession of that wire, the police will believe you are an accomplice! You'd be subject to arrest!" The wire was hidden under a bed. Adolph carefully instructed the children "do not utter a word of the existence of this item." After weeks of tension, Adolph finally disposed of the wire.

Then there was the Harmonyville blacksmith. Like most blacksmiths, the blacksmith in Harmonyville accumulated a large pile of junk metal and slag. One day, Adolph alone on his rounds led his wagon up to the blacksmith's forge. He looked over the metal. "I can buy the lot for six cents a pound."

The blacksmith sneered at the offer. He replied that someone else had already offered to purchase the metal at a much higher price than the one Adolph proffered. It was a price, Adolph knew, that was significantly above the wholesale price given junkmen at the foundry.

"You are a God-damned liar!" Adolph bitterly exclaimed. He whipped his horse and sped away.

One week later, Adolph's son Mike visited the same blacksmith. He was by himself. The blacksmith took no notice of the wagon although it had been at his farm recently. One peddling wagon looked like any other. Mike spoke amicably with the blacksmith. The two quickly came to terms. After consummating the sale, the blacksmith asked the young man to wait a moment. He wanted to relate a story.

"Another peddler came by here last week," the blacksmith confided to Mike. "That Jew peddler from Pottstown wanted to cheat me on the price," he recounted, "but I showed him!" Mike paid the farmer six cents a pound for the metal. It was the same price his father had offered. The blacksmith never knew that he was speaking to "that Jew peddler's" son.

For decades, whenever Adolph's sons got together, somehow in a deep voice one would inject into the conversation, "You are a God-damn liar!" In every instance, this caused uproarious hilarity.

To make a few more cents from a transaction, every trick, ruse or scam was fair play. Out peddling one day with a son, Adolph demonstrated the "proper technique" for lifting a sack of rags that a farm woman had brought from the house. "Here, tie the sack like this so it will dig into the scale," he instructed. The boy followed his father's command. He made a twist in the sack that caused it to show less weight on the scale. Another occasion, Adolph was hauling a load of bones to sell to an old white-haired man named Trinley who lived in nearby Linfield. He ordered his son to place stones into the load to make it heavier.

When peddling, Adolph avoided the mansions on the west side of town. The rich *goyim* who lived there, he believed, were the toughest customers. One day his eldest son decided to try his luck. At one estate the lady of the house instructed Sam to go to the garage where several worn out tires were available. The *chauffeur* weighed one tire and assumed all would weigh the same. Sam paid for eighty-eight pounds. Two weeks later, Adolph returned from delivering the tires to a buyer in Philadelphia. He reported to Sam that the tires he sold weighed 125 pounds. Since no additional tires had been collected, Sam realized he had underpaid the lady by thirty-seven pounds. He told his father he wanted to return to the lady and pay for the unpaid difference. Adolph looked at his son as if he had grown a second nose. "That is insane! You are completely *meshugas*!"

But while no rules applied when taking advantage of the *goyim*, woe to anyone who tried to reverse the score. To dig a connection from one of Adolph's houses to the water main, Adolph hired a plumbing contractor named Daub. The invoice Daub submitted called for the time of two laborers. "Why are two men needed to do the job?" Adolph inquired.

"One man wields the pick and the other man the shovel," Daub replied.

Adolph looked at Daub as if he were daft. "I won't pay for two men," Adolph retorted. "It is obvious they cannot work at the same time. The man who uses the pick can also shovel."

Committing brazen acts of unethical behavior against a fellow Jew was strictly out of bounds. However, even among Pottstown's small universe of Jewish peddlers some hanky-panky might be committed. One frequent target of this behavior was Mayer Pollock who arrived in Pottstown a couple of years after the first seven Hungarian families. Squeezed out of the most lucrative and accessible peddling routes by his relatively late appearance on the scene, the intrepid Pollock decided not to compete directly. Instead, he moved into the wholesale side of the junk business. Pollack purchased scrap metal from the other Jewish peddlers and resold it to foundries. The peddlers did not appreciate Pollock's self-insertion into a middleman role. This behavior ate into their own profit margins. Unfortunately, they could not figure out Pollock's key business connections. Most importantly, they did not know where he disposed of the scrap metal. All they could ascertain was that his key purchaser was located across the Schuylkill River in Chester County.

Adolph determined to end the Pollock monopoly on the wholesale side of the business. Early one morning, he waited unobtrusively on horseback in an alley near the South Hanover Street Bridge to Chester County. At his usual hour, the predictable Pollock with his team of horses and a load of junk passed the alley. Adolph followed Pollock at a respectable distance. Pollock's wagon traveled for almost ten miles along Chester County's country roads. Finally, he arrived at his destination, a foundry in Elverson. Adolph kicked his horse and rushed forward. He thumbed his nose at Pollock. "*Kuck zich oys!*" he called out, "Go take a shit for yourself!" From then on, Pottstown's Jewish peddlers cut Pollock out as the middleman for their scrap metal. But it did not halt Pollock's rise to become Pottstown's most successful Jewish entrepreneur.

Nor did Adolph's puncturing of Mayer Pollock's scrap monopoly affect the heartfelt collegial relations between the two men. Business was strictly business. What happened on the roads of Chester County did not enter the *shul* or the *chevra*. Riding in a car through town after attending Shabbat services years after the Elverson incident, the two men reminisced about their days peddling. High Street that season was suffering from an over abundance of potholes, a severe problem for automobile tires and springs. Pollack remarked, in Yiddish, about the bumps. "Our junk wagons were no smoother," Adolph replied.

Another of Adolph's peddler *lantzman* Adam Wolf was also a brother-in-law, his first wife having been the late Freydel Schwartz. Wolf was Adolph's close confidant and friend. Whereas Adolph peddled almost exclusively south of the Schuylkill, Wolf generally worked north of town in Berks and upper Montgomery Counties. Adolph was Wolf's elder by over ten years. Wolf looked up to him as more than just a mentor. The two were almost brothers and enjoyed a close bond. They frequently shared "can you top this?" stories from their long days on the road.

Late one evening the two men were sitting in the Markowitz home by a roaring fire. Empty whiskey glasses rested on a small table. Heavy snow lay outside. Peddling activities had come to a halt.

"Yesterday before the snowfall, I out on the road," Wolf recounted. "On my way back from Boyertown, I stopped at the Halfway House. They have the best pickled eggs. When I left the inn, it was already getting dark and the snow was coming down in thick feathery snowflakes, the size of silver dollars. I checked the hitch to the wagon, tightened the harness, and started back for home."

Wolf paused for effect and waited for Adolph to add a finger to the whiskey glasses. He took a long pleasing sip. "It was cold but there was no wind. I had on my overcoat and heavy scarf and mittens. The snow was still coming down and maybe three inches were already on the road. I mounted up and gave the horse a swish with the whip." Wolf looked intently at the glass in his right hand. "Believe me when I tell you Adolph, I fell asleep! I don't think we were more than fifty paces from the Halfway House gate." He waited for Adolph to deliver the inexorable "*nu*? so? What happened?" Wolf continued, "I felt the horse give a sudden jerk. I opened my eyes. We were right in front of my house on Cherry Street!" Wolf slapped his hands on the sides of the easy chair. "You know that must be a good four miles from the Halfway House! That horse brought me all the way home through town. And I don't remember a thing!"

"You are *meshugeh ahf toit*! Crazy as a loon," laughed Adolph as he passed the bottle to top off Wolf's shot glass.

Politics for Adolph was a shell game. Most of Pottstown's Jews were Democrats, and understandably so. But not Adolph Markowitz! He was a diehard Republican. After President Theodore Roosevelt's 1904 whistle stop in Pottstown, Sam noted his father's vocal support. He asked his father why he voted only for Republican Party candidates. Indeed, Sam's own middle name "Harrison" was derived from no Jewish hero of yore or from a long deceased ancestor, as Jewish tradition would dictate. Instead, Sam's middle name was given to respect President Benjamin Harrison, a Republican who would be challenged later in 1892, the year of his birth, by the Democrat Grover Cleveland.

"Both Democrats and Republicans are crooks," Adolph explained, "but during a Republican administration there is more money for me."

After the 1908 presidential election campaign and the successful candidacy of William Howard Taft, the teenage Sam rode a horse in the Republican victory parade up High Street. William Henry James Carter, a black Civil War veteran who never attended school, boasted to Sam "We drove the Jennings Bryan down Salt River, didn't we?" Sam never knew whether Carter even knew the Democratic candidate's first name.

The riddle of Adolph's long-standing support for the Republican Party was in sharp contrast to Jewish voting habits of the time. His behavior remained incomprehensible to his *lantzmen*. In their view, Adolph behaved like a Democrat but thought like a Republican. During his lifetime, Adolph's children broke with such convention of blind loyalty to one political party. But Adolph judged for himself what was in his best interest. If it meant siding with establishment Republican candidates like

Der pedler

Theodore Roosevelt and William Howard Taft over Free Silver Populists like William Jennings Bryan, so be it. He remained Republican loyal until the Depression finally caused him to side with a Democrat, Franklin Roosevelt.

Over the years, Adolph accumulated quite a bit of savings from his peddling. He moved the family again, this time to a red brick, two-story house on Walnut Street. The new home possessed a wide front porch ideal for sitting on warm summer evenings. From external appearances, the duplex appeared not remarkably different from the previous Markowitz residences. In the rear by the alley stood a stable that could accommodate two horses, wagon and harnesses. Across the alley fronting Beech Street, an old barn was converted into a warehouse for the accumulated junk. Adolph's elderly mother Lena occupied a one-room frame house next to the barn. Everyone referred to it as the "shanty" as at the previous residence. Old automobile tires, piles of wood, and other accoutrements of the junk business were piled in the back yard. Rose kept a few chickens in wire cages. She released them to peck for food under the strictest, most careful watch. Feral cats prowled the neighborhood. Rose kept the family on constant alert for any feline aggression on the poultry.

Inside, the Walnut Street home differed substantially from previous residences. Upholstered furniture in the living room was store bought, not procured third hand. Electric lamps in each room provided good reading light. The family no longer required the old kerosene lamps. They now joined similar unneeded items in the junk barn. Two bathrooms, one on the ground floor, one upstairs had the latest pull chain John Douglas Company toilets. Not only did the Markowitz house have up-to-date indoor plumbing and electricity, it also had a modern kitchen, including an impressive new-style electric stove and oven. Standing on four legs, the stove resembled another piece of furniture. Functionally, it dramatically surpassed the family's earlier wood and coal stoves. Instead of hardwood, a new invention, linoleum, served as the kitchen flooring. Its rectangular pattern gave the kitchen a thoroughly modern appearance.

The Markowitz residence was one of the first on Chicken Hill to possess a telephone. It was a black upright, two-piece "candlestick" rotary phone with a bell shaped mouthpiece. The party line number was 13W. Adolph proudly told his friends that he needed the phone to "transact business." With which of his rural customers he could have communicated by phone was unfathomable. None even had electricity. Calls for the entire neighborhood came in at all hours. In later years Adolph would send one of his grandchildren as messenger to inform neighbors of their incoming calls.

By the early 1920s, Adolph decided the time ripe to ease himself into retirement from Markowitz & Son. Adolph had added the "& Son" to the business when his youngest son Francis turned 16. He hoped Francis would continue the commercial enterprise. However, when Adolph retired, so did the son! While years of peddling had taken a physical toll, his health remained good. Thanks to his hard efforts and the "servitude" of his children for so many years, Adolph possessed a sizable bank account. The combination of money, available time, and undiminished ambition caused Adolph to move in another enterprising direction.

Next to the barn on Beech Street was a vacant lot. Adolph wanted to rent it. The junk business required space, particularly for the old farm implements that were collected. Such a convenient empty space would serve his purposes nicely. At Pottstown City Hall Adolph inquired as to the lot's owner. "There are no ownership papers recorded for that property," the clerk informed him. Adolph went down to the County Court House in Norristown. There, the recorder of deeds said the lot had never been titled. For five dollars Adolph had the vacant property titled in his name. From then on, the family referred to it as the *gefunah*, or "found" lot.

Because land ownership had been denied him in Europe, once Adolph had disposable income he exercised a flourishing passion for acquiring property. Acquisition of the land adjacent to the *gefunah* seemed a logical first step. He easily obtained the property on Beech Street. With steady income from the junk business, Adolph contracted to build a row of four frame houses. In partnership with the teenage Francis the only Markowitz son still at home, Adolph constructed a storefront with second floor apartments on the *gefunah* lot. He built other Chicken Hill edifices including the James Hotel.

With the exception of one family, all of Adolph's tenants were African-Americans. They were usually fresh arrivals from the Deep South, penniless immigrants as he had once been. Few could obtain good jobs; none received more than the most rudimentary education during Jim Crow. Because of the severe economic straights of the majority of his renters, Adolph constantly struggled with rent collection. With his tenants Adolph was fair but exceedingly stern. When one tenant did not pay his rent on time, Adolph walked into the kitchen, took a chicken right out of the family pot, and held the poor carcass hostage until settlement could be made on the amount of rent owed. When he faced hard times as a Chicken Hill immigrant, sympathy had not been shown him. Adolph was not about to offer what he had not received.

From his pauper's arrival in Pottstown, the peddler had come full circle. Adolph was not ostentatiously wealthy, but certainly he was well off, especially by the standards of Chicken Hill. After years of tenancy, he was now a landlord. Three sons graduated college. His other children and their spouses enjoyed mixed successes in small business. He survived to enjoy numerous grandchildren.

On November 1, 1940, while collecting rent arrears on one of his properties Adolph collapsed. Before his heart stopped his final earthly act was shouting at a tenant who was overdue on his rent. *Lantzmen* and family concurred that such an end, in Gods eyes and theirs, was quite appropriate.

Long after Adolph retired from peddling and shortly before his death, his grandson Norman Cohen was horseback riding in Chester County. He met an old farmer, Roy Wells. The two struck up a conversation.

"Perhaps you knew my grandfather. He conducted a lot of peddling in these parts."

"Adolph Markowitz? I knew Adolph Markowitz," Wells replied. "He used to stop at farm houses here abouts, but it wasn't just to buy junk!"

PART II

Dos Amerikanisch

Six

Dos bruderen

The children of Adolph and Rose consisted of six *bruderen* or brothers—five after the death of Harry at age 16—and two sisters. They were the *Americanisch*, the Americans. All were born in Pottstown. Rebnitza, Gaidos, the impoverished Galician *shtetls* existed only in stories told by their parents, uncles and aunts. Emperor Franz-Joseph, mentioned occasionally in newspapers, was a distant abstract personage. The children never fully grasped the hardships experienced by their parents during the ocean crossing. The children tolerated but did not fully comprehend those beliefs and traditions of their parents that seemed beyond normal Jewish religious practice. The Markowitz children understood and spoke Yiddish fluently. But they thought and dreamed in English. Christian children with whom they associated at school or on the streets were generally non-threatening. The Markowitz *bruderen* were of a new generation to whom history meant Washington and Lincoln, not just Maimonides, King David or the Prophet Isaiah. They spoke of math class and baseball, not pogroms or famine.

Each boy retained the physical traits of their father—square-shouldered, thick jawed, beefy yet dexterous hands. From their mother they possessed eyes that hinted of an Asian ancestry and a sly, almost contagious smile. None concealed their loyalty to the family and to each other. The Markowitz household was very much a *menner*, male-dominated milieu. Adolph ran a tight ship. When the boys were together women were relegated to the kitchen or other parts of the house. The head of the household was respected in every way.

Despite the lack of funds in the Markowitz home, schooling was imperative. For each child's admission to first grade—there was no kindergarten—a permit from the superintendent of schools was required. But with constant demands on Rose within the house and Adolph out on his peddling rounds all day, who had time to get dressed up and walk the six or eight blocks to the town hall? To avoid making the trip too frequently—the age difference among the children averaging 18 months—Rose obtained school admission permits by "twos." Thus, two children were registered together for the first grade. First, it was Yetta and Sam. Next came Mike and Ben. Finally, Robert and Katie. Despite the age differences, each pair attended the same grade in school.

The elementary school was located just two blocks from the Markowitz home. Between sixty and seventy pupils attended. Eight or nine students were Jewish, a similar number were black, and the rest were "white." Generally, peace among the groups reigned during morning and afternoon recess. On occasion though, fights broke out between whites and blacks or between gentiles and the few Jewish students. During the latter altercations, the Markowitz boys and the other Jewish kids were always on the losing side. One day Sam returned home with a bloody nose. Rose fixed him up as best she could. She pressed a clean rag to Sam's nostrils to staunch the bleeding and lectured him about "avoiding" confrontation.

Upon his return to the house, Adolph took a more sanguine view of the entire incident. Through bitter experience he knew the folly of going face-to-face with the dominant Christian society even in America. Sam's losing battle with the *goyim*, he believed, taught his son a crucial lesson. "It is best," he told Sam, "to pick your battles carefully. If possible, use your *kop*, your head, instead of your fists. It will save you more bloody noses in your life!"

"But if you must fight," he added, "knock the *kaker*, the shit-head, on his ass!"

While the children were in school, the teacher was obeyed *in loco parentis*. No complaints were brought home. Any punishment inflicted while at school was duplicated at home without appeal or discussion. More than once, one or another of the boys was reprimanded for what the teacher perceived as deliberate disobedience. The real cause was misunderstanding. The older children started school with only a meager English vocabulary. Yiddish was still being spoken exclusively at home. Excuses had neither any impact with Adolph nor with his own method of discipline. Yet, if there was purpose to the madness, it inspired the children to press harder to learn English and avoid such harsh treatment. Adolph's method generated respect for authority and obedience to teachers and elders.

With his sons Adolph could be brutal. His tool was a simple one. He wore it around his waist. The bad acts of each boy were recorded in a sort of West Point demerit system, building up to a point where they would get "straps" on their *toches*. The quantity depended on the number of demerits accumulated. After the beating the child was required to kiss the strap, which if not a belt, was usually a discarded piece of harness. God's admonition to Abraham as he raised his knife to his son Isaac

Dos bruderen

"Lay not thy hand upon the lad!" did not apply in the Markowitz household.

The boys compared their punishments. The prize for the worse punishment meted out by Adolph, they agreed wholeheartedly, was won dubiously by Robert. It was the result of a boat ride on Manatawny Creek that went awry. During his own youth, Adolph experienced an almost tragic swimming accident when one of his younger siblings nearly drowned. As a result Adolph feared swimming or any unnecessary activity around water. He constantly cautioned his children against swimming and warned them of the consequences.

Robbie disregarded his father's orders and went out on the nearby stream with his friends. The overloaded rowboat capsized. Upon his return home, the boy was unable to conceal his wet clothing. The punishment, 29 straps, was so severe that his older sister Yetta tried to interpose herself. Adolph brusquely pushed her aside with a swing of the strap. He continued inflicting his sentence on Robert. As a result of the incident, Robbie received from his brothers the nickname "Boat".

In contrast to the harsh castigations frequently delivered to his boys, this occasion was the only time in Yetta's life she received any physical abuse from her father.

Years later, when "Adolph's grown boys" were in town, they gathered at 719 Walnut Street. With their father present, they regaled each other with stories about peddling and the various farmers with whom they had dealt. Their humor, both in Yiddish and English, was irreverent and frothy. These tales kept them in stitches for hours, and visitors, when present, could not stop laughing. With much sarcasm and plenty of gossip the rapid fire staccato from Sam, Ben, Mike or "Shorty" and Boat shot thick and fast across the kitchen table. Yetta and her sister Kate remained silent.

Six evenings a week, but only five in winter, the kitchen table was cleared. Out came the shiny white oilcloth cover and a deck of cards. Adolph and his sons began playing *klabrias*, a complicated three-handed Hungarian card game using 7s through aces. *Klabrias*, they claimed, was impossible for the non-inducted to comprehend. Women were not allowed to play. Neither Yetta nor Kate ever indicated a desire to participate. Given the rowdy behavior of the boys, their reluctance was understandable. But Yetta felt slighted nonetheless for lack of an invitation.

Gossip and Yiddish expressions bolted across the kitchen. The players kept up a withering, even scandalous broadside of banter about *mishpoohah*, issues of the day, and the latest foibles of close relatives and friends. But none missed a beat when it came to the competition.

"*Bella!*" shouted one player. It signified the king and queen of trump worth 40 points. Another called out "*quartz bella!*" the king and queen of trump plus four in a row, 90 points. When looking for a particular card, a frustrated cardholder barked "*Nish du*, its not there!" *Shtuck* indicated the last trick had been taken. It earned 10 points. Two defenders loaded up against the declarer by *shmier*-ing good cards back and forth. *Nuch numblat* meant the player had *bella* but had been beaten to the punch before declaring trump. Three in a row was *tertz, quart* was four in a row. Spades were *shipa*, diamonds in later decades *ecstein*—named for Billy Eckstine, a bandleader of the swing era. *Herets* were hearts and *cretz* clubs. *Yus* was the queen of trump, the *minel* the nine of trump worth 14 points. Many pennies and the occasional nickel sweetened the pot and moved back and forth among the players. Each hand was avidly critiqued, in Yiddish of course.

Despite shared appearances, the Markowitz boys displayed dissimilar personalities. Mike was the middle son. As a child, Mike suffered from infantile paralysis, or polio. For hours on end when the boy was five years old, his mother massaged his affected leg to prevent further atrophy. As a result of the polio, Mike possessed a slight limp. This led to his nickname *Shorty*.

Family members snickered that Shorty was addicted to gambling. He certainly enjoyed taking outrageous chances. And like many gamblers he was a skinflint. Mike's gaming skills were questionable—although a good bluffer, he could not keep a poker face. His talent for escape, however, was indisputably Houdini-like. On one occasion, Mike was playing in a card game that was raided by the police. He escaped through a window, landing in a bush. It was an episode his brothers never permitted him to live down.

Mike never outgrew his adventurous risk-taking. One summer weekend Mike and his young wife Fanny took a motor trip with his sister Yetta and her husband. The two couples spent the night at a rural hotel. After checking out from their lodging, Yetta and her husband were waiting in the car. Dragging Fanny with him, Mike hurriedly rushed out of the hotel. They jumped into the waiting car.

"Step on it!" he shouted to his brother-in-law who was behind the wheel.

Yetta's husband did as he was told. He barely avoided hitting a parked car.

Mike who did not attend college was the first to admit his lack of any academic inclination or prowess. However, the long days peddling with his father honed Mike into a shrewd and competent businessman restrained only by a lack of ambition. Mike opened the Brockton Shoe Store in Norristown, 20 miles east of Pottstown. He eventually brought his own son into the business.

Although a year and a half older than Mike, Ben attended the same class in school as his younger brother. But there, any similarity between the two boys ended abruptly. Ben was the complete opposite of Mike. He was serious, hard working, and driven to succeed in any endeavor. Ben also displayed a generous and exceedingly family-oriented nature. Among his high school peers, few others were as popular. Classmates joked that Ben would become a senator some day.

He graduated in 1917 from Bucknell University with a pre-law degree. Yet Ben felt unenthusiastic about law school. He left consideration of his professional career behind and managed the Boston Sample Shoe Store in Plainfield, New Jersey. A cousin owned the store.

Ben might have remained content running a shoe store. However, events beyond his control caused him to rethink his future. The United States entered the Great World War in April 1917. Ben confronted a dilemma not uncommon among his contemporaries: how to stay out of the draft! Although not politically opposed to America's entry into the War, Ben felt strong pressure from his parents and other family members to remain a civilian and a buttress for family fortunes. Ben pondered his next move. Unless he could get into medical school, a contingency he had not even considered during his years at Bucknell, he was a sure candidate for military conscription. It was a hair brain scheme.

Ben's impulsive plan to attend medical school was indeed a gamble. While at Bucknell, he took neither pre-med nor science courses, nor had ever expressed any interest in the medical profession. Moreover, he was currently managing a shoe store! What medical school would take him?

With nothing to lose, Ben took his undergraduate transcript to the dean of Loyola of Chicago Medical School. Lena Molay, his fiancé, lived in that city and his brother Sam had studied at the University of Chicago. The meeting was short. Loyola's dean, a heavy-set man with thick jowls, gray beard, and wire rimmed eyeglasses, looked up from the Bucknell transcript. He studied the aspiring medical school candidate intently. He peered into the young man's eyes.

"Young man," the dean began. "I always wondered how a good student with no preparation in science would manage in medical school. If it is possible, you are the one to do it."

For decades, Ben rarely referred to his time at Loyola, except to say "the first year was hell!" Could serving in the army have been more difficult?

After completion of medical school, Ben did not return to Pottstown. He settled in Bloomington, Illinois. There, the young man launched a highly successful medical practice and became a charter member of the Illinois Society of Pathologists.

Two years younger than Mike was Robert, Robbie or *Boat* to his brothers. Like Ben, Robbie was admired by his high school peers. They elected him senior class president, quite an honor for a Jewish boy in Pottstown. Not only was Robbie popular, he was a bit of a daredevil—witness the boating incident on the Manatawny which earned him his nickname and the beating from his father. The cocky Robbie also possessed a "wise guy" assuredness that occasionally landed him in trouble. During his senior year at the height of his popularity, Mr. Engle, Pottstown High's English teacher for seniors, warned Robbie he was failing English class. Robbie's attitude reflected his disdain for authority and disrespect for Mr. Engle. "I am the class president," the young man retorted. "You can't fail me."

Robbie may have been senior class president, but he did fail English. He did not graduate with the rest of his class.

Deeply embarrassed, Robbie left town. He took a job driving a delivery truck for the Davis Grocery Company in Norristown. Unlike his brother Ben who by now had entered medical school, Robbie was drafted into the army. His stint in uniform was short-lived. The war ended while Robbie was still in training. Wearing the uniform of an army private, he returned to Norristown to pick up where he had left off.

Life behind the wheel of a grocery truck and living with his brother Mike and sister-in-law Fanny eventually wised up the cocksure Robbie. He tired of hanging out with high school buddies and having little money in his pocket. After just one year as a truck driver, Robbie decided to follow in the footsteps of his older brothers Sam and Ben. He arranged to finish the one class he flunked his senior year. With degree in hand, Robbie enrolled at Bucknell University. Like Sam and Ben before him, he enrolled with the intention to pursue a law degree.

That first autumn, Robbie earned a starting position on the freshman football team. Returning from an away game, the team bus went off the road and down the side of a mountain. Several players were killed. Robbie was hospitalized. On receiving word of the accident, his deeply anguished parents immediately traveled to the small central Pennsylvania hospital where the injured players were being treated. When Adolph saw his heavily bandaged son, orderlies had to restrain him. "What have you done to my son?" he shouted. Tears streamed down his cheeks. Robbie remained in the hospital for close to a month.

As a result of his injuries, Robbie lost most of his hearing. He also lost any real opportunity to pursue the law career he visualized. An individual with hearing impairment had no place in the legal profession. Quickly discarding any sorrow or self-pity for his misfortune, Robbie weighed his options. His sensitivity for people, sympathy for those less fortunate, and gratitude for having survived the bus crash led him in a new direction. With the advice of a respected professor, Robbie decided he would pursue a career as a social worker, a new profession at the time.

The youngest Markowitz child was Francis, eight years younger than the next youngest sibling Kate. Francis was the first son born after the period of mourning for his brother Harry who had survived Rebnitza and the journey from Europe but died at age sixteen in America. Adolph and Rose debated whether their newborn son could be named for a deceased sibling. Adolph promptly sent a telegram of inquiry to the authoritative Yiddish daily newspaper the *Forward*. The *Forward*'s *bintel brief* column served as the *de facto* governing body for such questions of religious practice. Eight days elapsed without word of a ruling from the *Forward*. With the day of the *bris* upon them, the couple could not wait any longer. Adolph and Rose decided not to name the child Harry. They went with Francis instead.

To his siblings, Francis was the spoiled child. How else could they rationalize that he had been given a pony by their father! Initially, Yetta deeply resented Francis. She knew, rightly, that she would have to care for her youngest brother as she had done for other siblings. Moreover, after Francis' birth, Rose's health began to decline. Although in later years, Yetta developed a special bond with Francis whom, in essence, she had raised, initially she was embittered by his appearance in the family.

Just how or why Francis received the nickname *Wushtie* is lost in time. He also suffered with the non-complimentary nickname *Fertzel*, a reference to small fart. Eventually, he outgrew *Fertzel*; he never outgrew *Wushtie*.

At the Passover *Sedar* there was little competition for who was the youngest Markowitz child. Francis sat next to his mother at the opposite end of the table from his father. Year after year Francis would be called upon to recite the "*Fier Kashes*", the Four Questions, always asked by the youngest member of the family who knew Hebrew. Francis dutifully asked the age-old questions *"Mah nishtana ha'lailah ha'zeh mi kol ha'leilos?* Why is this night different from all other nights?" From the Passover *Haggadah*, Francis read the Four Questions in Hebrew. Adolph answered them in Yiddish. It was one of the few occasions he spoke to his children in Yiddish.

Francis was the least studious of the Markowitz boys. Rebellious and apathetic about academic achievement, he performed poorly in most of his classes. There was no question whether Francis was college material. During his senior year of high school, Francis was on the verge of dropping out. This triggered consternation from Yetta. Now in her mid-thirties and with three children of her own, she still possessed strong maternal instincts for her kid brother. Their mother Rose had passed away a year earlier. Yetta felt, with justification, that she inherited the family's matriarchal mantle.

On her own and no consultation with their father, Yetta approached the high school principal. She asked that he reverse Francis' imminent academic suspension from school. She blamed his poor performance on his association with a colorful man named Yanesh, a chauffeur with the Potts family. Her allegations about Yanesh's negative influence on Francis may have been true. Family members sarcastically referred to Yanesh as the *nishgutnick*, the no-good-nick. But Yetta's effort to keep Francis in school until graduation met with no reprieve from the unsympathetic principal. Francis was tossed out of Pottstown High.

Francis left school and found work in the metal casting production unit at the Light Manufacturing Company. Despite his son's lethargic attitude towards peddling, Adolph still hoped that his youngest son would continue the now successful junk business. However, it became apparent even to him that Francis was not going to live up to the "son" portion in A. Markowitz &

Dos bruderen

Son. After a few months Francis tired of factory work. He left Pottstown and moved in with Mike and Fanny in Norristown. Eight years earlier, his brother Robbie had slept on the same bed in Mike's apartment. Like Robbie, Francis found a job driving a grocery truck. Mike's sales girl in the shoe store, Minnie Sacks, had a sister Ida. Although slightly older than Francis, Ida became his first girlfriend, then bride. With his marriage, Francis realized he needed more income than that of a truck driver.

In the 1920's, Friendly Five shoes, manufactured by the General Shoe Company, Nashville, Tennessee, was one of America's best selling brands of five-dollar men's shoes. With the assistance of an uncle, Francis obtained a salesman job with Friendly Five covering New York City. He and Ida moved to New Jersey. Unfortunately, the city was a graveyard for salesmen, particularly young, inexperienced ones with no New York connections. To supplement his meager income, Francis sold shoes on Saturdays for Willie Silberman in Perth Amboy. Silberman's wife Bertha was Francis' cousin.

Yetta fretted about her brother's flailing employment efforts. She took it as a personal affront, an indictment of her childrearing of the young Francis. "New York is no place for him," she told her husband. "Francis should have his own shoe business." She set out to make this happen.

The Schwartz Shoe Store at Tenth and Penn Streets in nearby Reading was for sale. With cash extorted from her husband and brothers, Yetta arranged for its purchase. Reading was an industrial city four times larger town than Pottstown. In Yetta's view, this meant four times as many potential customers. She was confident Francis would thrive in the shoe business there. Francis acquiesced and moved with Ida to Reading.

Although Schwartz's was a large well-furnished store, it suffered two significant drawbacks: poor location and stiff local competition.

Chicken Hill Chronicle

Unable to reverse the store's physical circumstances or carve out a customer base, Francis was overwhelmed. Ultimately, after just eighteen months the business venture was failed.

Francis then took Ida to Allentown. He obtained a sales job with Weiss Brothers, a shoe company run by another set of cousins. A few years later, that attempt too failed to pan out.

* * *

The oldest Markowitz son born in America was Sam.

To those he touched—and over the decades there were many—Sam's life was a lesson in open-mindedness. He believed that extremism, whether right or left, excessively conservative or liberal, was a threat to all minorities.

Yet, in his unique way Sam was an extremist. Sam did not preach tolerance. He practiced it. Raised on Chicken Hill in a predominantly African-American neighborhood, he was an early member of the NAACP (National Association for the Advancement of Colored People.) Late in life, he confided to a family member that he had marched with Dr. Martin Luther King. Jr. This was difficult to believe. Sam would have been over seventy years old during the Civil Rights movement of the 1960s. Moreover, he never mentioned this fact to his own children. But the concept of an elderly Sam Markowitz marching in Alabama would have been in character. Almost a half century earlier, Sam had fervently opposed America's entry into the First World War describing it as a capitalist war for profits. One afternoon while he delivered an anti-war soapbox speech in Cincinnati, a union activist took a shot at him. The bullet missed, however, the incident made the local papers.

Since Rose registered her children by pairs, Sam moved through Pottstown's education system in lockstep with his older sister

Yetta despite the twenty month gap in their ages. Thus, he was always among the youngest students in his classes. Sam demonstrated academic talent in courses such as Latin and German and received high marks from his teachers. Although friendly and outgoing, Sam's socialization skills lagged behind his peers, especially his younger brothers Ben and Robbie. Perhaps it was the price of being the eldest American-born son. Within the Markowitz household, none could advise the teenager how to behave in the social milieu of American schools. In junior high and high school, he exhibited a naïve, fussy personality, both gullible and insecure. In his senior year, Sam's classmates selected him as "most likely to remain a bachelor."

With his pending graduation from Pottstown High School in 1909, Sam pondered his academic future. His father encouraged him to continue his education and agreed to pay. But Adolph could not help with advice. What did a peddler from Rebnitza know about American universities? Without the benefit of guidance counselors or collegiate advisors, students were left to their own devices. Despite a plethora of nearby colleges, little information about them was available. None were seriously considered. For sure, a "swanky" college for the Markowitz kid was out of the question. Applying to an Ivy League school, Sam knew, would be "plain *chutzpah*."

The decision came to him. In the spring of his senior year, Stanton R. Smith, a Bucknell University senior, visited Pottstown High School. His purpose for the visit was to solicit interest in his alma mater. For $300 a year, Smith explained, a student could receive a college education, room and board at Bucknell University. Sam was convinced. Why not Bucknell? He applied and was accepted.

Out of a total university enrollment of almost 900, Sam was one of only eight Jewish students. A pea green freshman at seventeen, away from home for the first time, Sam was unprepared for his new environment. As a result, from the moment he arrived on campus his academic career and social interactions began to move in strange directions.

Because of the High Holidays, Sam reported to Bucknell ten days late. It was early October. The Allegheny Mountain foliage had reached its colorful peak. From the train Sam stared at the new landscape. He had never been to the Susquehanna River. Nor had he been to Harrisburg where he had changed trains. His father's *lantzmen*, Estreicher and Feldman, had stared in similar wonderment at Pennsylvania countryside from a similar train twenty-three years earlier. Sam thought about his family, especially his mother.

Whether the railroad ticket clerk was malicious or just inept, he routed Sam to Lewisburg indirectly. Instead of an early afternoon arrival as Sam had expected, his train reached Lewisburg after 6 p.m. Suitcase in hand, Sam got off. He looked confused and lost. At least he knew, unlike Estreicher and Feldman, he was in the correct town. But where was Bucknell? "Excuse me, which way to the university?" Sam asked the first person he saw.

Joseph E. Edwards, a senior divinity student and the son of a local Baptist minister, turned to the new arrival.

"The university office is already closed at this hour. You won't be able to meet the registrar until tomorrow." Edwards considered the young man standing with his lone suitcase. He smiled. "Don't worry. We'll take care of you tonight, and you can register with the college tomorrow," the upperclassman generously offered.

Edwards possessed a deeply pious, radiant, and compassionate personality which Sam found irresistible from the very outset. Sam realized that Edwards was different from anyone he had ever known. The older man enjoyed complete self-confidence. He was tall and sculptured with blond hair and blue eyes. Edwards possessed a *savoir faire* beyond that of anyone Sam knew back in Pottstown. Every word uttered by Edwards sounded to the smitten teenager as if it came from Moses on Mount Sinai. Within days Edwards recognized that Sam was homesick, forlorn, and ill adjusted to the transition to Bucknell. He perceived something else in the bumbling teen. Edwards sensed an intensity that if not bordering on genius certainly could lead to greatness. Edwards invited Sam to be his roommate.

Thus, within weeks of Sam's arrival in Lewisburg, Edwards became his mentor. The younger man blindly followed the elder. This included attendance at classes on Christian theology and even church services. Every Sunday morning, Sam felt privileged to sit with Edwards in the adult bible class taught by Professor Llewellyn Phillips, Bucknell University's most esteemed theology instructor. He attended the religious services that followed at the Lewisburg Baptist Church. Edwards remained Sam's guide and counselor throughout Sam's freshman year. Sam felt no remorse for his behavior. He knew, however, that summer vacation would bring the inevitable.

Sam could not hide the rumors that filtered home. One cannot live in a Jewish home, call himself Jewish, yet take off on Sunday mornings to attend services in a Baptist church! Moreover, such behavior cannot be kept secret from the community. Sam's record at Bucknell became choice gossip at the *shul*, and beyond. Even among Pottstown's non-Jews, the news was sensational, even shocking. Adolph was torn. It was a situation for which his whole being was unprepared. Out peddling from dawn until evening, Sam remained unruffled by the scandal he had created.

Adolph's effort to help his wayward son "see the light" proved fruitless. There was no reasoning with the boy. Adolph did not know where to turn for help.

Sam himself seemed confused. His introduction into Christianity catalyzed more questions than answers. "If the traditional rabbinical code is the law Jews should follow," he pondered, "why is it so blatantly disregarded?" If in America the code no longer has authority, "should not some other procedure be developed?" It was all so theological. To Adolph such words were those of a *meshugener*, a crazy man. "What has this American college done to my son?" he asked his closest friends. They just shook their heads. None had an answer. None had sons attending college.

As summer drew to a close, Adolph decided his son would not return to Bucknell. How could he? Instead, he sent Sam to Pittsburgh where he would labor for a relative. Adolph hoped the sojourn in Pittsburgh would cure his son of his philosophical ranting.

At the urging of parents, Sam consented to discuss his conflicted moral feelings with rabbinical authorities. Seeking answers, he met with various rabbis in the Pittsburgh area. None of their responses satisfied him. Sam felt their answers smug and condescending. All failed to explain what he called the hypocrisy of contemporary Jewish life. In frustration, Sam gave up any hope that Judaism held the key to resolving his tortured search for meaning. After a year of working for his uncle, discouraged in his quest to resolve his internal dilemmas, Sam returned to Lewisburg. Completely infatuated with his mentor, he moved in with Edwards, now married and a minister at Hope Baptist Church.

With Edwards' encouragement, Sam drew tighter to the Baptist movement. At ease in Lewisburg's gentile environment, Sam turned his back on his Jewish roots. He was baptized and warmly welcomed into the fold. After some training, Sam received a license to preach. By autumn 1911 Sam returned to Bucknell for his sophomore year. Tuition money from home was not needed. Sam received scholarship funding provided by the Northern

Baptist Convention. For spending money, he conducted biweekly church services, delivered sermons, and baptized babies at a small country church. The news trickled back to Pottstown. Letters from family members desperately pleaded with Sam to return home. The beseeching was in vain. At *shul,* Adolph recited the *kaddish,* the prayer for the dead, for his son.

However, cracks began to appear in Sam's convictions. Doubts gradually tormented the young preacher. During the summer of 1913, Sam served as a temporary staff member of the New Covenant Mission to Jews of Pittsburgh. While walking Pittsburgh's streets on this proselytizing mission, vague questions gnawed his confused mind. He began to have serious regrets about his chosen path. But he remained loyal to Edwards and to the Baptist church. Back at Bucknell that fall, Sam studied the Gospels Matthew, Mark, and Luke with Professor Phillips in a class taught in Greek. New questions entered his mind. Certainly, not all Baptists were angels, and not all Jews devils. "Was religion a hoax?" he asked himself. Was it "a product of avaricious priests? Was it possible that he had been "misled?"

After graduation, Sam put his religious activities on hold. He took a one-year teaching position at Spring City High School, seven miles from Pottstown. The school board knew his background and assumed he had converted. The pastor of the local Lutheran church was of the same species; hence a convert in the community was no novelty. Adolph had not reconciled to his son's apostasy. He had by now, however, stopped reciting *kaddish* each day. He now said it only on Shabbat. On days he knew his father would be peddling, Sam surreptitiously traveled to Pottstown to visit his mother. He kept to Chicken Hill's back alleys. Why risk being spotted by nosey neighbors or acquaintances?

Sam's year of teaching in Spring City and his non-involvement in religious activities provided him the necessary distance to review his recent past and ponder his life's choices. His thoughts constantly returned to religion. "Why," he asked, "if Joseph Caro's *Shulchan Aruch*, written in the sixteenth century, was the compilation of Jewish law, did Jews not live by it?" At *chevra* meetings a frequently heard expression when discussing Jewish law was "*Schtait geshribben*, it is written!" (as in the *Shulchan Aruch*.) Jews paid "lip service" to the law. Yet, very few followed the law as written. Sam pondered his difficult questions. His simple conclusion: "No Jew could possibly follow the law" as Joseph Caro laid it out.

His journey into Christianity, Sam decided, had been a terrible mistake. He did not blame Edwards or Lewisburg's Baptist leadership for his chosen direction. Instead, he reproached himself for being so trusting of their guidance. But with this insight, what was he to do? Where could he go to seek advice? Some Bucknell classmates were doing graduate work at the University of Chicago. Sam decided to join them. But they could offer little. After more extensive soul searching, Sam was still no closer to determining his future life direction. He felt as if he had reached a dead end.

Then, the flash hit him. He would become a rabbi! He informed his family. Adolph was astonished. Now he knew his son was *meshugeh*!

Sam made it his full time quest to gain entry into a rabbinical seminary. Sam appealed to the leadership of the Judaism's Orthodox, Conservative and Reformed movements. He consulted with his brother-in-law who had recently been ordained at the Jewish Theological Seminary. When rabbinical authorities heard his story, however, they offered no solution. In their view, his notorious past precluded rabbinic study. There could be no restitution. A few laughed in his face. There would be no question of allowing Sam to "return to the fold" in *this*

Dos bruderen

manner! From each contact, he received the same negative response. A rabbinical career would not be possible.

Sam's desperate trek took him to Julius Rosenwald, President of the Sears Roebuck Company and a major contributor to the nascent Hebrew Union College in Cincinnati, Ohio. Rosenwald listened intently to the young man's plight. He was impressed by Sam's zeal but not wholly convinced about his common sense. Rosenwald paused while he considered what he would advise. "Although this is against my better judgment," Rosenwald confessed, "I'll try to assist you."

Rosenwald succeeded in gaining Sam a conditional enrollment at the Hebrew Union College. Sam would be a rabbinical student. The terms were severe. Sam would attend on a one-year probationary basis. If he slipped up, he would be dropped from the rolls. College leadership remained skeptical about the experiment. Nor did Sam's outspoken criticism of America's entry into the World War provide much encouragement. But like his brother Ben who was undergoing his own trial by fire at Loyola Medical School, Sam persevered.

In 1979, Sam's nephew Norman Cohen participated in a tour group that spent two weeks behind the Iron Curtain. The tour visited an old synagogue in Poland. Its community devastated by the Holocaust was now in the nascent stages of a recovery—what little recovery could be permitted under communism. One of the members of the tour group, a department store manager from Philadelphia, seemed especially awed by the experience. "This reminds me of the man who taught me how to be a Jew," he remarked. He made his comment to no one in particular but loud enough to be heard by many in the group. Someone asked to whom he was referring. "My former Rabbi back in Philadelphia, Samuel Markowitz," he said. He could not know that the person next to him was Sam's close relative.

Seven

Yetta

The first Markowitz child to be born in Pottstown was Yetta. Her birth less than a year after her mother's harrowing Atlantic crossing, symbolized the family's transition from Europe to America. Of all the Markowitz children, Yetta remained most transfixed between two cultures, American and *shtetl*. On one hand, she experienced and enjoyed America's relative freedoms; on the other, she dutifully, and later sullenly, served her parents' old world social mores. Yetta found the chasm difficult to traverse. Two societies pulled her in opposite directions. She never seemed fully comfortable in either.

America proffered limited opportunity for women. A talented woman might advance towards a career or even a profession. Perhaps even marry someone not selected by her parents. Girls from other Jewish families did accomplish much. Given the steep hurdles, however, few women cracked open male-dominated professions and academic institutions. But success was possible, especially with strong family support.

The *shtetl* world of Yetta's parents rested upon traditional Jewish values brought over from Galicia. Although Yetta possessed a deep-seeded desire to emulate the academic success of her younger brothers, she enjoyed no foundation from which to launch her own dreams. In its view of the role of women, Adolph and Rose's patriarchal world was sexually rigid. With a boost from her family, Yetta might have achieved success. Her mind was as sharp as any of her brothers. But it was a hopeless prospect. Adolph's vision did not include female academic accomplishment and leadership. He remarked repeatedly, even in the months just before his death, "I don't believe in college education for women."

Paradoxically, Yetta's father greatly respected schooling for all his children, daughters included. Adolph was not unreasonable about educating his two daughters. Yetta attended although did not complete high school. Many of her peers could claim less. Later, she attended the Pottstown Business School, a private institution run by a family named Kelly. This was more education than the daughter of immigrants could expect to receive. Adolph had little difficulty comprehending that young women could benefit from learning secretarial skills. But her father's motives were clear. "To get a husband," he constantly told his eldest daughter, "is more important for you than education."

Through her brothers Yetta witnessed academic achievement. Adolph encouraged his boys to pursue higher education. Three eventually earned university degrees. One became a doctor, a second a PhD Rabbi. The other two boys, Adolph acknowledged, were not college material. But Adolph considered a university education for his daughters a frivolous luxury. Sam, Ben, Robbie, Mike, and even Francis had their opportunities. Yetta, the family's eldest living child, aspired for such a chance. It never came. She felt unfulfilled. She could not cloak her resentment and frustration within the social constraints of her sex. Her anger smoldered for decades. She repeated often and with scorn her bitterest tirade. To any who would listen, she spat out how "unfair it was that my brothers received a college education but I was unable to graduate even high school!"

During her childhood, Yetta constantly fretted over the family's peddler status. Money in the immigrant household was scarce. Little consideration was given to "appearances." One rainy day, Yetta went to school wearing old, dull looking rubbers salvaged from her father's junkyard. They were not even proper mates. If her mother had not insisted, Yetta would never have put them over her shoes. Upon arriving at the school, Yetta quickly rid herself of the offending footwear. She surreptitiously placed the unmated pair in an unlit cloakroom and pushed the horrible potential embarrassment from her mind. But Yetta knew she would have to retrieve the rubbers or receive a scolding. That afternoon, Yetta sat in the dark cloakroom and, without looking down at the offending pair, placed a pair of rubbers over her shoes. Walking home from school that afternoon, Yetta realized she was wearing a pair of shiny, almost new rubbers. In her discomfiture, she had not noticed any other rubbers in the cloakroom.

At school the next day, an announcement was made to the entire student body. "Will the person who took the wrong pair of rubbers yesterday return them to the office. They can claim the old pair that was found." Mortified with shame, Yetta never made the exchange. She also never wore the rubbers again.

As a young teenager, Yetta craved more attention from her busy father. "Why can't I go with you papa?" she asked her father as he pulled himself onto his peddler's wagon. The boys Sam and Ben were seated in back. "I can help you peddle."

From the wagon seat Adolph looked down on his daughter. He face showed only meager sympathy but growing impatience. "You have to remain here to help your mama take care of Robert and Mike," he curtly told her. When Yetta did not move, Adolph grew angry. He added caustically "How could *you* peddle? This is man's work." Such behavior! Shaking the reins, Adolph continued to mumble to himself. It was Rose's doing, he believed. "What ideas is she putting into Yetta's head?" He shared his annoyance with Rose upon his return that evening. "That my daughter should go be a *pedler*, what *meshugahs*! Why do I even expend breath on this topic?"

Rebuked, the sullen Yetta drifted off to assist her mother with chores. Around the kitchen table that evening and many evenings after, her brothers regaled their daily adventures on the road with their father. With their yarns, a half smile of pride escaped from Adolph. He was pleased that his young sons so enthusiastically welcomed the family labors. While her brothers chatted away, from the seat next to her mother a vacant expression registered upon Yetta's vacuous face.

Yetta felt sorry for herself. But it was resentment, not self-pity that ate away at her heart. While the boys enjoyed their outdoor peddling adventures, Yetta was stuck assisting her mother and grandmother with housework, food preparation, and care for the younger children. When she was not at school or doing homework, the house served as her own personal prison. After housework, little time existed to socialize with girls from other immigrant families or cousins who lived down the street. Worse, precious little took place within the four walls of the house that deserved mention at the family dinner table. Yetta's few close friends acknowledged that they accepted their fate to labor as their mothers were doing. They possessed no yearning for taking on the outside world. They dreamed not of riding beside their fathers on a back road to Pughtown or Warwick Furnace, witnessing the change in seasons from the seat of a wagon, or engaging in spirited negotiation over the price of scrap iron. Instead, all they spoke about revolved around a future as wives and mothers. "If God wills it," one of her friends confided, "my future husband might even secure enough money to hire servants!"

* * *

At the dawn of the twentieth century, housework consisted of tough physical toil. It had changed little during the previous hundred years. And as throughout recorded history, the lion's share fell on the women in the family.

Most burdensome was the kitchen. Until electric and gas appliances made their appearance, women in America typically cooked over coal or wood stoves only marginally improved from the time of its invention in the eighteenth century. It was dirty work. Stove ashes from old fires required removal. Paper and kindling demanded a proper set. To heat water a fire was kept lit throughout the day. To direct smoke out of the kitchen, prevent accidental burns, and reduce the constant risk of a house fire, homemakers carefully watched and adjusted flues and dampers.

Stove temperatures were a matter of guesswork, since neither thermostats nor thermometers were available. Stoves were cast iron and required constant rubbing with a thick black wax to prevent rust. In order not to run out of wood or coal at inopportune times, a sufficient supply needed to be on hand. On average, housewives spent four hours each day laboring with these cumbersome iron contraptions—in addition to the time dedicated to myriad other responsibilities necessary to assure food reached the table.

However, maintaining a stove throughout the day, six days a week—no food preparation occurred on Shabbat—was just a portion of the daily labor for the homemakers. Food preparation required countless hours. Housewives purchased fruit, vegetables, flour, sugar, coffee beans, and milk products from vendors. Live poultry and fish required extra time. To prepare poultry, Rose or Yetta took the living bird to the *sochet* for proper slaughtering. Afterwards, the bird was plucked, cleaned, boiled, and cut apart. Fish entailed scaling as well as gutting and cleaning. Guts and other organic byproducts required disposal, often in the garden as fertilizer. It was messy work to which Yetta as the eldest daughter was generally assigned.

Using unwritten recipes passed down from previous generations, Rose supervised food preparation. Bread was baked. Coffee beans grounded. Vegetables chopped apart and boiled. For all this labor, the boys and men who benefited from their labors shared not a dime of compensation nor extended many words of appreciation.

Cleaning and maintaining the home was a Sisyphean task even more arduous than food preparation. Stove and hearth fires produced thick smoke and gritty ash that permeated every corner, curtain, and closet. Kerosene and gas lamps emitted their own noxious odors and grime. Lamp glass required wiping, wicks needed trimming. In summer dust and dirt from the unpaved street penetrated even closed windows. Rain and snow resulted in tracks of mud despite assiduous care to leave footwear outside on the porch. Floors were scrubbed and rugs beaten. Rodents, a constant menace even in an immaculate home, thrived when the conditions were less than perfect. Mosquitoes and other insects entered the house almost at will.

Yetta was a young teenager when the family moved into a house with indoor plumbing, a heaven sent blessing. At the previous two Markowitz residences water was obtained from wells behind each house and perilously close to existing outhouses. The women manhandled the pump handles heavy and stiff with rust.

They filled buckets and carried them into the house. During long dry spells, well water thickened into an unappealing odorous green stew. Cold snaps froze well pipes and thick ice coagulated around the pump handle. To obtain cooking and drinking water when the well was inoperable, there was little to be done except hike to a public cistern near the bottom of Chicken Hill and, of course, stagger back with the weighted buckets. Over a year, each housewife and assisting daughter carried water buckets scores of miles. Without drains or sinks to allow wastewater elimination, the pattern went into reverse. The used water was dumped in the back yard, the alley, or down the outhouse hole.

Yetta considered laundry days the worst. She hated them passionately. Without mechanical devices, muscle power provided the wash cycle agitation. The evening before dirty laundry was placed in a tub to soak overnight in lye soap and warm water. The next morning the laundry was scrubbed on a stiff washboard. Rose or Yetta then removed the laundry to a second vat of boiling water and stirred the clothing with a pole. They lifted the wet clothing by the pole into the original tub, dirty water now replaced with fresh. After rinsing twice, the clothing was wrung out and hung on clotheslines in the back yard. In inclement weather, clothesline was strung across the dank unfinished basement and the clothing hung there. During winter, there was little choice. In such damp conditions, trousers might take days to dry. Adolph lacked appreciation for the challenge of drying laundry in the basement. For the next week, through innuendo and snide Yiddish he expressed his unhappiness with the musty odor of his flannel shirts.

As the eldest daughter, Yetta toiled unceasingly with housework and childcare. In contrast, Katie who was nine years younger escaped most of the drudgery. By her teenage years, all but two of the boys were already out of the house and the family occupied its most modern residence yet with both electricity and indoor plumbing.

Unlike her older sister, Kate did not fret about foregone educational opportunities. Like her brothers she attended Pottstown High School. She participated in school functions and was socially engaged with friends both Jewish and non-Jewish. Passive, unambitious, and unmotivated, Kate did not fret about college.

In jealousy or perhaps just out of spite, Yetta treated her sister miserably for many years. She made her feelings towards Kate transparently clear through snide comments, excessive criticism, and constant belittling. Why Kate put up with such treatment and took the abuse, no one in the family ever figured out. Nor could anyone understand why neither Adolph nor Rose took any action to curtail the abuse hurled by one daughter against the other.

For many years Kate's best friend was Pauline Friedman whose father had a china and glass store on High Street. Pauline's elderly parents were friendly and quiet and utterly dedicated to their only daughter who herself was courteous, unassuming, and delightful. Yetta complained continually and caustically to Katie about her *shmegegi* idiot friend. She ragged Kate about Pauline as if her friend and the rest of her family had leprosy. The venomous language hurt Kate deeply. Yetta was unsuccessful in breaking up the friendship. But she succeeded in poisoning relations between the two families.

Another cruel incident demonstrating Yetta's ill-will towards her sister occurred a decade later. By then, Yetta was married with three young children. She lived many blocks from her parents. In late 1922 their mother took sick. The illness was severe. To receive care and attention, Rose was moved to Yetta's house. The end came in February 1923. One son, Robbie, was away at Bucknell University. With Rose on her deathbed, Sam and Ben composed a telegram, maximum of ten words, instructing Robbie to get back promptly to Pottstown. "Mother seriously ill, calling for you." Mike in Norristown was contacted and he hastened to Pottstown.

At the moment of their mother's passing, however, Kate was not in the room. She had been out with friends and did not get the word of her mother's sudden turn for the worst. Kate walked into the somber room. Yetta turned to Kate. A shadow of revulsion and pent up hatred clouded her eyes. With venom as deadly as an adder's, she acerbically taunted "Katie, where were you? Now you have no mother!"

In ways large and small Yetta displayed her contempt for the sister she evidently wished she did not have. Before important Jewish holidays, Yetta prepared *bulkies* (her version of a Hungarian word for cinnamon coffee cakes) to send to her brothers wherever they were residing. Prior to the holiday of Purim, she baked *hamantoschen* to distribute to them. Yet, it never occurred to Yetta that she had a sister to whom she could also send cake and *hamantoschen*.

Yetta's rage towards Kate never mellowed. She never accepted Kate's marriage to Morris Benstock whom she considered a gambler. It was a rare feeling she shared with their father. Adolph perceived Benstock as shiftless and incapable of making a living. Later, Yetta transferred her vindictiveness to her sisters-in-law, Jewel (Sam), Fanny (Mike), Bea (Robbie), Ida (Francis) and her brother-in-law's wife Hannah. Even after fifty years, her ire did not wane. When the family received word that her husband's only brother Herman passed away, Yetta's only comment was "She (Hannah) killed him!" Yet for some unfathomable reason, Yetta liked one of her sisters-in-law. Lena, nicknamed Brick, Ben's wife, somehow escaped Yetta's ire. Yetta never had a harsh word for Brick. The feeling, however, was not mutual.

One of Yetta's few close companions was her teenage cousin Golda Weiss. Golda had just immigrated to America. For Yetta,

Golda was the sister that Katie was not. For Golda, Yetta was her pillar of adjustment to life in America. Yetta taught her cousin English, escorted her to school, assisted with homework, and quickly introduced the newcomer to life in America. The girls shared their hopes, dreams, and frustrations. The two were inseparable. Golda was the maid of honor at Yetta's wedding. The companionship remained tight into their respective marriages.

The mutual good feelings however did not last. After her marriage Yetta left town with her new husband Abe for New Hampshire. In the meantime, Golda and her new husband Ben Berger were set up in a Pottstown shoe store assisted by her successful brothers. Following her husband's unimpressive and unsuccessful business efforts elsewhere, Yetta and her young family returned to Pottstown. Likewise with financial support from her brothers, Yetta's husband opened his own shoe store. Golda resented her cousin's return. She felt the new store created unnecessary business competition for her own family. By opening the second shoe store, Golda claimed her cousin and her husband caused "bread to be taken out of my family's mouths!" Golda broke off the friendship.

Yetta was deeply hurt by Golda's rejection and animosity. "There are enough customers in Pottstown for many shoe stores," she contended. Golda may have been right, however. The two shoe stores competed for decades.

Despite her own emotional intensity and deep resentment towards others, Yetta could not comprehend her cousin's passionate reaction against her. Yetta appealed to her cousin to soften. She appeared unannounced at Golda's front door, usually with a freshly baked cake. She approached Golda at *shul* during the High Holidays. It was no use. The one-sided rift solidified into deep estrangement.

Years later, Yetta was traveling by car with Golda's brother Morris. She raised the issue of the estrangement. Morris was visibly uncomfortable with the topic. "Why is Golda so upset with me?" Yetta persisted.

Sheepishly, choosing his words warily, Morris replied that Golda's reaction was "human nature."

"I don't understand," Yetta said. She asked Morris to elaborate.

Trapped by her persistence, he diplomatically tried. "Golda regarded you as her older sister. She looked up to you. Perhaps she feels that when Abe opened the store, you were not sensitive to her interests, to her family's well-being."

Still, Yetta failed to understand the root cause behind Golda's bitterness.

The feud was not patched up until proprietorship of both shoe stores passed on to the next generation.

Yetta directed her deepest rancor towards her father. Ties between the two had never been close. Adolph's worldview strictly segregated the roles of men and women. He possessed an inflexible attitude about women outside the home. "Of course, I raised my sons differently than my daughters," he once told a *lantzman*. "Without a man to earn the money, how can a woman put bread on the table for her family?" On the other hand, his daughter perceived this narrow-mindedness as a personal attack. To whom else would her father be referring when making such remarks? Around her father, Yetta spoke little. But behind his back she castigated him bitterly and mercilessly.

The estrangement only worsened. After her mother's death, Yetta and her family moved in with Adolph. There was little choice. Who else would take care of the "old man?" The youngest son

Frances, a teenager of sixteen, was still at home. All the other Markowitz siblings had left Pottstown for greener pastures. Katie and Morris Benstock resided on Natrona Street in Philadelphia where Morris operated a sandwich stand. Mike and Fanny owned a shoe store in Norristown. Sam, Ben, and Robbie, all university graduates, were well on their way towards success in their respective professional careers.

Thus, onto Yetta's shoulders fell all the housekeeping and childrearing burdens she so despised. All the memories of slaving through daily chores with her mother resurfaced. This time, things were worse. She had her own family, her own children, to raise. No one else picked up the slack. Bad enough, Yetta felt, that she must labor on behalf of her passive, underachieving husband. Now, she was forced again to serve as the underappreciated housekeeper for her father.

The situation was corrosive. Fights broke out over the smallest, most insignificant issues. When Yetta's temper reached a boiling point, Adolph stormed out of the house. "*Strasheh mich nit*! Don't threaten me!" he shouted, lapsing into Yiddish to get his point across.

Two years later, Adolph married the widow of a *lantzman*. He did not hide the fact that it was a marriage of convenience. "*Nu?* What would you have me do?" he asked his daughter.

With the appearance of a stepmother, Yetta and her family left her father's house for good. From then, she refused even to speak with her father. The rancor deeply scarred the family. Despite their close proximity on Chicken Hill, the close ties of the grandchildren to their *zaideh*, and Adolph's own financial self-sufficiency compared with Yetta's relatively impoverished household, the two stubborn Markowitz family members refused to communicate. Social intercourse was conducted through her husband, the children, and occasionally her brothers. While the broken ties with his eldest daughter distressed Adolph, he steadfastly refused to press for any reconciliation. For her part, Yetta's anger smoldered like a smoking volcano, ready to erupt at any moment. She rebuffed for years any effort by her husband or other family member to bring the two parties together.

In more contemporary times, Yetta's emotional suffering would likely have been recognized in psychological terms. Had psychiatrists been available, perhaps her mental distress could have been addressed. Alas, psychiatry for the masses did not yet exist. Mental illness, if recognized, meant dementia or insanity. Inevitably, it led to placement in an asylum. Except for her sisters-in-law who formed a solid consensus, few people claimed Yetta was insane. But she was profoundly troubled.

One might ponder another cause for Yetta's anger. Had Adolph's constant drumbeat about landing a husband further traumatized the young Yetta?

When Yetta turned 21, an old maid by the standards of the *shtetl*, the pressure on Adolph and Rose to married off their eldest daughter intensified. Unfortunately, tales and evidence of Yetta's incendiary personality already pervaded Pottstown's incestuous Jewish community. Identifying possible grooms from among Pottstown's few eligible Jewish bachelors proved difficult. Yetta's own unhappiness matched the parental desperation. It was a volatile mix.

In one episode, Adolph and Rose arranged for a matchmaking meeting with a man named Berman from rural Montgomery County. In tow with her parents, a sullen Yetta made the trip by wagon to Green Lane to meet the potential suitor. Berman who looked the part of the country farmer greeted the party and played the gracious host. Yetta noticed immediately that Berman wore the same style old-fashioned suspenders used by her father. She had no intention of spending the rest of her life living on a farm or looking each day at a *yeshuvnik* husband who wore the same rustic clothing as her father! She rejected Berman outright. That torpedoed the matchmaking. The indignity involving Sam's entry into Christianity scandalized the family and also turned off any other potential suitors from around Pottstown.

By age 22, Yetta's life, to her parents at least, seemed to be washed up. Adolph was undeterred, however. He would not permit his daughter to become a spinster in the Markowitz house! He decided to extend his search for a mate for his eldest daughter. He targeted the *bintel brief* (A Bundle of Letters) section of the widely circulated New York Yiddish newspaper, the *Forward*. The *Forward*'s lonely-hearts column generally offered advice to perplexed readers who solicited help. Letters inquired "should I marry a woman with one leg shorter than the other?" or "should I return to Russia to fight in the Revolution?" It also served as a national anonymous matchmaking network for America's Yiddish-speaking population.

"Dear Editor,

Please help me out of my situation. We live in a small town with only few Jews. There are no eligible bachelors. My wonderful daughter, a real beauty, is a *kalleh moid*, (girl of marriageable age.) She has a *Yiddisher kop*, properly educated in *bentshen* of all prayers, well brought up in a proper *Yiddishkeit* home. She also is taught in secretary skills and is very capable of housework.

I seek for a *shidech*, her betrothal, a *mensch* who will make for her a good husband and she a good wife. The family has done well in *die goldene medina* and this is our first child born in America. She talks English better even than the *shiksehs*!

Dear Editor, I will be thankful for you to be *shadchen* matchmaker for me.

> Respectfully,
> Rose"

Although Adolph crafted the letter, he would not allow *his* name, even anonymously, to appear on a *bindle brief* letter!

Following its publication a few respondents answered the letter. But only one, an Abe Cohen of Louisville, Kentucky, resident of Manchester, New Hampshire, expressed serious interest.

Eight

Der zigar maker

In hindsight, the marriage of Abraham Cohen to Yetta Markowitz joined two terribly mismatched people. Initially, however, nothing out of the ordinary was apparent in their betrothal or marriage. Neither the Cohen nor Markowitz families greatly surpassed the other in wealth, class, or religious fervor, although in the later regard, the Cohen patriarch displayed an orthodoxy far beyond the morally ambiguous Adolph Markowitz. Born in Europe, Abe came to the United States as a young child. Of life prior to his arrival at Castle Garden, he remembered little. Each party to the marriage started life with Yiddish as their first language. Both bride and groom were *Americanisch*. Each was the eldest of siblings to reach adulthood. Each helped raise younger children. Moreover, at the time of the wedding in 1913, both were on the older side for matrimony. Abe was 28, Yetta 23. Certainly, the two seemed ripe for the *hupah*.

* * *

Abe Cohen was the eldest surviving son of deeply religious parents whose orthodox practices and religious bigotry influenced intensely the attitudes and beliefs of the son. He claimed as his birthplace Grodno, Lithuania. Grodno was a profoundly medieval Jewish city that contained famous yeshivas and ornate synagogues. More likely, Abe was born in the small village of Skidel, about 20 miles from Grodno. In Skidel his grandfather, Abraham Kotkin, ran a successful lumber business. Through his maternal grandfather, Abe's family heritage reached back through a long line of esteemed scholars and rabbis back to twelfth century pre-Inquisition Spain. One of his ancestors was the great medieval scholar Zachariah HaLevi. The lineage was prestigious. But Abe himself could not be mistaken for a bright leaf off the family tree.

In Russia's Pale of Settlement, Sima Kotkin identified few good prospects. With encouragement from his parents, he departed his Lithuanian *shtetl* to seek his fortune in America. At age 19, Sima was handsome, ambitious, and unencumbered by family obligations. The year was 1877. Sima arrived in New York City equipped only with a slip of paper giving the address of a *lantzman* who might consent to assist. Although confident he would do well in America, Sima was penniless, linguistically-challenged, and alone. But he possessed a deep unshakable faith in God's divine guidance. From the moment Sima walked down the gangway of the steam vessel, he knew America was a land that truly enjoyed God's blessings.

The American Civil War ended just a dozen years before Sima's arrival. The massive migration of Europe's "tired masses yearning to breathe free" would soon commence. The mass exodus of Eastern European Jews to America was a decade in the future. Americans in the 1870s gazed confidently westward towards the Great Plains, the Rocky Mountains, and beyond. The frontier beckoned "come west, young man!" In his own way the young

Der zigar maker

Litvak was also a pioneer, although Sima did not settle beyond Brooklyn Heights.

The teenager found accommodations in a small tenement apartment with five other single, sternly orthodox immigrant Jews. Like him, his roommates intended to make their fortunes in the New World. Living conditions were cramped but the rent was affordable. The men shared housekeeping responsibilities. They prayed each morning and kept to a strict kosher diet. That was how they were brought up in Europe. Different behavior was unthinkable.

Sima arrived in an America still reeling from the after affects of the financial "Panic of 1873." The country still suffered from a severe economic recession. Jobs that offered a living wage were scarce. Still, for the six young Jews living in a small tenement apartment in Brooklyn, the future shone far brighter than the recent past. With advice and support from his more "worldly" tenement mates, Sima took on an occupation that would mirror the profession chosen by his future in-law Adolph. He began peddling.

Sima worked out a deal with a local slipper company. In exchange for half the net profit, he would sell felt slippers door-to-door and to small fabric stores in Connecticut. Early each Sunday morning, Sima departed Brooklyn with a heavy sack of inventory slung across his back. He took the first Fulton Ferry of the morning across the East River to Manhattan. He hiked up First Avenue, crossed the Harlem River to The Bronx, and followed the old post road to Connecticut. Sima was determined to squirrel away every penny. The luxury of train fare to journey to Connecticut was unthinkable. "*Di klugeh gai'en tsu fus, un di naren foren!*" he said. Wise men go on foot and fools ride.

"SLIPPERS, SLIPPERS FOR SALE," he called out. His voice was a heavily accented baritone and carried far. Well aware of his limited English vocabulary, Sima nonetheless was unafraid to shout. "SLIPPERS, SLIPPERS, A GOOD PRICE!" At the outset, Sima's appeal for customers utilized perhaps two-thirds of his total command of English. But the young man persevered. Connecticut Yankees welcomed him into their homes. They offered him dinner and provided the young man with a place to sleep. They found him a gregarious fellow, a quick wit, and gracious to everyone he met. His English improved swiftly.

On rural roads around Stamford, Norwalk and even far-flung Danbury and Bridgeport, the slipper peddler hauled his load at a frenzied pace. He admired the region's industrial capacity, the fertility of its farms crowded with livestock, the corn and wheat fields stretched beyond the horizon. This might some day be a good place to settle, Sima thought. As he strutted, he hummed. He sang lullabies, Yiddish ballads and melodic Hebrew prayers he absorbed as a boy in the *chedar* in his village. "*Scheyne meydele kum tantzen Di redele dreht zich Di Mame kocht lochsen Der Tate freyt zich* . . . ." The tunes reminded him of holidays, his mother, and his grandparent's hearth in Skidel. He missed family but tried not to dwell on the distance between New England and old Lithuania. His heart wandered, but his mind was focused on the task at hand. He was in America to sell slippers and earn money.

The pace had to be quick. Time was short, particularly, since he was not riding the train. Whether or not he sold out of slippers, Sima had to return to Brooklyn by Friday evening before sundown, before Shabbat. If he ran late, he would be forced to expend a princely portion of his week's earnings to take the train.

In contrast to his future in-law Adolph Markowitz with his own peddling adventures in Pennsylvania, the cerebral Sima perceived no quandary between Jewish law and economic considerations. Shabbat remained sacrosanct. If slippers were unsold on Friday,

Der zigar maker

Sima left them with a trusted contact or carried them back to Brooklyn. For Sima, there would be no request to God for *selihot*, forgiveness, for violation of the tenants of Shabbat.

Time moved rapidly. Sometime during his three-year sojourn in America, Sima submitted paperwork for U.S. citizenship. It was routine, his friends assured him. To finalize the naturalization, all he need do was visit the local courthouse. In the press of work, however, Sima never completed the naturalization process.

After accumulating some savings, Sima decided to return to Lithuania. America was wonderful, a true golden land, but it was not home. Once back with his family, Sima married Dora Rachael Epstein daughter of Nachman (ben Shimshon) Epstein, a distant cousin. Three children were born to the couple. The family was rigorously religious. Shabbat and holidays were celebrated with fervent passion. Jewish life encompassed the family like a thick wool blanket on a frigid night. *Mishpoohah* lived all around. There was no reason to consider a change in their lives. Lithuania was their home.

Sima's life and that of his young family might have remained cemented to the Lithuanian *shtetl* but for one predicament, a financial one. More content to reading Talmud and following God's precepts in leading an orthodox life than in conducting business, Sima had difficulty maintaining his commercial ventures. Within five years, he lost all the money earned in America. Now with a wife and children to support, his options narrowed considerably. Piety may have been better placed in Lithuania than in America. Penury, however, was not. Sima reflected with his wife on his options. "I must go back to America, for good I think. When I have money I will send for you."

Rachael acknowledged her husband's decision. She understood. There was no angst in her voice. "Then you must go."

During his second passage west across the Atlantic, Sima shared mutual experiences with another Jewish returnee to America. The two discussed employment possibilities, the best places to seek jobs, getting past the immigration authorities at Castle Garden. Sima mentioned his earlier sojourn in America.

"*Oy Gevalt*," the fellow exclaimed, "you neglected to get your citizenship papers or a passport! Since this is your second entry, the immigration officer won't let you enter."

Sima's face drained of all color, "What am I to do?"

The man offered specific advice. "This is how you behave," he said. "Whatever you do," he explained, "act like a complete greenhorn, don't speak any English, and for God's sake don't use your real name!" Sima considered the guidance.

Upon reaching Castle Garden, Sima entered a long snake line of anxious arrivals. From the pier a corridor led into a large prison-like hall. Sima did not remember the building. It was not the same one he had entered a decade earlier. Sunlight came through a cupola giving the hall an eerie affect. Uniformed guards stood everywhere. At the time of his previous arrival in America, few immigrants were crossing the Atlantic. Sima remembered the entry process then had been little more than a formality. He answered a few questions from a New York State examination officer, received a cursory check by a physician, and then was released to catch the ferry to the Battery

Evidently, times had changed. Sima carefully observed the milling families. There seemed to be hundreds. Despite warm weather, most wore coats and extra clothing. How else could one carry the few possessions brought over from Europe? He caught the words of caution from husbands to wives, from mothers to children. Tension in the hall weighed heavy. The unfortunate whim of an official, a misinterpreted remark, the evidence of glaucoma in an eye caught by the medical officer, or possession of the identical name of someone else who happened to be on a no-entry list might turn an arriving immigrant into a departing passenger on the next ship to Europe.

A low hum reverberated throughout the hall. No one wished to be heard by too many ears. Everyone seemed to speak in whispers, except for those who had reached the examination windows. There, flustered, tired immigrants underwent a battery of questions, delivered in staccato blasts from overworked officials. Interpreters stood along side the nervous arrivals. They tried to keep up with rapid fire questioning, the anxious responses. Every few minutes, a teary-eyed unfortunate was escorted into a holding room. These were the unlucky ones who would be returning to Europe. Howls of sorrow followed as other family members pleaded with immigration officials. Please allow their loved ones to enter America. The officials rarely relented.

Eventually, Sima reached the head of the line. He tried to chase the stress of the long waiting line from his face. It was no use. He knew he looked exhausted. Finally, he stood in front of an immigration examiner. "Name?" the immigration official barked. The officer had not even looked up from his paperwork. Sima paused a moment. He planned for this moment, knew what his next action was going to be. But when the moment came, he paused, unable to pull the trigger. A shudder raced through his body. Was he doing the right thing? Did he have to give up his name, his identity? Would they really know that he had already been to America a few years earlier? That he had taken out immigration papers? Sima noticed the shiny silver INS medallion on his blue cap. This was a federal official, not a New York State one. Perhaps, Sima feared, he will be harsher. The examiner's eyes found Sima's. It was the moment for decision. "Cohen, Simon Cohen." His voice sounded like a croak. Where did his voice go?

The decision was made. Sima knew it was a common surname, unlikely to raise any suspicions.

In America, the name Kotkin had just been erased from his life.

The tired inspector already inundated that morning with hundreds of arrivals barely glanced at Sima's face. He looked down and recorded the name on a list. He stamped a document and handed it to Sima without any further questioning. Sima Kotkin possessed a new identity. His new name was Simon Cohen.

In 1890 Simon sent passage money for Dora Rachael and the four children to join him. Abe age five made the harrowing crossing in steerage with older sister Katherine, older brother David, and infant brother Herman Max. The family reunited on the New York City Battery.

Most new arrivals moved immediately into New York's ethnic enclaves such as Manhattan's Lower East Side and Crown Heights in Brooklyn. Many never left the city. Neither Manhattan, nor Brooklyn, nor the Bronx, appealed to Simon. All were too crowded with immigrant competition. Simon already had enough of New York.

Kotkin *lantzmen* urged Simon to bring the family to Louisville, Kentucky. A Jewish community of almost 7,000 thrived in the city. This he did, reaching Louisville just months after a devastating March 1890 tornado severely damaged the city's tobacco row. With money he recently saved, Simon established a small peddling business. It operated out of a dry goods shop on east Market Street. On the side, Simon conducted a "furs and peltries" exchange. He learned the profession from an uncle in Lithuania. Simon purchased pelts from trappers still active in the Appalachian Mountains. He processed the furs and sent the finished product to furriers in New York. Simon rented an apartment at 514 E. Jefferson. It was only half a block from the new B'nai Jacob synagogue, next to the Crown Shirt Manufacturing Company.

While resident in Louisville, Simon never allowed his strict religious compass to drift. He possessed the same narrow, pious beliefs he held in Lithuania. Decades later even when he left Kentucky, his religious attitudes did not waver. Upon retirement Simon relocated with his wife and single daughter Katherine to Pottstown to be in close proximity to his son and grandchildren. Pottstown proved to be insufficiently religious for his orthodox views. After just one year, Simon again moved his family, this time to Brooklyn. It was the same neighborhood where he had resided more than four decades earlier. Simon died in 1921. His widow moved to St. Paul, Minnesota, to live with her son Herman, now a Rabbi.

Almost two decades after Simon's passing, former Pottstown resident Babe Friedman traveled from the Pennsylvania coal region to attend a funeral in his hometown. After the service he met Norman, one of Simon's grandchildren. They discussed common acquaintances.

"Norman, I want to tell you about your grandfather Simon," he said. "One evening Emmanuel Schwarz was having a house party. It was a big affair. He invited every Jew in town—with the exception of my father Hershel." Friedman's voice quivered as he recounted his story. At the time, Hershel Friedman operated a shoemaker shop on South Hanover Street. He was one of Pottstown's two chronic Jewish alcoholics and was often publicly drunk. Babe continued his story. "Cohen entered the house during the party. He went straight up to Schwartz and pointed his long, boney finger at Schwartz's face. He proceeded to lecture Schwartz loudly and with no concern about who might overhear. 'A Jew,' he said, 'never must shame another by ignoring him!'"

Simon's compassion had its limits, however. Another occasion exemplified the extent of his religious zealotry. Adolph's youngest son Francis asked Simon if he might pick a flower. Simon scolded the boy. "You're not religious enough to have a flower!"

Unlike his younger brother Herman who thrived in the world of books, Abe disliked school. He hated the regimen. Abe loathed sitting for hours in a classroom, forced to miss life's true pleasure: playing and watching baseball and football on the Louisville sandlots. As a result, Abe never progressed beyond seventh grade. For his father that was no serious issue. Simon himself never proceeded pass the *talmud torah* back in Lithuania. His son could labor for a living. From a young age, Abe obtained modest earnings as a newspaper boy for Henry Watterson's afternoon daily *Louisville Courier Journal*.

During the 1890s the Louisville Colonels baseball club played in the Federal, later the National League. The Colonels competed against such teams as the Cincinnati Reds, the Boston Beaneaters, the Brooklyn Bridegrooms—later Brooklyn Superbas, the Baltimore Orioles, and the Washington Senators. Each game day, one newspaper boy received free admission to the ballpark and exclusive right to sell penny papers. All the paperboys wanted the sales monopoly.

To reach the new Eclipse Park, home field for the Colonels at 28th and Broadway, a horse drawn trolley ran from downtown. The fare was a nickel. Newspaper boys paid the nickel fare and rode. As the trolley slowed to a stop, the boys jumped off and raced to the gate. The winner entered the ballpark. The losers sold their papers outside.

Der zigar maker

Not only was Abe reluctant to part with a precious five cents, he saw little reason to ride when his two ten year old legs loved to run. For the season opener at Eclipse Park, Abe decided he would run the distance instead. From the *Courier Journal* offices, Abe grabbed his share of fifty newspapers. The other boys dutifully rushed to the nearby trolley stop. Abe tore straight for Eclipse Park, two miles away.

That first week of baseball season, young Abe consistently reached the gate first. The gatekeeper noticed that the same winded paperboy arrived first every game day. He admired the kid's spunk and agreed to give Abe the exclusive right to sell papers in the park. This alleviated the need for Abe to sprint all the way to the ballpark with his newspapers. But he continued to run.

After selling his load of penny papers, Abe glued himself to a bleacher seat—there were plenty of vacant ones. He refused to miss any action on the field. Abe worshipped the Louisville Colonels. He revered its star slugger Honus Wagner, outfielder-manager Fred Clarke, and the eccentric pitcher Rube Waddell who played a couple of seasons in Louisville before going to Pittsburgh. Seven decades later the gray-haired Abe could still rattle off player statistics from those magical seasons during the 1890s. Players noticed the skinny blue-eyed kid who was a constant presence throughout the season. They occasionally invited him down to the field after the game. The youngster witnessed the flowering of the Louisville Slugger baseball bat with its rounded end and thickened diameter. He met the bat's inventor, thirty year old John Hillerich who explained how he had created the white ash bat in his woodworking shop in collaboration with Louisville's Lewis Rogers "Pete" Browning, the "Old Gladiator."

When the Kentucky Colonels finished the 1898 season, Abe did not return to the local public school. The paperboy was too old to continue selling papers at the ballpark, or elsewhere. For Abe, it was just as well. A year later Louisville played its last major league game, defeating Washington 25 to 4. Weeks later a fire razed the wooden grandstands from where Abe had viewed so many games. Besides, Simon had plans for his fourteen-year old son. Abe would learn a trade.

At the turn of the twentieth century, Louisville was the world's tobacco capital. Its tobacco district stretched for over a mile along Main Street, centered between Eighth and Twelfth Streets. Kentucky tobacco growers brought their cured production to the city's auction houses. The odor of cured tobacco wafted throughout the city. Residents recognized by smell the variety of tobacco being unloaded blocks away. Tobacco warehouses contained thousands of hogsheads of tobacco—each five-foot tall hogshead barrel contained between 1,000 and 1,500 pounds of tobacco. Buyers examined the exposed hogsheads before the bidding opened. Business spilled onto Louisville's streets. Wagons drawn by teams of horses carried up to four hogsheads. Every day but Sundays and holidays thousands of workers and hundreds of wagons jammed Louisville's tobacco row. Locals claimed a pedestrian could walk from Second Street all the way to Tenth or Twelfth Streets on the top of the hogsheads without ever touching the ground. Almost 200,000 hogsheads were traded annually. Adjacent to the dozens of tobacco warehouses were manufacturing plants and scores of small and medium-sized cigar and cigarette companies.

Simon arranged for his son to apprentice to a cigar manufacturer "D. Coblens and Brothers." on First Street. The brothers, Daniel and Felix, were quite willing to assist their friend Simon.

Before being considered proficient in their profession, cigar workers underwent an arduous apprenticeship. Teachable youngsters like Abe were highly prized. They gained knowledge quickly, usually possessed dexterous hands, cost the company almost nothing, and complained little. Moreover, young boys were unlikely to engage in union activity, a growing worry for many executives in the cigar industry. Before being considered qualified, apprentices learned to 'strip' the tobacco. 'Striping' required cutting the stem from the tobacco leaf. An improper strip wasted tobacco and ultimately made for an inferior cigar. The apprentices received instruction on 'selecting,' the separation of tobacco leaves by color, size, texture, and quality. The apprentices also underwent training on the proper inspection of the finished cigar to ensure an even roll and its correct packing in boxes or wrapped bundles.

The most talented workers who mastered stripping, selecting, inspecting, and packing apprenticed for at least one additional year to an expert cigar roller. Rollers were considered the elite of the cigar floor. Accordingly, they received a higher rate of compensation. Cigars came in hundreds of sizes and shapes. Each type of cigar also possessed its own particular flavor based on its wrap and filler. Thus, cigar rolling required extraordinary skill. A cigar roller began by selecting and blending the proper amount of filler leaf for the particular cigar being made. The roller placed the correct amount and type of filler tobacco in the palm of the hand and wrapped it with the correct size and type wrapping leaf. Each wrapper leaf also required careful selection to ensure the proper color, texture and flavor for a smooth aromatic burn. Using a knife, called a *chaveta* by many in the cigar industry familiar with the Cuban cutting instrument, the roller wrapped and trimmed the leaf evenly around the filler and clipped excess leaf from the cigar's lighting end.

Abe labored full time as an apprentice. After three years on the cigar floor, he acquired the entire range of skills to be considered an expert cigar roller. His wages went directly to his father who allowed him a meager monthly allowance.

By age 17, Abe had grown to almost six feet. On weekends when not laboring at the cigar bench, the lanky teenager played baseball and basketball for the Louisville Young Men's Hebrew Association (YMHA). He was a pretty good left-handed pitcher and won more games than he lost. Baseball was a different game in the 1900s than it would become in later years—more stealth and guile, less power and pure speed. Abe was no exception. He had a fair fastball and knew how to throw the change-up. His out pitch, however, was a spitball that broke just as it reached the plate. The spitball was perfectly legal, as was the scuffing of the ball by the pitcher to cause it to tail one way or the other. Since a ball was constantly reused, it became routinely scuffed anyway by hits and groundouts.

Conceived just seven years earlier by James Naismith at the YMCA in Springfield, Massachusetts, basketball was still its infancy in 1900. The first collegiate game was played only in 1896. Although he preferred baseball, Abe enjoyed the new game. On the basketball floor, the pace of action was languid—a lot of passing, very little shooting. When a traveling Yale University team came to Louisville, the YMHA defeated them 2 to 1. (Basketball really was a different game back then!) Decades later Abe contended he had scored both points for the YMHA side that day. Since there were no witnesses around to contradict him, his claim was difficult to dispute.

As Abe reached his late teens, cigar making and an affinity for baseball and basketball were not enough to keep him in Louisville. Simon recognized that his son possessed itchy feet. Perhaps it was an inherited trait. "If you wish, you can leave," his father conceded. "Go ahead and seek your fortune."

Possessing cigar-making skills and a nascent passion for adventure, Abe left home in 1903. He was seventeen years old. He made his way south.

Der zigar maker

For a cigar-maker, the Ybor City district of Tampa, Florida, was the place to be. Called "the cigar capital of the world" Ybor City was named for Don Vicente Martinez Ybor, a Cuban who opened the first cigar factory there in 1886. In just over a decade the district became the world's leading cigar manufacturing center. Ybor City's *La Septima Avenida* bustled with business and traffic. Thousands of immigrants sought jobs in the new cigar factories. Irish, Germans, Slavs, Spaniards, Jews, and Afro-Cubans rubbed shoulders at the rolling tables. After work, they made their way to their own clubs and overcrowded boarding houses. African-Americans and Italians generally held the maintenance and transportation jobs. Spanish workers dominated the rolling floor. They and Cuba's proximity gave the industry a "Spanish" air. Wrapper selectors were called *resagadores*, packers *escogedores*. Women worked at the stripping tables and boxed the cigars. With his experience as a roller, Abe easily found employment at one of Ybor City's larger factories. He shared a room at a Jewish boardinghouse.

Thanks to his accumulated skills, Abe earned about $27.00 for every 1,000 top quality cigars he rolled. This was good money. With little on which to spend his earnings and plenty of free time when not behind the cigar bench, Abe developed an affinity and talent for gambling. Upstairs at the boarding house or at one of Tampa's small Jewish clubs, Abe practiced the fine art of bluffing at poker and melding at pinochle. As in baseball and basketball, he achieved a proficiency made more effective by his calm demeanor, straight face, and lack of pretense. Plenty of willing partners certain of their superior card skills sat across from the tall boy from Louisville. More often than not, Abe left the table with no less cash than when he started the game.

After three years rolling cigars by day and playing cards in the evenings, Abe felt ready to move on. He departed Tampa for the Midwest. After knocking around Illinois and Missouri, he proceeded to the American Southwest. With his cigar making credentials, jobs were easy to find. Almost every state seemed to have a cigar industry. Abe passed a few weeks or months in one place, grew bored, and boarded a train to the next city or state.

In the summer of 1907 Abe arrived in Oklahoma City. Oklahoma was still a U.S. territory; it would receive statehood later that year. The city bustled with activity. Cowboys fresh off the range, roughnecks servicing the new oil fields, Chickasaw and Choctaw Indians from nearby reservations, recent immigrants, aspiring homesteaders, wheat farmers, former Buffalo Soldiers, peddlers, gamblers, hooligans, snake oil salesmen, con artists, aged lawmen, and drifters roamed the streets and crowded the many saloons. New arrivals occupied every inch of available hotel or boardinghouse space. The streets were dirt. There were no sidewalks. An oil well operated on the lawn in front of what was to become the state capital building. Cattlemen herded steers through the main streets of town. Livestock pounds were situated on the town's outskirts. On occasion pistol shots rang out, particularly on Saturday nights and following the completion of long cattle drives by teams of dusty, thirsty cowboys.

By being frugal and a careful gambler, Abe accumulated one thousand dollars. He kept the money hidden in his satchel. It was September, the time of the World Series and a prizefight involving a Jewish boxer. Abe wagered his fortune on the Cubs—more the better, he said, since the Cubs were opposing the Tigers with that Georgia bigot Ty Cobb—and on the Jewish fighter going a certain number of rounds with the champion. After waiting painful days for the newspaper to publish the final results, he won both ends of the bets.

With two thousand dollars in hand, Abe bought a saloon including building and inventory. Before making the purchase Abe frequented the establishment as a patron. He carefully observed the bartender whom he noticed took drinks but placed all receipts in the till. Abe kept the bartender. He himself never went behind the bar. Instead, he preferred to keep close watch on his business from the customer side. The saloon enjoyed a brisk if not rowdy commerce. In one corner, a poker game was in perpetual operation. Cowboys entered his establishment still wearing spurs and holsters. They spent their money quickly. Farmers in town for supplies were more cautious in their spending habits. Fights were rare but tempers did flare. Then one afternoon the bartender was fatally shot by an angry, inebriated customer. Abe promptly sold the saloon and decided he had had enough of Oklahoma City.

Traditional religion was deeply ingrained into the young man. During his travels, Abe consumed only kosher food and observed the Shabbat in proper orthodox fashion. Only after Shabbat ended did he light his first cigar of the week. In years of travel Abe developed extensive familiarity with almost every Jewish boardinghouse and hostel from the upper Great Plains to the Deep South. By the 1900s, Jewish families resided in most of America's significant settlements. Invariably, they heartily welcomed Jewish travelers who sought lodging or a meal and shared gossip and stories. Among Jews who crisscrossed the country, the locations of these islands of Jewish repose were shared back and forth over dinner tables with other travelers.

Years later, his brothers-in-law enjoyed toying with Abe. They were convinced they could show him up. "Abe, where can a Jew find a place to stay in Cairo, Illinois?" Or "Where can I find a kosher meal in Wichita, Kansas?"

Abe was amused by the test. It hardly pushed him to think. Abe not only provided the name of the local Jewish boardinghouse, he also gave the address and the name of the proprietress. When he could not provide a name, he noted that no Jewish boardinghouse existed in that particular town when he transited.

Gradually, Abe migrated to the northeast. He passed through Louisville and visited his family. Herman, his studious brother, had reached his late teens. In neither appearance nor personality did Herman resemble his older sibling. He was inches shorter and less hardened in body. Instead of wanderlust, Herman possessed a dedication to books and rabbinic Judaism. Already, he was preparing to enroll at the Jewish Theological Seminary in New York where he would begin rabbinical study. Simon approved of his son's aspirations, although he preferred that Herman move in a more doctrinal direction of Jewish study. Founded just two decades earlier, the Seminary formed the bedrock for America's nascent Conservative movement. Abe's stopover in his hometown was warm but short-lived. Louisville held no attraction for the man who had seen more of America than anyone else he knew. Simon did not ask his son to remain.

Abe repacked his satchel and headed to the train station. He passed through Ohio, Pennsylvania, and New York. He arrived in Manchester, New Hampshire. For no particular reason, the young man decided he would remain. The town was pleasant and had a small, active Jewish community. Nor was it far from Boston. He could travel by train and be in the city in less than two hours. Abe returned again to the profession he knew best. He found a job with the R.G Sullivan cigar factory. He developed a settled routine, for the first time since his Ybor City days. But now Abe was almost 27. He keenly felt the need for companionship. Few eligible Jewish women were available in Manchester. Abe was unenthusiastic to return to Kentucky to be matched with someone selected by his parents. He began to scan the Yiddish newspapers from New York. The papers usually reached Manchester a day or two after publication.

One notice intrigued him. It was a matchmaker letter in the *Forward* from a mother in Pennsylvania. Abe weighed the opportunity. He responded to the letter with one of his own. An exchange developed. He agreed to travel to Pottstown, a community he could not recollect traversing. There he met the Markowitz family. Rose took an immediate liking to the tall, handsome, soft-spoken, blue-eyed man. Adolph did not seem to care as long as his daughter was married off.

Yetta appeared to be resigned to her fate. Although not overwhelmed by her suitor, she was not unhappy with him. Abe was polite, awkwardly charming, and rigidly proper in the courtship. At least marriage to him, she felt, would allow her to escape Pottstown! Most important, Cohen did not remind her of her father!

The couple was married on June 24, 1913. Abe's brother Herman served as best man. For the wedding reception, Adolph rented Pottstown's Auditorium Hall, the former Prince's Theatre, at High and Charlotte Streets. There was dancing.

High Street Pottstown, Pennsylvania

McClintik-Marshall Company, Pottstown

Pottstown train station ca. 1880s

(Pictures courtesy of Pottstown Historical Society)

Last Jewish remnant of village of Rebnitza Its cemetery 1994
(Photo by author)

(Photo courtesy of Faye Phillips)

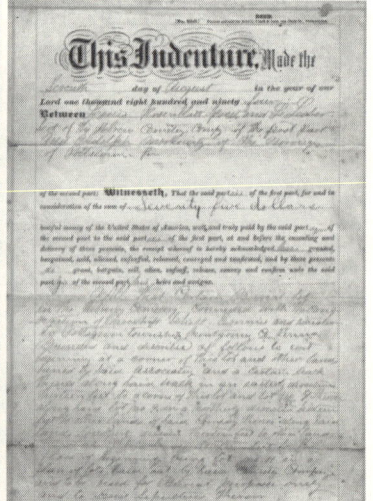

Former synagogue on Chicken Hill, rear view
(Recent photo by author)

Deed to cemetery plot belonging to Adolph Markowitz August 7, 1894
(Courtesy of author)

Pottstown ca. 1910 Looking northeast across Manatawny Creek,
High Street on right
(Photo courtesy of Pottstown Historical Society)

Markowitz Family 1915
Seated from left: Kate, Adolph, Rose, Francis, Lena, Yetta Cohen
Standing from left: Mike Robert, Benjamin,
Sam, infant Norman, Abe Cohen
(Author's collection)

Rachael Epstein Cohen, Simon Cohen ca. 1905
(Author's collection)

Yetta Markowitz Cohen, Abe Cohen 1913
(Author's collection)

Russell, Norman, Sylvia, unknown child, Lillian 1928
(photo courtesy of Sylvia Cohen)

Prince's Market *(Photo courtesy of Pottstown Historical Society)*

Former Markowitz home at 719 Walnut Street
(Recent photo by author)

Marching with Torahs, Decoration Day, ca. 1920s
(Photo courtesy of Faye Phillips)

Pottstown High School Football Team 1930
Record: 2 wins, 5 defeats, 3 ties (all 0-0)
Norman Cohen in first row
(Author's collection)

Second Lieutenant Norman
B. Cohen 1944
(Author's collection)

Yetta and Abe Cohen 1959
(Author's collection)

Nine

Der kremer

After their marriage Abe took his bride to Manchester, New Hampshire. Abe returned to his job in the R.G. Sullivan Cigar Factory. Yetta settled down in her new life as homemaker. Their first son, Norman Benjamin, made his appearance the following summer. A Doctor Weeks delivered Norman at home. Homebirth was nothing extraordinary. At the time only the most affluent families—which the Cohen family most certainly was not—had their children delivered in a hospital.

Until forty years later, nothing about Norman's birth was noteworthy. Norman's cousin Albert, Mike's son, needed passports for his family in a hurry. It struck the middle age Norman that perhaps he also should be prepared for a similar contingency. He sent a request to the Department of Vital Statistics in Manchester for a copy of his birth certificate. The office responded that no such birth record existed. His birth had not been recorded. Norman asked his mother why his birth was not registered.

"Oh yes," she responded dispassionately. Her tone discounted the potential seriousness of the matter. "There was a reputation about that Doctor Weeks. According to the papers, he got into some trouble later for not registering deliveries." Norman's mother neglected to address why years earlier she did not take the registration of her first born child into her own hands. What can explain her failure to fulfill one of America's most basic twentieth century bureaucratic exercises, the validation of the birth of a child?

Yetta gazed across the Merrimack River in the late summer of 1914. Many conflicting thoughts distressed her. She had not acclimated well to the land of New England Yankees. She never felt comfortable in the region's Puritan environment. There was the distraction of the Great War, which had just broken out in Europe. Along with millions of Americans, she was concerned for family left behind in Europe. Indeed, at that moment the Austro-Hungarian army was conscripting all able-bodied men from Galician *shtetls*, including, she feared, her cousins.

A more pressing and immediate concern was the family's need for money. Abe did not earn much of it rolling cigars. The newborn infant represented an additional expense. It had been only seven years since Yetta assisted her own mother with caring for the infant Francis. The memory was etched deeply in her mind. Of course, she still knew what to do. But the prospect of additional years of childrearing drew no joy from her soul. The toil of caring for children would be onerous. Manchester offered the new mother no support mechanism. Yetta had no family and pitifully few friends to call upon for help. And her husband, she knew, would provide slim comfort and support. The new mother entered a period of serious depression.

Manchester itself demoralized Yetta. The town served as a constant reminder of where her life seemed to be heading. She never forgave her father for pressing her into a marriage with Abe Cohen, a *nebbish* cigar-maker. What kind of profession was that? To Yetta, the thought of a lifetime as the wife of a cigar roller was beyond unappealing. It was almost nauseating. Moreover, as long as Abe rolled five-cent cigars and children appeared in the usual fashion, theirs was destined to be a life of near poverty. How irksome this was, Yetta thought, particularly when her cousins and brother Mike were becoming increasingly successful in their various shoe businesses. If she could do nothing about the marriage, Yetta determined there was plenty she could do regarding her husband's profession!

While the infant Norman slept in the corner of their one room apartment, the new Mrs. Cohen pondered her options. She appealed to her brothers for their assistance in finding a more meaningful and prosperous career for her husband. Perhaps, she wrote, Abe could become a *kremer*, a storekeeper like Mike in Norristown. Ben responded promptly with an offer of some start-up money. Most likely, Ben drew some of the money from Adolph's own bank accounts that by now were fairly impressive. Uncles Mendel and Emmanuel offered additional assistance. With the promised money in writing, Yetta told her hapless husband that his days in the cigar factory were at an end. The young family of three departed New Hampshire for good and moved to Bayonne, New Jersey.

In Bayonne, Abe opened a tiny shoe store. It was located in a working class neighborhood filled with the flotsam of recently arrived immigrants and refugees from New York City's boroughs. In contrast to their high hopes though, little money entered the till. Moreover, Abe quickly discovered he was unhappy running a business. For one thing, he no longer could observe Shabbat as he felt it should be respected. But how could a retail store survive, let alone flourish in a *goyish* environment, if not open

Friday evenings and Saturdays? Also, the new businessman hated making the hard sales pitch usually required to assure completion of the sale. Although skilled from his gambling days at keeping a poker face, Abe was a miserable failure when it came to convincing a customer to lay down cash on a pair of shoes. Few customers walked in the door, many fewer left with shoes. The Bayonne store lasted less than a year.

With more help from the family, the Cohen family relocated to Norristown, Pennsylvania. Abe and Yetta tried again. Abe was staked to a modestly furnished downtown shoe store. Bizarrely, his business competed directly with Mike's established and better stocked Brockton Shoe Store. Why the couple opened a shoe store just down the street from Mike's, and why Yetta's brother did not take some action to prevent the inevitable commercial disaster, is anyone's guess. Once again, Abe's venture was a failure.

Yetta attributed their frustrating commercial efforts to not having *mazel*, luck for business. To anyone who would listen, she related the story of a customer to whom Abe was trying to sell a certain pair of shoes. After extensive effort and many fittings, Yetta explained, the customer walked—no sale. When Abe closed the store for the day, she and Abe went to Mike's store. They observed the same customer purchasing from Mike the identical style pair of shoes at the same price! "How could it be anything but *mazel*?" Yetta rhetorically asked. Abe had nothing to say. His forlorn expression told everything. It was becoming obvious. *Mazel* or the paucity of it had nothing to do with Abe's lack of success.

Like their Bayonne effort, the Norristown store did not work out. When the one-year lease on the store was up, Abe determined enough was enough. It was the best business decision he made, so far. This time the couple with child in tow decided it would be best to move back to her hometown. Frankly, they had little choice. Abe and Yetta were broke.

Four years after their marriage, the couple returned to Pottstown. With a small loan from his father-in-law, Abe rented half of a double house at 628 Beech Street on Chicken Hill. His parents, Simon and Rachel, moved to Pottstown and rented the house next door. Abe's in-laws resided a couple of blocks away. Just two blocks up Hale Street stood the *shul*. A few months later, a Jewish family by the name of Coverman moved into the other half of the duplex. Next door in a single-family house lived an electrician, Bill Fillman and his wife Rose Moser Fillman whom Yetta highly admired. Mrs. Fillman was raising her orphaned nephew and niece, Ted and Sis Kemp. The young Norman frequently attended their birthday parties and other social occasions. However, Norman spent most of his time with Mary Williams, a girl who lived across the street. The friendship ended when Mary bit the boy on the arm.

Abe and Yetta considered the Beech Street house almost extravagant compared to their previous residences. This was a result more of Chicken Hill's low rents compared to New Jersey and Norristown than of fine lodging choices. In reality, the home was modest even by the working class standards of Chicken Hill. The family enjoyed few of the amenities found in *bubbeh* and *zaideh*'s warm and comfortable home. Unlike the furniture in the Cohen house, the furnishings that belonged to Yetta's parents were not overdue for the junk heap. Since Adolph rented the first Markowitz residence on Warren Street, twenty-seven years earlier, his household had progressed markedly. The Cohen home, on the other hand, was better suited for recent immigrants—which in a sense they were. The floorboards on the front porch were uneven. The ends bent upwards like little Dutch clogs. Exterior walls cried for paint while the interior walls were everywhere shaded with soot that refused to come off even after the most assiduous scrubbing. Wind entered unfettered through poorly insulated window frames. The front door would not properly close. The kitchen, as Yetta continually made clear to her husband, was ancient. Smoke from the stove leaked unabated from the flue. The smell of old cooking grease could never be completely eradicated despite Yetta's constant cleaning efforts.

Still, the house possessed indoor plumbing, electricity and living space for a growing family. When the weather was not inclement, the backyard served as Norman's play area and Yetta's small vegetable garden. A clothesline was strung over the garden across the yard from fence to fence. From the back door to the alley, a narrow footpath treaded between hoed soil and old junk left by Adolph when available storage space behind his own house was at a particular premium.

Next to the alley behind the house stood a small wood shed. In a futile attempt to keep it warm in winter, newspaper, cardboard, and other insulating material lined the inside walls. It also made the shack a terrible fire hazard. Among other purposes, Yetta used the shack when she needed to singe chickens before removing the feathers, a process called "flicking." She performed this vital ritual inside the shack to keep out of sight of gentile neighbors. The gentiles generally dipped foul in boiling water, an act forbidden by Jewish law. On one occasion while flicking, Yetta briefly returned to the house to retrieve something. From the yard her son had been watching her. The newspapers on the walls suddenly burst into flame. The boy ran into the house. "Fire, mother, fire!" Yetta rushed back to the shed and extinguished the fire with a bucket of water. No harm came to the chicken.

In a single frame building on the corner of High and Charlotte Streets, Abe rented a small storefront. The rent was surprisingly affordable. The landlord was eager to deliver a lease. The reason for the low rent soon became clear. Preceding Abe's rental, the store was a feebly maintained shoe business, notary and real estate office run by a man named William Edelman. "Edelman's, the People's Store," was emblazoned on the storefront display window. Although in business over a quarter century, Edelman's had seen better days. A lonely, dusty pair of men's tipped calfskin oxfords, priced at $2.00, sat in the window. Next to the oxfords was an even dustier pair of men's blucher, Piccadilly toe shoes with its $2.50 price clearly marked. Outmoded ladies Dongola flexible shoes were also priced at $2.50. A small sign announced boys' shoes for $0.50, $0.65, $0.75, and $1.00, although the store window displayed no samples. "Slippers, $0.10 All Sizes," was hand written on another small sign. It was a very low price. The back room, however, contained little slipper inventory.

Already quite familiar with "problematic" commercial circumstances, Abraham Cohen sensed trouble. He swiftly cleaned up the store and introduced more fashionable shoe lines. Despite its prime corner location and more trendy shoes, hardly anyone entered the store. Businessmen from neighboring shops sought Abe out. They surreptitiously questioned him about "business ethics." Abe was confused. He had been in business only a short time. But it seemed his reputation was already on the line! Strange, he thought. He had just taken over the store. Why was everyone on High Street so jumpy? And why, he wondered, were there so few customers?

Abe introduced himself to the other High Street merchants. He asked about Edelman. To his horror, he discovered the cause of the apprehension from businessmen and customers. Before the store was turned over to Abe, Edelman earned a notorious reputation for unsavory business practices. To be blunt, one businessman told him, the name 'Edelman' on the window hurt business. A former Edelman customer provided a clue. She told Abe that she had bought a pair of wedding shoes from Edelman. "Before the wedding I tried on the shoes at home," the woman explained. "They were too tight. I brought the pair back for an exchange." Edelman evidently did not have a larger size available.

"Rather than return my money," she went on, "the owner told me that exchanging the shoes would assure me of an 'unhappy marriage!' He told me also he did not have the heart to be the cause of such misfortune! What nerve!"

It did not take long for Abe to take action. The name of the store had to be changed. "Edelman" was scraped off the window. After discussion with his father-in-law, Abe selected "Royal Shoe Shop." The name sounded upscale. Best of all, the name had not yet been incorporated or registered in the State of Pennsylvania. Changing the store's name to "Royal" was one of Abe's better business decisions.

At the outset following the store's rebirth as Royal Shoe Shop, it appeared that Abe's new venture might very well succeed. Support from family members helped immeasurably. His brother-in-law Mike helped Abe obtain the exclusive Pottstown agency for the popular W.L. Douglas brand of shoes. While a clerk watched the store, Abe traveled with his peddler father-in-law on the horse drawn wagon to farmhouses throughout Chester County. Whether or not Adolph consummated a deal in scrap or junk, Abe offered the farmer a discount on his next shoe purchase for permission to tack a W.L. Douglas sign on the barn. He also carried in the wagon a supply of felt boots to offer for sale. Many of his farmer customers originally met the "shoe man" during these peddling jaunts with his father-in-law. Abe also was an early riser. If he noticed snowfall, he rushed to open the store at daybreak to accommodate farmers and working men who needed waterproof footwear.

The store operated at a modest profit for one year. Then, two events happened that reversed the promising beginning. The year 1919 turned out to be a poor time to be a struggling retail shop in a factory town. Following the end of the Great War, the country's economic situation turned sour. The crush of discharged soldiers caused unemployment to rise sharply. Customers suddenly were short of cash. Abe cautiously avoided offering credit and sales declined. It also became common knowledge throughout Pottstown that the building's owner intended to sell the property. The High Street grapevine indicated the new owner planned to demolish the structure and construct a theatre. Since the property seemed doomed for ultimate destruction, Abe panicked. He asked the owner to write up a month-to-month lease. Understandably eager to relocate, Abe focused his attention on finding a new store location.

On the sidewalk one day, he met an acquaintance. Howard Isaiah Dampman was a fellow Chicken Hill resident who often conversed with Abe as the two walked each morning to their respective High Street stores. Dampman owned a haberdashery, a first-rate High Street property next door to the Woolworth 5 & 10. He liked Abe, and the feeling was mutual. The two spoke about general issues of the day. Abe mentioned his eagerness to relocate the Royal Shoe Shop. Dampman brightened. "I want to sell the property," he confided to Abe. "Would you be interested?"

After a short discussion, Abe made an offer right there on High Street. The two businessmen agreed on a price and shook hands. Dampman set up an appointment to close the transaction at the Binder Real Estate offices the following Saturday at 10 a.m. Abe was elated. He rushed home to tell Yetta the good news.

That Thursday afternoon, Abe was purchasing his usual first cuts of *brust* (brisket) at the kosher butcher shop of Adolph Printz. One of Pottstown's wealthiest Jews, Printz also served as the president of the shul and led the drive to construct a new synagogue that would replace the existing Hale Street structure. Behind the counter assisting customers was Printz's son Joe. Joe Printz recently passed the Pennsylvania bar exam. He had just opened a Pottstown law practice. Abe asked Joe if he would represent him at the settlement. Joe agreed. Since Saturdays were generally busy at the store, Abe inquired of Joe if the time of the appointment should be changed.

Printz replied absolutely not. "If the man said 10 o'clock Saturday, then that is the time the appointment should be." Abe deferred to his guidance. He said he would meet Joe at Binder's.

At the appointed hour, Abe entered at the Binder Real Estate office. He found it quiet, except for the ticking of a Regulator clock. Sitting behind his desk Binder looked up. "What can I do for you?" Binder asked.

"I'm here to close on the Dampman property," Abe said.

Binder looked puzzled. "Joe Printz told me you were no longer interested in the store. He changed the time of the settlement to 8:30. Joe's father purchased the property."

Binder's statement hit Abe like a ton of bricks. He stared at the real estate agent for a moment, mouth agape. The color fled from his face. His knees buckled. Before he could collapse, Abe fled Binder's office.

Over the next week, Abe made several attempts to convince the elder Printz to sell him the property. He even offered Printz a nice profit. On a couple of these visits to Adolph Printz's house, Abe took Norman along. If Abe thought the presence of a child would soften Printz's heart, he underestimated the cold-heartedness of the elder Printz. It was all to no avail. Abe never got the property.

In hindsight, the moral chasm between Simon Cohen's son, the cigar-maker from Louisville, Kentucky, and Adolph and Joe Printz was too immense for Abe even to comprehend, let alone overcome. However, his father-in-law understood perfectly. The Markowitz patriarch appreciated the swindle for what it was. While he held little respect for his *shmo* of a son-in-law who had been taken by a real *goniff*, his anger and resentment towards Adolph and Joe Printz as a result of the double-cross inflicted on his daughter's family deepened immeasurably. He despised Abe's efforts to change Adolph Printz's mind with what amounted to a bribe. He considered Abe's appeals to Printz both naïve and demeaning. His antipathy towards the Printz family carried over into synagogue affairs. While Adolph and Joe Printz garnered greater say in Jewish community affairs, Adolph's own involvement at *shul* waned. He also refused to patronize Printz's butcher shop.

An unintended result of Abe's struggle with Adolph and Joe Printz was that the young Norman received a first rate education about business ethics. Behaving as if unaware of the disdain felt towards him by Norman's grandfather and unmindful of the distress he heaped on Norman's family, Adolph Printz treated the young Cohen boy with unusual warmth. He greeted Norman at *shul* and often offered the boy a piece of hard candy kept in an inside pocket.

One afternoon after school Norman walked by Printz's house on some long forgotten errand. Sitting in a rocking chair on his porch, Printz called out "Norm Cohen, come over and sit with me." Norman dutifully sat down on a cushion next to him. Printz kindly patted Norman on the head and gave his earlobe a soft pull. In an effort to impress the boy with his business acumen, the elder Printz related a story from the old country. It was a tale he frequently enjoyed relating. As Printz spoke, his rocking quickened, his thick hands gripped the armrests more tightly, and his magnetic brown eyes latched onto Norman's.

"When I was a young man in Europe, I took a sack of grain one day to sell in the market. After a few minutes a *goy* came by and bought the grain. After paying me he asked 'Would you mind watching the grain for a short time while I go make another purchase in the market?' I naturally agreed. As I waited for the first man to return, a second man came over to me. He asked about buying the same sack of grain." A broad smile crossed over Printz's face as he prepared to hit the punch line. "I then sold the same sack of grain to the second man and quickly left the market!"

More nervous than ever that the building would soon be sold, Abe decided to break the lease. He refused to await the circumstances of the rumored sale. At the same time, Sam Hoffman was seeking a Pottstown site for a new business. He quickly picked up the lease that Abe dropped. Hoffman could not believe his luck. To obtain a corner location at High Street's second busiest intersection! Hoffman sensed or knew the stories floating around town about the owner converting the property into a theatre were exaggerated, premature, or simply untrue. The New York Cut Price Department Store became a Pottstown landmark. Eventually, some years later, the Strand Theater would be built on the corner. But its construction occurred only after the New York Store had enjoyed a profitable run at the location. Later, Hoffman relocated his department store to an even larger site on the corner of High and Penn Streets.

When Abe opened the former Edelman store, he found a black Corona typewriter in the stockroom. Abe assumed it was an oversight. He wanted to return the Corona to Edelman. Yetta adamantly vetoed the idea. "What's ours is ours!" she retorted. The typewriter stayed. When the store was turned over to Hoffman, Abe left the typewriter on the same table he had found it. When she discovered what her husband had done, Yetta was outraged. She refused to accept her husband's decision and constantly nagged him about the typewriter. "Why didn't you take it?" she berated on and off for months. It hurt her no end that Hoffman received not only the property but also wound up with the Corona.

Following the fiasco with Dampman, Abe staunchly opposed the purchase of any real estate. He emphatically asserted that he preferred to rent. However, at Yetta's insistence and with funds from his father-in-law, Abe reluctantly took a mortgage on a twin property at 147 and 149 West High Street. The rundown three-story building had served as the office and workshop for the Storb Granite Company. For multiple reasons including its somewhat morbid past as site of a tombstone manufacturer, the property was less attractive than Dampman's which, ironically, later became the Tubis Shoe Store. Fewer customers patronized West High Street stores than similar businesses on the busier east side of Hanover Street. The building required immediate repair. Abe rented the 149 side of the building to Chris "the Greek" who converted it into the Crystal Restaurant. The Royal Shoe Store occupied the 147 half. The Cohen family, now two children, left their Beech Street house and moved into the second and third floors above the store.

Six months after the move, Abe received a telephone call from Jesse L. Evans, Pottstown's most respected lawyer, and, at the time, also Pottstown's solicitor. Evans asked Abe to come to his office on an important matter. Abe was nervous, as was Yetta. "What had he done?" he asked his wife. Peevishly, she retorted "you must have made an error in the property tax." Abe, perspiring even though it was a cool day, put on his hat and coat and hurried to City Hall.

Upon returning from the Evans office, Abe ran upstairs to speak with his wife. His voice resonated with excitement. "Evans wanted to know about the circumstances of the Dampman property," Abe related. "He said he heard some facts about the case and asked me if they were true." When Abe affirmed the facts, Evans asked him to appear at a hearing. "He told me the Legal Society wants to have Joe Printz disbarred. But for this to happen," Abe added, "I have to press charges. I told Evans I would not do it."

In a community as small and close knit as Pottstown's, few incidents such as a double-cross perpetrated on a High Street businessman escaped attention or gossip. When friends from the *shul* heard about the Legal Society's effort to punish Printz for his unethical behavior in the Dampman transaction, they swiftly approached Abe. They gathered in the rear of the shoe store and interrogated the shoe man as if the case had already gone to court. "Why are you letting Joe Printz off the hook?"

Surrounded by his colleagues, Abe rolled his eyes and threw his hands in the air. The cigarette smoke hung in a cloud around their heads. To him, the reason seemed obvious and required no explanation. "You must avoid shaming a fellow Jew in public," he lectured. Doing so "would bring shame to every Jew before the *goyim*!"

To Abe, it did not matter whether the *goyim* were Irish Catholics, Quakers, Baptists, Indians, immigrant Italians, African-Americans, or wealthy Episcopalian Blue Bloods from Philadelphia's Main Line. To file charges and possibly go to court against a fellow member of the *shul* would not only embarrass both plaintiff and defendant but, more importantly, spark ridicule from the Christian community. Abe envisioned smirks from non-Jewish businessmen and bankers passing him on the street. He visualized transparently wry smiles that on the surface were innocent but actually were lashed with anti-Semitic hatred. While he searched for the correct shoe size in the stockroom, he feared customers would speak in lowered voices about the simpleton Jew businessman cheated by his crafty Jew lawyer. Pitiless neighbors would talk. The sordid story would circulate among grocery vendors and shopkeepers. He would become a High Street laughingstock. That was a prospect Abe could not stomach.

Yet Abe's response also mirrored another segment of his character. His defensive justification for not taking action against Printz reflected his narrow, even bigoted beliefs towards both Jews and non-Jews. These he long unflinchingly shared with his father, Simon Cohen. Jews could commit crimes like anyone else, and just like anyone else they deserved punishment. The shoe man did not understand or perhaps just refused to accept, that simple paradigm. This was an attitude completely at odds with that of Adolph Markowitz. When informed of the incident, Adolph caustically urged his son-in-law "*zei nit kain vyzoso*! Don't be a damn fool!"

Both Abe and Yetta possessed an attitude that *goyim* were less intelligent than the Jews. Such a view was never expressed beyond the home. It was a silent bigotry, never matched or reflected by deed. On the contrary, the *religion* of the *goyim* was always respected. Yetta was especially sensitive to the feelings of her neighbors. Washed clothes were never hung outside to dry on Sundays. To desecrate their Sabbath, she believed, would be a *shanda*, a shame to the *goyim*. Because her neighbors observed the Sabbath in the same manner as she was taught, no work of any type was exhibited on their holy day of rest. Before Christmas, Yetta visited the homes of Christian neighbors to wish them a good holiday season. In the shoe store Abe altered the display window to give it a Christmas holiday appeal. However, the parents drew a firm line with participation by the Cohen children in religiously slanted school Christmas pageants. In contrast to respecting those with clear religious beliefs, Abe also possessed an intolerance of people who in his opinion "lacked religion." There were plenty of such people in Pottstown, even among Jews.

From his Kentucky upbringing, Abe possessed another narrow-minded prejudice. The Louisville of his youth possessed a culture of strict racial segregation and unbending discrimination. Even ordinary conversation was laced with racial epitaphs. Bigotry emerged casually, randomly, subtly, and impulsively. As with most Jewish members of the community, the Cohen household was devoid of explicit bigotry. Yet, all too frequently,

Abe displayed biases ubiquitous of the times—times when throughout America minstrel shows were the rage. Stinging parody and iconic caricature reflected the highly racist period. Expressions such as "African-Americans" were not used in the 1920s. Nor did one hear the term "blacks" very much. The words used by whites to describe people of darker skin were much less respectful.

On Chicken Hill, most neighbors and playmates for young Norman were *shvartza*, blacks, or *schutzim*, male gentiles. Abe did not employ the word *shvartza* in an especially derogatory manner. But in his mind, it certainly was not a compliment. Before attending elementary school, Norman never heard the word 'nigger' until uttered by a white teacher. His parents prohibited such words in the home. Norman was careful not to emulate, even accidentally, the more racist elements that pervaded those times. Even at a young age, he realized that being Jewish also made him an easy target of abusive remarks. That was another lesson commonly fostered in a Jewish home.

With such sensitivity about how the *goyim* viewed them, the couple worried constantly about how they fit within Pottstown's *goyish* society and culture. Although surrounded by immigrants, Abe and Yetta were of a generation with little or no memory of a home country before America. Respect and appreciation for American traditions, its holidays, a shared history, pride in being Americans never wavered. But confidence in this identity, as Jews, came at a price. Abe and Yetta overlooked or intentionally ignored the challenges faced by their children when confronted by bigotry and intolerance.

* * *

Following the Great War, car sales skyrocketed. Everyone began to talk about cars. Those with money rushed to automobile dealerships which sprouted up like late summer dandelions.

For many of Pottstown's working class, automobiles were still too expensive. Yet, many factory workers joined the craze. Some old-timers who did have savings—including Adolph Markowitz—refused to join the car buying frenzy. They preferred the "reliability" of horse-drawn travel. But these individuals were the exceptions. Cars were the new fad. They were "in vogue." Pottstown's streets began to fill with cars.

Like most of America Abe developed a fascination with the automobile. He acquired his first car the year the family moved into the upstairs floors of the Royal Shoe Store. In 1919, Yetta's cousins Sam Fuerman and Ben Berger joined with Abe to purchase three Chevrolet Model 490 touring cars from Sam Daub, the local Chevrolet agent. The $650 price each paid supposedly reflected a "volume" discount. Yanish, the Potts family chauffeur who later became the "bad influence" on Francis, taught the novice Abe how to drive. Five-year old Norman sat in the back seat, eagerly digesting all of Yanesh's instructions.

Except to visit relatives, the Cohen family rarely traveled beyond Philadelphia—though not because it could not afford to do so. The scarcity of funds in the house did not mean there was no money. Expenses were low and the shoe store did generate positive cash flow. Abe never felt constrained, when he so desired, from getting behind the wheel of his automobile. With his cronies he took in ballgames in Philadelphia or met his brother-in-law Mike for lunch in Norristown. The shoe store did not require his constant presence. He could afford to take days off, except Saturdays. Not infrequently, Abe disappeared in his car for hours. Yetta enjoyed no such luxury. Raising a family kept her busy. The family soon reached four children with Sylvia in 1923, and the last child, Russell, in 1926.

Although a car was nice to have, did Abe really need one? The family lived above the store, Norman walked to school, and Yetta never learned how to drive. But like many then and generations of car owners since, Abe was immensely proud of car ownership. He loved to cruise up High Street where other businessmen could see him behind the wheel. He kept his Chevrolet as clean as Pottstown's dirt streets and alleys would allow.

Until later in the 1920s, every brand of automobile promoted one basic model. The Chevrolet touring car was a beauty. It had four doors and plenty of legroom. There were no side windows. The Chevrolet's only glass was the split windshield that could be folded back when the soft top was down. When raining, everyone exited the car and rushed to snap the canvas curtains in place. The curtains were stored beneath the rear seat. The car had only one windshield wiper. Located on the driver's side, it was manually operated. With one hand to steer and one hand for shifting, the driver had no hands left for wiping the fogged-up windows. When the curtains were down, a full cargo of passengers in such an enclosed humid space caused the windows to fog quickly. Leaning across his father's lap, Norman operated the wiper and used Abe's handkerchief to swab the fogged windshield.

When he was behind the wheel, Abe possessed an unusual trait that lasted many years. Cars did not have much horsepower. As the underpowered Chevrolet slowed, especially after making a turn, Abe applied a little "body English" to provide it additional momentum and, supposedly, prevent stalling. He twisted his body into the turn, as if attempting to roll a strike on a newfangled bowling alley—not that the Cohen family ever went bowling! Particularly when climbing steep hills, Abe repeatedly pumped his torso back and forth. It was a motion akin to *davening* at *shul*. As the car crawled ever more slowly upwards, his pumping became more feverish.

When Joe Lerner had trouble using the hand crank on his newly acquired Model T, willing "supervisors" emerged from every corner of the neighborhood. From these self-appointed experts, one learned the correct amount of spark and ignition to apply on the hand controls while the starter was cranked. Turning the lug wrench-sized hand crank could be dangerous. Located beneath the closed hood just under the radiator, the crank required a lot of torque to turn, especially in cold weather. One had to be especially careful not to grip the crank too tightly. Because of the kick, a person could easily break an arm or loose a thumb. After watching Joe Lerner's ordeal with his hand crank, Abe appreciated even more his safer self-starter, even if it was not overly reliable.

Sunday drives were a risky affair. Luck rode with the family if it got home with only one flat tire. Abe enjoyed taking the family to Sanatoga or a picnic spot on Ringing Rocks Hill. He was not perturbed by the tire problems, until about the third or fourth time. Changing a flat was a straight-forward operation, albeit slightly more complicated than in modern times:

> To prevent rolling, place a rock or two under non-flat tires. Remove the lug nuts by turning them counterclockwise with a lug wrench. Put the jack under the axle and lift the car. Remove the entire wheel. Take a portion of the tire off the rim. Remove the inner tube nozzle. Pump it and locate the hole as air exited the tire or remove the nail, a more obvious situation. Rough up the area of the hole with sandpaper. Apply rubber cement. Place a rubber patch on the hole. Blow air on the hole to dry the rubber cement. Replace the inner tube. Reaffix the tire to the rim. Put the wheel back on the axle. Tighten the lug nuts clockwise. Hand pump to about 15 pounds of pressure. Check the tire pressure with a tire gauge. Lower the car. Remove the rocks from behind the other wheels.

Performing the entire operation in less than 15 minutes was considered exceptional. Abe rarely got close to this standard.

In the early 1920's, Dodge Brothers began to manufacture a four-door sedan with glass windows, a self-starter, and a heater! Imagine driving on the coldest winter day wearing just short sleeves! The Dodge looked like a boxcar with a high center of gravity. The Dodge brand had a certain cachet about it and appealed to Abe. The Cohen family was not loyal to Ford. Abe rarely offered positive words about the Model T. He considered Henry Ford an anti-Semite, which in fact he was. Despite Abe's assertions that "sedans will never be popular since owners will become tired of replacing glass," he replaced the Chevrolet with a Dodge sedan. The windows on his Dodge never shattered.

Soon after he purchased the Dodge, Abe took the family to Plainfield, New Jersey, to visit Yetta's Uncle Emmanuel. There they also met her Aunt Esther, Esther's son-in-law Willie Silverman, and Willie's wife. Willie Silverman drove the same model Dodge as Abe's. After a few hours with the Schwartz family, the Cohen family followed the Silvermans to their house in nearby Perth Amboy. At an intersection, the Silverman car collided with another Dodge, again the same model and color. It happened right in front of Abe. Both cars overturned. Willie was unhurt but his wife required hospitalization. Abe and Yetta sat for a long time in the hospital to comfort Aunt Esther.

Yetta had a cousin Harold "Honey" Klein who was five years older than Norman. Klein's father purchased a one-ton Model T panel truck for his grocery store's deliveries. The young teenager took Norman along on his delivery runs. When out of sight of his family, Klein allowed Norman to sit behind the wheel. In order for Norman to see out the windshield, Klein placed a pillow on the seat. Since Norman's legs were too short to reach the floor, Harold operated the pedals. He pushed the accelerator and maneuvered the breaks. At times the speed of the panel truck frightened Norman who begged Klein to slow down. But when asked to give the truck less gas, Klein only laughed.

One day, Harold Klein and Norman were making a delivery to a wealthy bungalow on Ringing Rocks Hill, one of the area's steepest climbs. The motor gasped and the truck stalled almost in sight of Ringing Rocks Park. Model Ts did not have fuel pumps. Instead, the gas flowed with gravity into the engine from the gas tank located under the hood in front of the windshield. If low in gas and ascending a steep hill, the engine would be higher than the gasoline in the gas tank. Like most of Pottstown's streets the dirt road up Ring Rocks Hill was deeply rutted. The road's narrow right shoulder dropped off into a forest. On the left side the hill stood like a fortress wall. Klein instructed Norman to find rocks to place behind the rear tires. He somehow manipulated the truck moving it back and forth on that constricted space while Norman quickly moved the rocks to the down slope side of the tires. Somehow, Klein turned the car completely around. Norman got back in. Klein proceeded to finish the drive up the hill in reverse.

The backbone of the new Royal Shoe Store was the "Enna Jettick" brand of women's shoes. Manufactured by Dunn & McCarthy Inc., Auburn, New York, Enna Jetticks were then the country's best selling women's shoes. They would remain so for years after. Royal Shoes held the Pottstown franchise in conjunction with Mike's Brockton Shoe Store in Norristown and David Glick, Mike's brother-in-law. Glick had a shoe store in West Chester, about twenty miles south of Pottstown. Since the Royal Shoe Store possessed little other competitive advantage with other shoe stores, holding the franchise to the fashionable Enna Jetticks was critical in attracting customers.

One year, Dunn & McCarthy ran a sales contest. The top prizes were three new automobiles to the three company accounts with the largest percentage increase in sales. To make the contest fairer, the stores were divided into three different population categories. Pottstown qualified in the smallest population group. Dunn & McCarthy offered the prize winners the choice of either the Ford or the Chevrolet. Later, the company announced that if all three contest winners agreed, the company would upgrade the prize to the more expensive Plymouth.

This was a contest the three brothers-in-law could not resist. Abe arranged with Mike and Glick to provide him their weekly fill-in orders. That way the Royal Shoe Store's own shoe orders to Dunn & McCarthy showed a significant jump. When the ordered shoes arrived in Pottstown, Abe himself delivered them to Mike in Norristown and Glick in West Chester. The three businessmen were gleeful that the contest was all but won.

Abe won the car, but he lost the account. The bookkeepers at Dunn & McCarthy were not blind. After the contest, the company figured out what happened. One day in the mail, Abe received a letter from Mr. Paden, the Enna Jetticks salesman. The letter stated Dunn & McCarthy would no longer service Royal Shoes. The company, Paden wrote, had "taken Royal Shoes off the books." Abe grew angry. He crumbled the letter. "The devil with him!" he swore. For Abe Cohen this was an unusually harsh expression. For the Royal Shoe Store, the result of Abe's latest episode of poor business judgment meant a new line of women's shoes had to be found.

Ten

Pottstown

In February 1923 Rose passed away in the front room of the Cohen apartment above the shoe store. During Rose's last months Yetta tirelessly cared for her mother. Yetta's nasty retort to her sister Kate when their mother died cannot be easily forgotten. Perhaps she could be forgiven. Adolph was not present when the bitter words were spoken. Had he been so, he would have been enraged. The bad blood between father and daughter would have been even worse.

After Rose's burial, Abe and Yetta arranged to move the family back to 719 Walnut Street, Adolph's house. The old man, they felt, required the presence of family. Initially, the Walnut Street house seemed crowded. Kate and Francis still lived at home. But Katie would be leaving in a few months. The date for her marriage to Morris Benstock was already set. She and Morris would live in Philadelphia, his hometown. At sixteen Francis was eager to move out of the house. Eight-year old Norman shared a room with Francis. Young Lillian shared Kate's room until her aunt left for Philadelphia.

In addition to his growing real estate endeavors, Adolph still operated his junk business. The assets of A. Markowitz & Son filled the entire back yard and overflowed onto the alley like a crashing wave. Piles of junk were everywhere. Scrap, newspaper, and old furniture packed the stable. There was barely enough room to squeeze through the stable door. Worn-out tires possessed value, especially if they were repairable. The backyard was piled high with them. Old inner tubes were thrown onto a separate heap. With the surge in automobiles had come a new phenomenon—car wrecks! Stacked against the rear fence were old axles, broken wheel rims, bumpers contorted into crumpled shapes, bent fenders, punctured radiators, even an engine block or two. Cars, specifically the damaged car parts that were increasingly a natural consequence of driving, kept Adolph's scrap enterprise going. What a playground for his grandson! Norman and his friends passed hours constructing forts and castles out of the scrap and tunnels with the tires.

Although Adolph and Yetta's relationship remained severely strained after months of stress over Rose's deteriorating health, the two attempted to make the best of the situation. Abe rented out the former apartment on High Street. The income covered the mortgage on that property. The Royal Shoe Store did not move. It remained at 147 W. High Street during the 1920s. There, it continued to struggle while other High Street shoe stores on the better side of Hanover Street enjoyed prosperity.

High Street witnessed numerous parades. On Memorial Day—many people still referred to it as Decoration Day—flags hung from every High Street lamppost and store window. An arch to honor the community's 140 young men who had served during the Great War was erected across High Street between Sterns Fish Store and the Pottstown Bargain Store. At each base stood a statue, on one side a soldier, on the other a sailor. For years the Memorial Day parade was Pottstown's biggest event, even larger than the July Fourth fireworks in Manatawny Park. The Pottstown High School marching band often led the procession, followed by a variety of area drum and fife bands in fancy military uniforms. White-haired Civil War veterans wearing faded blue uniforms, polished medals, and Kepi caps strode purposefully with the help of canes. Some rode in open cars or perched on the back of flat bed trucks. Each year there were fewer. The parade spectators, many of whom were grandchildren or great-grandchildren, loved the grizzled Civil War vets. They waved, clapped and cheered enthusiastically. Younger Spanish-American War and Great War veterans marched in more martial step. They wore blue infantry or olive-colored field uniforms. Before he left town for good, Robbie who served briefly in the army during the War but never went overseas, participated in these parades.

On other occasions, less pleasant processions took place on High Street. By the mid 1920s Ku Klux Klan marches occurred with disturbing regularity. Spectators were less boisterous during the Klan rallies. If a Klan march took place during business hours, Abe promptly closed the store. He did not want any trouble. During one of these marches, Maurice Miller got into a fight with a Klaner. Fortunately, it was broken up before the Klaner's colleagues joined in. Another time, rumors spread among the crowd that because of the height and limp, a Klaner in the front row of the march must be Doctor Elmer Porter, Pottstown's leading citizen and it's wealthiest. Since Doc Porter always treated the Cohen family well, neither Abe nor Yetta believed the story. Despite its high profile marches, the Klan was not strong in Pottstown itself. But it was robust elsewhere in the area. In nearby Spring City and Royersford, Klan rallies and cross burnings were not uncommon.

It was impossible for Abe and Yetta to believe the worst about Doc Porter. One day Mrs. Labor's cow escaped from her Chicken

Hill barn and wandered into a farmer's field to graze. The farmer took the cow into his own barn. He refused to return it to Mrs. Labor until she paid for the grass the cow had eaten. The widow who was Jewish did not possess the money being demanded. Abe suspected the farmer made the malicious demand out of anti-Semitic spite. In any case, Labor sought assistance from Doctor Porter, at the time Pottstown's burgess. "Go home and don't worry," Porter reassured her. "Things will be taken care of." That night, Porter sent his workmen into the farmer's barn. They escorted the cow back to Labor's barn. It was additional, if not conclusive evidence to Abe and Yetta that Doc Porter could not possibly be a member of the Ku Klux Klan.

The 1920s were a time of growing media excitement, especially in sports. Horseracing, boxing, and baseball garnered immense attention and generated intense debate. From his early days at Eclipse Park in Louisville, Abe remained devoted to baseball. Although the shoe store usually kept him busy, he loved to take in ballgames in Philadelphia—preferably Connie Mack's Athletics at Shibe Park. The Phillies who played at Baker Bowl were usually so putrid. Abe was free on Sundays. Unfortunately, until the 1930s, blue laws still in effect prohibited Sunday baseball in Philadelphia.

Abe occasionally took Norman to the ballpark. Although both were A's fans, one of their favorite players was Walter Johnson, then at the end of his illustrious pitching career with the Washington Senators. Abe carefully analyzed for Norman everything about Johnson's pitching including the secret to his amazing fastball. He once remarked about another Johnson characteristic—Johnson's large shoes.

Even though Abe could not attend major league games as often as he liked, his knowledge of the game and its players was second to none. Yetta's cousin Chaim Klein knew this. He frequently sought to trap Abe by asking baseball trivia that no one had a right to know. At *shul* after services Klein buttonholed Abe with some well rehearsed baseball minutia. Other worshippers gathered around. Many of Klein's questions did not make sense. They were too obscure or irrelevant. Abe patiently played along. Just like when his brothers-in-law sought to trick him with questions about Jewish boardinghouses in Missouri and Nebraska, he confidently gave the answers to Klein, almost always correct. He sometimes even amended Klein's questions when they became too convoluted. Witnesses enjoyed Klein's discomfiture, daring him to come up with *real* trivia.

During the decade many major national news stories stood out. One in particular caught Abe's attention. In early 1925 Floyd Collins, a backwoodsman with a reputation as a discoverer and explorer of local caves was trapped in a rural cave in Kentucky. The event became a media circus and carnival. Mobs of people flocked to the entrance of the cave where Collins was stuck. The entire country followed the story. From the pulpit to the barbershop, it was the big topic of discussion. Every day for two weeks, Pottstown's newspapers provided the latest bulletins on the rescue efforts. *The Pottstown News* covered the story relentlessly. "Cavern Explorer Close to Freedom," "Little Hope for Cave Explorer," "Collins Alive Tests Indicate." Dozens gathered in front of newspaper offices. They awaited the most recent word from rural Kentucky. Ecstasy overwhelmed the crowd when errant word came that Collins' feet had been freed. Then despondency returned when word came that debris continued to pin Collins to the cave.

The Cohen household closely followed the rescue efforts led by twenty-one year old Skeets Miller, a cub reporter with the *Louisville Courier-Journal*. Because of his youthful connection to the newspaper, Abe was particularly mesmerized by the drama. He spoke of little else.

"Have you heard the latest? They're drilling a hole to free Collins," he told customers who entered the store and were as hungry for the latest news as Abe was. A week later, Abe was still at it. "They say that Miller may have gotten Collin's leg free. He should be out of the cave anytime!" During the saga, Abe hardly slept.

Unfortunately, the optimistic reports were wrong. Various attempts to free Collins from the tight passage failed. After languishing two weeks in the cave, Collins died and so did the attention. With the live drama, however, a new fangled invention truly came of age—radio.

Radio soon held a tremendous grip on popular culture. Autumn meant the World Series. On game days a house on Walnut Street placed a radio on the front stoop. There, Abe and eleven year old Norman listened to part of the 1925 World Series. It was the second straight World Series appearance of the Washington Senators, or Nats. They were playing the Pittsburgh Pirates. Game Seven was at Forbes Field. The Pirates had rebounded from a 3 to 1 deficit in games to tie the series. Rain was coming down at the ballpark. His voice cracking with deep emotion, broadcaster Graham McNamee described Walter Johnson's heroic pitching. The mud on the pitcher's mound was ankle deep. "Johnson is carrying the Senators on his shoulders!" Abe exclaimed. Johnson already had won games one and four and was now attempting to seal the Series. But two costly errors by the Nats shortstop Roger Peckinpaugh late in the game caused four unearned Pittsburgh runs to cross the plate. Johnson lost the game. Norman was heartbroken. He cried for hours that evening.

PART III

Norman

Eleven

Yingl

Yetta and Abe returned to Pottstown in 1917. Norman was three years old. Their *yingl*, their child, almost did not make it to four.

Men gathered around a gaunt brown horse lying on the sidewalk. Smashed portions of a child's toy lay splintered under the horse's neck. The poor animal twitched a few moments, gave one last kick. Then it was still. Behind the horse still attached by its traces was an overloaded milk wagon. Slouched by the wagon the burly milkman wiped his brow with an old handkerchief. His hair and forehead were moistened with sweat, as much from shock and tension as from the high summer temperature and Pennsylvania humidity. His calloused hand shook uncontrollably. He stood and tried to unhitch the harness but arm strength seemingly had abandoned him. He stared vacantly at the scene in front of him.

One by-stander gesticulated wildly. He pointed to a toddler a few yards away. "Did you see that?" he asked the others who quickly rushed to the scene. "That kid was riding a kiddy cart on the sidewalk. I saw it all!" He had their rapt attention now. "The milk horse began to behave funny. It stumbled then collapsed right onto that kid's cart crushing it beyond recognition! Somehow, the boy jumped off the kiddy car just before the horse fell on it!" More people gathered. Soon a policeman appeared on the scene.

Norman sat on a nearby lawn. The scene frightened him and he began to cry. A neighbor consoled the boy. Another rushed to Yetta's front door. "It is a miracle, a miracle," the witness repeated. "That kid leapt off, just seconds before the horse crashed to the ground!"

Soon after Norman's fifth birthday, his Uncle Robbie enrolled the boy in the local public school for first grade. It was the same elementary school all the Markowitz children attended. That first day, Robbie pulled his excited nephew to the schoolyard on an old toy wagon. Recently discharged from the army, Robert still wore his army tunic with its tall stiff collar and polished buttons. As he rolled by, Norman shouted enthusiastically to no one in particular "Look! I am going to school!" Heading to the same destination one lad whose eagerness to begin classes was evidently lacking, returned a singularly perplexed look.

How proud Norman was to be going to school. No longer would others have to read the comics to him. "Hare-breath Harry," "Mutt & Jeff" and "Blondie" were his favorites. Although odd, Norman began to associate school with Robbie and not his parents. His father Abe was busy in the store. Yetta was too occupied with housekeeping and Norman's infant sibling to deal with such mundane matters as school. No one perceived the irony. Similar household pressures constrained Rose Markowitz when she registered *her* children for first grade.

Located one block up Beech Street from the Cohen house, Jefferson Elementary School consisted of two two-story buildings. To the new pupil, its classrooms seemed immense. The largest rooms he had ever seen. Through the south facing windows sunlight flooded across the classrooms and caused a severe mid-afternoon glare. There were no curtains or blinds. Since "Cohen" came early on the class's alphabetical roster, Norman was seated halfway back in the first file, next to the window.

Norman's first grade teacher was a middle age spinster. Her face was sharply angular with a deep widow's peak. Compared to his mother, she seemed to Norman as ancient as a matriarch from the land of Canaan. Maybe, Norman wondered, she was even as old as *bubbeh*, his grandmother. Yet, her soft smile and puppy dog eyes entranced Norman who was smitten. After school that first day, Robbie appeared to take his nephew home. Before leaving the building, he took Norman to the fifth and sixth grade classrooms upstairs. Amazed, Norman told him the desks and chairs were intended for giants!

"No giants," Robbie laughed, "just fifth graders."

About two-thirds of the pupils in Jefferson Elementary were African-American. This reflected in rough proportionality their status as Chicken Hill's dominant racial group. Of the rest, most were the children of Pottstown immigrants, particularly Polish and Italian Catholics. Only a handful of Jewish kids attended Jefferson Elementary. None were in Norman's class. Despite the ethnic makeup of the school's students, the teachers were lily white. All were women, unmarried for the most part, although the pupils did refer to some of the older teachers as Mrs. instead of Miss. None of the teachers lived in the neighborhood. Nor did any of their family members attend Jefferson Elementary. For them to be a resident of Chicken Hill was considered just short of preposterous.

During recess and after school most of Norman's playmates were African-American. They were his classmates. He sat next to them throughout his years at Jefferson, the same kids who lived on Chicken Hill and played in the neighborhood alleys and vacant lots. However, during the years Norman attended Jefferson, only a few made it past sixth grade. Fewer still made it through junior high. By high school, there would be only one, Dick Ricketts. He was Pottstown High's star athlete in three sports and an incredible running back. However, Ricketts failed to graduate. He was forced from school his senior year for getting his girlfriend pregnant.

Robbie became very close to his nephew. He taught Norman how to catch a baseball, pitch pennies, and play cards. He carried Norman on his shoulders and related war stories to the gullible kid, although he had never made it onto a troopship before the war ended and thus had no firsthand war stories to tell. On weekends, Robbie played tennis with his cousin Itch Klein at the Hill School courts on Beech Street. Norman was the ball boy.

One late summer afternoon, Robbie took Norman on an outing. It was a muggy, painfully bright lethargic afternoon punctuated with buzzing cicadas and grasshoppers. It was the kind of Pottstown afternoon that enticed boys and young men to water. Despite the lack of a breeze, the scent of an on-coming thunderstorm filled the air. Uncle took nephew swimming at an amusement park in nearby Sanatoga where Sprogel's Run had been widened and deepened. Robbie loved the water, although Norman was too young to have known of his infamous outing on the Manatawny that led to his nickname Boat. This was to be the young boy's first time in water over his head.

"Promise you will not let me go," Norman pleaded. He held onto Robbie with both arms around his neck.

"Okay, okay, I promise," replied Robbie.

Perhaps the slickness of the muddy water on skin made Robbie's shoulders more slippery. The boy lost his grip and fell, arms and legs thrashing, into muddy Sprogel's Run. Carried onto the ground endless moments later, Norman coughed up mucky water. He looked around. The surrounding adults seemed to be scolding him. Not so. It was Robbie the strangers were scolding. The boy never spoke of the incident to his parents. Eventually, he pushed it from his conscious memory. If Adolph ever heard of the incident, there is no telling what punishment he might have inflicted on poor Boat.

* * *

Stubbornness must have been an inherited trait. If so, there was little doubt from which side of the family it came. Yetta constantly looked over her son's shoulder at whatever he was doing. One evening Norman was practicing writing for his second grade homework. His mother asked him to spell the word "it." The boy refused. Not because he did not know how to spell the word. Of course he did. Something else bothered him. Even at a young age, Norman sensed his mother's pleasure with seeing him act like a trained dog. Her constant overbearing behavior disturbed him although he would not have been able to describe his feelings. He resented his toddler sister who did not receive the same haughty treatment. Norman sealed his mouth. He knew speaking back to his mother would have angered her further.

Yetta nevertheless became irate. She gripped Norman by my shoulders and shook him viciously. "IT, IT" she shouted repeatedly. With her spelling of each letter she pressed her fingers harder into Norman's skin. Luckily for the boy, "it" is a short word. The fierce treatment did not let up. Yetta continued to treat her eldest son caustically. She attacked him at every opportunity.

When Norman was 13 or 14, his two-year old brother Russell performed some infantile act. Norman made a silly comment. His mother berated him savagely. She peered into his face and in absolute seriousness asserted that his brother was *"er bis kleiger don ere,"* smarter than you! "If Dad had his way," Norman kept telling himself, "she would never hit me."

But in the Cohen home Abe rarely had his way, especially when dealing with Norman. Yetta's violent temper imposed her will upon everyone in the family. At the tiniest infraction, at her insistence, Abe reluctantly took a strap to Norman. Intently, she watched the punishment being meted out. As Abe punished Norman, his mother's eyes deepened. She seemed to look right through her son. "Harder, HARDER," she shouted as the strap was put to Norman's *toches*, his rear end, just as her father Adolph did to her brothers. Abe intensely disliked performing this onerous chore. The anguish was etched on his face. But he said nothing about it to his wife, at least in Norman's presence.

As he grew, Norman gave constant thought to running away. Paradoxically, the more he daydreamed of escape from the constant grief, the less determined he became to take such action. Gradually, the boy withdrew into himself, into an introverted world where the hurt did not exist, the pain vanquished.

The teacher in one of Norman's early primary grades at Jefferson Elementary sent a note home with the boy. She suggested to Yetta he be advanced a grade. It was evident, the teacher explained, the boy was the most advanced child in the class. Yetta came to the school the following day. "Your son understands everything," the teacher said. "Unless we move him up a grade, Norman will exhibit boredom with class work. He might easily get into mischief." The recommendation hit his mother like a rock. She reacted as if struck dumb. Until that moment, Yetta assumed her son was among the *least* academically inclined students in his class, not the most advanced. She could barely croak a response.

But her doubt was transparent. Yetta's reaction startled the teacher who for a moment wondered whether she was meeting the right parent.

After meeting with Yetta, the teacher immediately sought out the school principal. She described the tense meeting with Norman Cohen's mother, especially the empty stare that followed the initial exchange. "Wouldn't you think a parent would be proud of their child's ability?" she asked. The question hung between them. Cigarette haze hovered over the principal's desk. Finally, the principal took a long, deep drag on his half finished cigarette. He exhaled more smoke to the existing cloud. He tapped the precariously arched ash into an already overloaded ashtray. He shrugged, rolled his eyes, and conjectured out loud whether his counterparts face similar issues at Lincoln and Washington Elementary Schools.

Despite her strained reaction and vapid response, Yetta did not challenge the teacher's proposal to advance Norman. No recommendation from a teacher could be ignored. Moreover, Abe, for once, was adamant. "If the school wants it," he barked, "we must do it!" Yetta acquiesced. She agreed to let her son move one grade ahead.

As a result of being moved up, Norman was always the youngest student in his class. Especially in high school, the one-year age difference with classmates seemed enormous. He was always smaller than the other boys. Being the youngest student in his classes contributed to his shyness. He constantly displayed timidity and signs of an inferiority complex. This included a fear of answering questions in class, even though he almost always knew the answer sought by the teachers.

At home Norman developed a fear of opening his mouth. No one paid attention to the small boy sitting invisibly behind the grown-ups. It was not only his mother. Other adults ignored him.

Norman dreaded sharing problems with uncles or older cousins whom he most admired. He felt comfortable in their presence. However, he did not want to embarrass himself by mentioning his pre-adolescent problems. He listened and observed but remained silent as the Sphinx.

In 1920 within the silent film profession, a very heavy-set comedian named Roscoe "Fatty" Arbuckle was the popular topic of a famous sex scandal. After listening to the conversations of older children at school, the six year-old Norman baldly announced to his parents that he knew the story of Fatty Arbuckle. With serious continence they glared at their son. Norman rushed ahead. "Since Arbuckle was a very heavy man," Norman said, "he killed a girl by sitting on top of her." Silence, then chuckles. Norman received laughs but no explanation.

One day Robbie appeared at the house in his full army uniform. The Great War had ended a year earlier. Pottstown was full of returning veterans. Fathers, uncles, and older brothers of other children had war stories a plenty. Norman asked his uncle "How many Germans did you kill?" A laugh, but Robbie offered no explanation. Norman's face reddened in embarrassment. Had he said something wrong? All he wanted was something to relate, a tidbit of information he could share with the kids on the playground. He yearned to respond to playmates that dramatized with highly exaggerated expression the numbers of Germans killed by their family members. They told yarns and stories with pride, or perhaps mischief that were communicated at dinner tables by proud former soldiers to eager ears.

Every day in school and on the streets the young Norman confronted questions and issues of assimilation. He felt different from his peers. He tried to fit in but had difficulty. Usually, older boys ignored him. Often they teased him, occasionally viciously and bitterly, and called him names he did not comprehend at first. Eventually, Norman perceived a stigma that could not be dropped, the mark of Cain beyond his control. A sign hung from his neck. The sign said "Jew."

During the summer, Pottstown's retail stores closed Wednesdays at noon. The businessmen referred to it as a "summer half-holiday." For the Cohen family the free afternoon meant a picnic and possibly swimming. One pleasant afternoon, Abe drove the family to a new park and swimming pool that had opened in Royersford, about 9 miles from Pottstown. Abe parked the car and the family walked to the park entrance. Suddenly the family reversed course and returned to the car. Norman was perplexed. "Why are we going back to the car? Why can't we go swimming?"

His father snapped back "There is a sign posted 'No Jews Allowed.'" Norman had not noticed the sign. It struck him as odd. "How do they know we are Jewish?" he asked. Both Abe and Yetta frowned. It was a legitimate question, Norman thought. He deserved an explanation. His parents briefly looked at each other. Abe turned, grinded his teeth, and shot his son a fierce look. "Get in the car," he ordered. But there was no other response. "Children's foolish questions do not deserve an answer," his mother said.

Norman's grandfather Adolph was the only adult who gave young Norman the attention he craved and the self-assurance a pre-adolescent boy requires. Although Adolph still occasionally went out on his peddling rounds, he had by now entered semi-retirement from the junk business. Instead, he practiced his new profession. It matched his business acumen with his "take no prisoners" attitude towards the world. He was a landlord. It assured him both a steady income with minimal labor and time for his grandchildren.

Norman was Adolph's eldest grandchild and the relationship was special. When the grandson beseeched him with questions about any topic—cars, games, his junk collection, words in Hebrew or Yiddish—Adolph listened patiently and answered completely. During Norman's younger years, the two had their own pet games. Norman rubbed Adolph's bald head and exclaimed 'bald a moonshine!' How or why he coined that phrase neither grandfather nor grandson could remember. Adolph then growled like an angry dog and snapped at Norman's hand with his mouth. With Norman mounted on his back, Adolph crawled on hands and knees and tried to buck the youngster off. The bronco generally succeeded in throwing its rider onto the sofa. When Norman fell, Adolph smoothed his sense of failure. "Come here and I will pick you up," Adolph said kindly. It was his favorite expression with his grandson.

Adolph was a master storyteller. He enjoyed telling *bubba maisses*, literally grandmother tales. With his friends, he recited these stories in Yiddish, occasionally throwing in Hungarian or German words and expressions to tweak the story in just the right way. With exaggerated facial expressions, a polished resonance, and embellished hand movements to demonstrate some point, Adolph mesmerized his listeners. From his *lantzmen*, he always seemed to spawn a hearty laugh, even more so when whiskey was available. To Norman he always used English. One story went like this:

> "A boy asked his father to teach him about business. 'Okay,' his father said, 'let's get started. Climb to the top of that step ladder,' the father instructed. His son dutifully did as he was told. The father then held out his hands. He told the boy to jump. As his son jumped, the father backed up and allowed the boy to fall to the ground. With a hurt expression and a couple of bruises the son looked up at his deceiving father. 'Why didn't you catch me?' the son asked.

That is your first lesson in business,' his father replied. 'Never trust anyone, not even your father!'"

Years later, Norman realized that his grandfather cleaned up many of his tales for the boy's consumption.

Despite the cordial bond with his grandfather, Norman also observed a sinister, almost perverse side to Adolph's character. It was a disposition tempered in the *shtetl* and buffeted by a tough life. His grandfather was a hard man, Norman realized. This realization was chilling to a boy familiar solely with Pottstown's streets.

One afternoon while the two sat on the porch, Adolph told Norman about a horse he once owned that was not performing to his satisfaction. While the poor beast was pulling a load of heavy junk up a hill, he continued to whip the animal. The horse stopped, twirled around and dropped dead in its harness. Adolph then explained. "It was not a loss, however. In fact, it was for the best. I collected the insurance on the horse, an amount fit for a much better mount!" The story sent a shiver of gloom through Norman's body. How can his grandfather be so kind to his grandson and so cruel to an animal, he wondered.

Norman accompanied his grandfather on his many errands in town. On these jaunts Adolph constantly shocked the boy in both word and deed. One Friday evening as Norman's parents labored in the store, Adolph served as Norman's babysitter. The two walked down Chicken Hill into town. On High Street, between Evans and Charlotte Streets, they passed a hotdog vendor. Norman glanced at the vendor's cart. "Norman, do you want a hotdog?" Adolph asked.

Norman was stunned. His grandfather was offering him a non-kosher hot dog! Norman could not comprehend why his grandfather asked such a question. Adolph knew well Abe's thoughts about eating *traif* food. Although the hot dogs in the vendor's cart looked succulent indeed, Norman could not bring himself to go against his father's strict orders. "I'm not hungry," he told his grandfather who sagely suspected the truth and, for once, did not pursue the issue.

Norman's home life did not produce many pleasant memories. Few evenings passed peacefully. Yetta invariably took the offense, Abe played defense. Yetta complained constantly about everything: Abe, his activities at the synagogue, or his evenings out with his friend Jake (Yonkel) Markowitz—no relation. She also complained about her eldest child. So pervasive were the criticisms that seemed to cover every aspect of his existence that Norman long repressed most of them from his memory.

Family finances were the most common grounds of bickering between the parents. Every other family in Pottstown, even those on Chicken Hill, must have enjoyed prosperity, Norman reasoned. Otherwise, why would all the other boys have marbles, bicycles, skates, etc. Norman had none of those things. For the gentile boys to have such items, he understood. But with Max Lerner and Mush Estreicher, two Jewish boys who were his best friends, there was a difference. Did their fathers possess some secret ability to accumulate money? Norman was perplexed. Why did his father never seem capable of mastering this art? There was always food on the table, Norman realized. Abe proudly owned a car, never older than a few years. Yet, the family never seemed blessed with much more. Norman gave up asking for anything from my parents.

In the spats that dictated family life, Norman was a spectator, sometimes a pawn, and too frequently a target. His sisters too young to understand sometimes cried from the shouting. When the yelling became too bitter, the acrid words not taken back, Abe abruptly stormed out of the house. The door slammed sharply behind him. He escaped usually to the residence of his pal Jake, anything to get away. This left Norman to take the brunt of his mother's continued anger.

Norman conceded one point. His father never drank. Fathers of other working class families with similar problems often drowned their problems at neighborhood speakeasies—with predictable results. At the Cohen home Abe remained stone sober. Moreover, Norman believed, it had nothing to do with Prohibition. Abe certainly enjoyed sharing schnapps with cronies at *shul*. But he never entered the house with even a whiff of alcohol on his breath.

* * *

When the Cohen family moved in with Adolph following four years living above the shoe store, Norman once again was back among Chicken Hill friends who attended Jefferson School. He again was master of the alleys and dirt streets, the vacant lot where neighborhood boys played baseball and football at the appropriate seasons, and the corner grocery stores where he ran errands. It was only a five-minute walk to the *shul*. And he now lived under the same roof as the only adult who seemed to care about him, his grandfather.

From the neighbor's property a large cherry tree overhung Adolph's junkyard. In season it produced large, succulent black fruit. When the branches were heavy with cherries, Norman longed to sample them. However, even though the branches extended onto Adolph's property, the boy did not know whether he was entitled to take any off the tree. He longed for the cherries but never reached for them or touched them. I should ask grandpop for permission, he told himself. Adolph would have assented. Most likely, he would have eagerly assisted his grandson. But Norman feared his mother's wrath if she found out. And find out she certainly would. He remained too reticent to go around her. He never tasted the cherries from the tree. The birds got them instead.

Roughly fourteen Jewish families resided on Chicken Hill. Half lived on the 500 block of Beech Street. Among them were the Phillips family, Maurice Miller, the Bresslers, the Fuermans, and Ben Berger. During Norman's daily treks and errands through the neighborhood, he observed members of these families and the other Jews of Chicken Hill. They knew him well. They were the parents of his friends. He called them 'aunt' or 'uncle.' They called out "Hey Norman. How's your grandfather?" "Can you run a quick errand to the store? I'll give you a nickel." The pennies and nickels Norman received in these endeavors were not reported to his parents. Other mothers and housewives, he was certain, would never enlighten his mother as to the tips. On occasion, the boy enjoyed a meal with them. None ever treated him harshly or unfairly. Norman could not remember ever being scolded outside his home.

In the years before his Bar Mitzvah, Norman frequently accompanied his father to *mincha/maariv*, afternoon/evening services at the *shul*. Before Pottstown had a full time rabbi, Abe often led these services. If someone in the community had a *yartzeit* in memory of a loved one, making a *minyan* of ten men, the requirement for holding a service, was no problem. On ordinary weekday evenings however, a *minyan* often proved difficult to achieve. If to make a *minyan* an eighth, ninth or tenth man was required, Abe sent his dutiful son down the hill to fetch additional worshippers. Beech Street, an obvious first target for the additional men, was just two blocks away. On these missions Norman moved up Beech Street like a postman delivering the day's mail. Norman knocked on front doors. When the neighborhood fathers or grandfathers saw Norman approach or heard him knock, they knew the mission. "They need a *minyan* at *shul*," he quickly said as the door opened. He knew once the words left his mouth, the men would feel obligated to rise from whatever they were doing, even if in the middle of a meal. The men put on their coats and hats and walked briskly up the hill to the *shul*. Making a *minyan*, everyone understood, was an important obligation.

However, Norman scrupulously avoided Maurice Miller's house. He had once seen a Christmas tree inside their window!

Abe always appreciated the appearance of the *minyan* makers and warmly thanked them afterwards. As a favor to those pressed for time, he *daven*ed swiftly. He rushed through the *amidah* prayer at breath-taking speed. But he never skipped a Hebrew word nor cut out any prayer. After the service if time was not pressing, a bottle of schnapps and shot glasses might emerge from some mysterious closet where Prohibition did not apply.

Only white families lived on their block of Walnut Street. The corresponding block on Beech Street, just one block up, was predominantly black. For the boys segregation did not extend to the schoolyard or the neighborhood streets. As far as the kids were concerned, if you got along, you were welcome. Despite the occasional fight or harsh words between individual boys over some petty issue, the Chicken Hill neighborhood did not have serious problems with kids or gangs. Understandably, Norman possessed a closer affinity for the Jewish boys his age. Morris (Mush) Estreicher lived two blocks away on Walnut between Washington and Warren Streets. Max Lerner resided just two doors down. They were Norman's best buddies. Although Mush lived farther away, Norman felt closer to him than to Max. Norman and Mush had constant contact at the *shul*. The Lerner family did not attend services regularly.

During school recess, Norman usually played with only one white boy from his class. Fred O'Dell's father taught at the Hill School. It was understood that when Fred was older he would go to that school. Norman's other playmates at Jefferson Elementary, all African-Americans, included Richard "Dick" Ricketts, Francis Banks, and Carter—the kids always referred to him by his last name. Even teachers seemed unaware the boy had a first name. After school Norman also played with Archie O'Neill who lived across the street and Sparky who lived on the short block of Walnut Street next to the Hill School. Archie was the youngest of many brothers, some of whom were adults and had their own families. When Archie was nine, a brother already served on the Pottstown police force. Sparky had an older sister who passed away from measles. She was laid out in their living room. Black crepe hung on the front door. It was the first time Norman ever observed a corpse. Other boys ran with the group but these were the ones who invited Norman into their homes.

Most of Chicken Hill, including Walnut Street, was unpaved. Residents referred to the surface as dirt, although that depended on the season. Winter snow swiftly deteriorated into a gray mush broken by sodden brown horse droppings and yellow horse piss. At these times just crossing the street became an ordeal. Following heavy rain, the streets turned into a thick goop with the consistency of syrup. Wheel ruts formed in the spring mud hardened and remained for months. In summer the streets baked into a shell as hard as cement. A trip or minor fall onto the "dirt" street could leave an ugly abrasion, sometimes even a broken bone.

Few wagons and fewer cars routinely reached Walnut Street. Those that came by maneuvered around the boys playing in the street. Rarely did a car need to honk. When a car got stuck, the boys offered to push. "Mister, we'll push your car for a nickel," one boy might say. Sometimes the nickel materialized. But most of the boys did not ask for money. Most drivers who came through the neighborhood knew the parents well. If word got out to the parents that their boys were exploiting the misfortune of others, there could be hell to pay.

When school was out, if chores were completed, and no more errands were left to run, the boys were free to do what they wanted. Shooting marbles was a popular pastime. A stick was used to make a circle in the street. Boys "in the game" placed a certain number of their marbles in the center of the circle. They took turns "shooting" other marbles in an attempt to knock out as many marbles as possible. Norman was always a spectator, standing alongside the occasional sister of one of the gang. The other boys had marbles.

Some intersections such as the one at Walnut and Hale Streets had better streetlights than other neighborhood intersections. At these locations the boys played "kick the wicket." The game utilized the same rules as baseball but without balls or mitts. Each street corner served as a base. The batter placed a piece of wood similar to a broom handle on his instep and kicked it as hard as he could. From there, the same rules as baseball applied. A missed catch of a hard piece of wood smarted a little on the hands. Sometimes the boys received cuts or bruises. No one was ever hurt enough to leave a game in the middle. The ballplayers feared only one thing. On warm summer evenings bats seeking a hearty meal of insects fluttered around in the glow of the streetlights. The boys then stayed far away. They were afraid the bats might fly into and get tangled in their hair! Although no one could recollect ever seeing such an event, all were adamant that the risk from bats was real.

Occasionally, a biplane flew overhead. Of course, that stopped the game mid-stride and launched comments of awe and envy. "Boy," someone would say, "I betcha it's goin' a mile a minute!" The boys stared at the plane until it passed from view.

Nearby, close enough to cast a shadow on Chicken Hill's streets was the Hill School. The exclusive private prep school for boys was strictly off-limits to neighborhood kids. A high wooden fence surrounded the school. "No Trespassing" signs ominously were displayed on the gates which also had the school emblem with the words "whatsoever things are true." Norman starred frequently at the school's Gothic structures, its finely manicured lawns. Students walked between buildings. Each wore a tailored navy blue blazer. They seemed so sure of themselves, thought Norman who so wanted to visit this mysterious school perched on a hill and attended by rich kids. Naturally, Norman's parents constantly reemphasized that he was not to approach or enter the school grounds.

Mr. Saylor was an older African-American who did some caretaking and gardening in the neighborhood. Adolph used Saylor's services to cool down and curry his horses at the end of a long day of peddling. Saylor, a short man, seemed overly cautious when around horses. Norman suspected that he was afraid of them. One day while Saylor was combing one of Adolph's horses, it pulled away from the tie rope. The horse took off up the alley. Whenever a horse escaped from its stable or slipped from its harness, the owner and available passers-by yelled for help as they pursued the horse. Shouts of "loose horse, LOOSE HORSE!" then filled the neighborhood. The escape of his grandfather's horse provided Norman a chance. He ran to the Hill School gate and entered the school grounds yelling "LOOSE HORSE!" For a few minutes Norman observed the forbidden sights. A thrill passed through him. As he ran through the Hill School grounds, he hoped no one would stop him and ask how a horse could enter a fenced area.

During Christmas break when students were away, the Hill School allowed visitors onto the campus. What an opportunity this was for Norman to return to the barred territory! Near the campus center was a pond called The Dell. Locals were permitted to skate. Norman mentioned to his mother that Adele Wilson, the niece of a neighbor, Mrs. Finn, wanted to go skating. She had new shoe skates. Norman had none. "Why don't you rummage through your grandfather's junkyard for ice skates?" After a long search, Norman found one women's skate blade and one men's size skate. Both were rusty and lacked the clamps to attach to shoes. Norman was undaunted. He was not about to give up. He tried to attach the blades to his shoes with a thin rope. He hobbled to the edge of the pond and went onto the ice. Of course, the experiment was a fiasco. The skates wobbled and Norman's ankles painfully turned inwards. That episode ended Norman's exposure to ice-skating.

The skating incident bothered Norman deeply. The young boy did not know the financial condition of Adele's parents. He assumed her father worked in one of Pottstown's factories. The row house they lived in was "low end." That winter Solomon Borger's mother hosted a birthday party for her son. Norman wondered why he could not have a party for his tenth birthday. At that moment, Norman gladly would have moved from his home to live with Adele and her family or with Sol's family if only a pair of shoe skates or a birthday party were included in the deal.

Next to the property that later became the Sunnybrook Restaurant was a picnic area. Above it a steep grassy bank rose to a lot. It served as an ideal sledding run. After a snowfall the lot and hill attracted scores of children. From the flat area a kid could belly flop onto a sled and fly down the bank to the picnic grounds. Norman did not have a sled. Sometimes, he persuaded a kid into allowing him to jump on his back after the kid made the initial start and before he reached the embankment. One time, an obliging boy consented to Norman's request. As the boy picked up speed for the drop off, Norman made the jump onto his back. Unfortunately, the sled was not strong enough for the weight of two passengers. It caved in at the runners. Since Norman was on top holding on to nothing more than the back of the boy's coat collar, he lost control. Like a snowball his momentum carried him down the hill. Somehow Norman's clothes survived, although he could not fathom why. The skin of his face though took a beating.

Each morning at home the breakfast routine was identical. Yetta usually did not get out of bed until Abe and Norman were out of the house, the first to work, the second to school. Adolph occasionally joined them, but he was an early riser and usually gone by then. Abe prepared the same oatmeal and coffee breakfast each day. He was not one to waste motion or time in the morning. On days he did not go to *shul* for the morning *shaharit* service, he *daven*ed at home. He stirred the oatmeal with his left hand—Abe was left-handed—and held the *siddur* the prayer book with his right. Bending mechanically back and forth at the waist, he read from the *siddur* softly but swiftly. When he ended his prayers, the oatmeal was ready. It was always very lumpy.

Abe did the family meat shopping. Almost everyday the family had *brust*. "It has to be first cut," Abe always repeated at the butcher counter. Despite Printz's unethical behavior towards him with regards to the Dampman real estate transaction, Abe still patronized Adolph Printz's butcher shop. Grandmother Cohen taught Yetta how to prepare and cook the meat. Norman never tired of a piece of meat so soft he could cut it with a fork. It was one of the few dishes Yetta prepared well. For lunch the family usually ate vegetable salads. Abe disliked uncooked vegetables; he called it "eating grass." Unlike Norman, he did not come home from the store for lunch. So for lunch Yetta served salads to her heart's content.

On Fridays, Yetta prepared either chicken or goose for Shabbat dinner. Each Thursday afternoon, Abe went to the Obermeyer farm to buy live birds. With a keen eye, Abe carefully examined each bird Obermeyer presented. He selected the healthiest, plumpest available. On the way home, he stopped by the *shochet* for the bird's proper slaughtering.

Abe was carrying a live goose under his arm one autumn day as Norman and he walked to the *shochet's* house. Suddenly, he slipped on some ice and landed on his *toches*. But Abe still held onto the live goose. In one quick motion he bounced back onto his feet unhurt. Norman unintentionally let out a laugh. His father's slip brought to mind the figure of Ichabad Crane. Norman's class had just read Washington Irving's 'The Legend of Sleepy Hollow.' He thought his father's fall and swift recovery was hilarious. He did not mean to poke fun at his father. At the time a popular comedian, Joe Penner, carried a duck in the same manner. To uproarious laughs, Penner repeated 'Wanna buy a duck?' But Penner did not have the slip in his act. Abe angrily told Yetta of the incident. She sternly rebuked Norman for laughing at his father.

The usual Saturday meal consisted of chicken left over from Friday evening, except for when Yetta needed *schmaltz*, or chicken fat, for cooking. Then, she rendered a goose or chicken. The fat was placed in an old whiskey bottle. Usually, Norman took the live birds to the *shochet* to be slaughtered. Mr. Klein who was also the *hazen* at *shul* charged ten cents for slaughtering a goose but only a nickel for a chicken. He performed the act in a shed behind his Warren Street house. Once Klein reached into Norman's burlap sack and found a dead chicken. Norman returned home with both five cents and a dead chicken. Since the chicken had not been properly slaughtered by the *shochet*, the family could not consume it. The bird was not a total loss. Abe immediately sold it to Chris the Greek who served the non-kosher chicken in his Crystal Restaurant.

Being raised in a religious household, Norman thought that his family's lifestyle was the way all Jews lived. He was wrong. When he attended *chedar*, Hebrew school, he observed the behavior of his peers. Following their example, Norman became brave. With increasing brazenness, he started eating *traif* food, violating Shabbat, eating without a *kippah* on his head, etc. His parents did not find out about his new habits, or so Norman assumed. A few years later, Rabbi Farber who had recently arrived in Pottstown confided to his *chedar* students that he was aware they ate *traif* hotdogs. "But I am not angry with you," he told the trembling *chedar bochers*. "Because of the *hametz* (leavened) hotdog roll, at least refrain from doing so on Passover," Rabbi Farber admonished. The boys complied with the Rabbi's instruction. But that was Norman's license to eat *traif*.

Despite Norman's caution not to flaunt his "lapses" from a strict kosher diet, Norman's parents were not unaware of Norman's nascent adolescent rebelliousness outside the house. Abe reluctantly tolerated his son's lapses into eating *traif*. What else could he do? He never brought up the subject with his son. But this did not mean he condoned such behavior. Norman's mother also pretended not to notice.

Yetta continued to exercise total control over other aspects of Norman's life. When Norman reached the grade at school where all the boys wore knickers, he still wore shorts, the only kid in the class still to do so. In a real sense, the first pair of knickers symbolized the change from boyhood to adolescence. For the older boys at Jefferson Elementary, the first day at school in knickers was as important as any in the calendar, a combination of Christmas, birthday, the arrival of the circus, and the beginning of summer vacation.

Each day Norman walked to school in mortification. His short pants, Norman felt, shouted to everyone that he was different, that he was still a boy. The humiliation went deeper since his father had a store on High Street. No case could be made that he was too impoverished for knickers. "Please," Norman implored his mother, "all the other boys already have their long pants." His entreaties met with stony silence or a brusque retort. "Your pants are still in good shape. When they are worn out, then we'll consider what next." She kept him in shorts for an eternity. Despite constant wear, the shorts refused to show any age. Norman thought he was cursed with the only pair of indestructible pants ever made. He continued to plead with his mother for long pants. Eventually, Yetta caved in to her son's beseeching. She rationalized that with colder weather coming, longer pants might help prevent illness.

Norman's first pair of knickers was brown corduroy and buckled above-the-knee in the common style. Most boys, however, preferred knickers that buckled or fell below-the-knee. Once out of sight of parents, the bolder kids unstrapped the above-the-knee buckles and let their knickers down a few inches. Norman did not care about fashion. He loved to hear the swishing sound made by the pants legs when he walked. For the first time, he felt grown up.

Later, the fad in school was "white ducks." They became as common as blue jeans in later years. Norman pressed his mother. Yetta reluctantly took her son to the New York Store. She asked Sam Hoffman, the owner, to show her white ducks. Hoffman brought out a pair Norman's size. Yetta examined them carefully, turning them over multiple times. She passed her hand on the soft white fabric. She turned to Hoffman. "These pants will become so *shumtzig*, so dirty, in no time! I would have to wash them every Monday and Thursday!" She handed the pants back to Hoffman. Norman looked mournfully at Mr. Hoffman who just rolled his eyes and shrugged his shoulders.

Norman never got his white ducks.

Twelve

Bocher

In the mid 1920s, Norman moved from boyhood into adolescence, a *bocher*. Francis already moved out of the house to work in Norristown. Adolph remarried. The arguments between Yetta and her father persisted. As long as the two remained under one roof, relations between them remained strained beyond repair. Adolph Markowitz was not a man to keep thoughts to himself. The failings of his daughter and by implication his son-in-law could not escape his attention and criticism. With another matron in the house, Yetta knew it was time for the Cohen family to leave. Her family sensed her anxiety to depart.

Abe found a house about six blocks away at 77 N. Franklin Street. Business in the shoe store had improved. Abe succeeded in saving enough money for a reasonable down payment. The Security Trust Company handled the store account. It offered a manageable mortgage with a low interest rate. Yetta enthusiastically approved the purchase.

The red brick house had ten rooms, an unimaginable number. Two separate stairways led to the second floor. Yetta had one of the stairways torn out. "Who needs two stairs when only one can be climbed at a time?" she frequently commented. Despite doubts about his daughter and son-in-law, her father approved the logic.

The house contained too much space for two adults and four children. The solution was to find a tenant for the third floor which had its own bathroom. Yetta rented the room to a young couple. They were friendly and courteous and paid their rent promptly the first of the month. The couple gave the impression they were starting out in life. Starting out was true enough. Yetta discovered they were not married. They were living in sin! That was the end of renting out the third floor. When the tenants left, Yetta madly scrubbed the entire third floor with lye soap. She especially scoured the commode.

Next door lived the Morris Miller family. Before Pearl, their first-born child, the Millers also had tenants. Mrs. Miller was a kind woman. She willingly kept an eye on the Cohen children as they played in the neighborhood. Her friendly behavior was not fully reciprocated. Yetta constantly found fault with the Miller household. Each evening she conveyed to Abe her displeasure with some action by Mrs. Miller. Soon the two women were not on speaking terms, although Morris and Abe continued a cordial relationship.

The Millers were among the first families in the neighborhood to own a radio. On the Miller's front stoop, Abe and Norman joined with a dozen others in listening to the second Dempsey-Tunney prize fight, the one with the famous "Long Count." It was a crisp September evening. The awestruck audience gathered around Miller's radio actually felt the excitement from Soldier's Field in Chicago. Tunney seemed to dominate the fight. Then in the crucial Seventh Round, the "Manassa Mauler" pounded

Tunney to the canvas. "Take THAT you son of a gun!" shouted one of the neighbors. With the knock down, the fight seemed over. "We were momentarily convinced that Gene Tunney had been knocked out," Norman recalled.

But Dempsey delayed moving to a neutral corner. The referee waited five interminable seconds before starting his count. Tunney rose at the count of nine. He then proceeded to win the fight with a unanimous decision. Abe shook his head at the end of the fight, mumbling over and over "I don't believe it!" At the shoe store the next day, Abe kept up a running dialogue with customers and cronies who stopped in to chat. When it came to sports, Abe's friends knew that Cohen knew his stuff. Whether boxing or baseball, they respected his views. At junior high school, the fight was the only subject of discussion among the boys. "Boy did we argue about *the fight*!" Norman said at dinner that night.

In the other half of Miller's double house lived the Ash family, an elderly couple, a son and daughter-in-law. The son was a chiropodist who attended Hahnemann Medical School in Philadelphia. He later opened his medical practice in the basement. Occasionally, Norman ran errands for Mrs. Ash. Usually, she sent him to the Great American Grocery (later the Acme) on Chestnut and Evans Streets. He received the customary five cents tip. This remittance was Norman's unreported overnight loot to be shared the next day with friends.

Three doors away lived the in-laws of Newton Baker, a member of Woodrow Wilson's Cabinet and a Presidential appointee under President Calvin Coolidge. The Empire Hook and Ladder fire station was across the street. The clanging of fire engines going out on a call occurred at all hours. In May 1927, a fireman stuck his head out of a second floor window to shout for the entire block to hear "HE LANDED IN PARIS!" Charles Lindbergh had succeeded in his attempt to fly the Atlantic. People rushed out to the street. Everyone was excited by the news. The firehouse also had a radio.

When World Series came around and radios were still rare, *The Pottstown Mercury* erected a 50 foot square green pane in front of its building. The pane showed an outline of a baseball diamond. A large white ball controlled by wires moved between the pitcher's mound and home plate. When a ball was hit, the moving ball followed its path. The scoreboard specified whether the hit ball was a groundball, fly out, pop out, single, etc. A crowd gathered to watch the first pitch and follow the early innings. But by the middle innings, the green panel drew little interest. Most men preferred to find a barbershop at which to hang out, a friend's front stoop, or a corner bar where near-beer (3% alcohol) was served—and perhaps listen to Grantland Rice's play-by-play on a radio.

Eventually, everyone had radios. Zenith, Philco, and Atwater-Kents were the most popular brands. On summer evenings when front windows and doors were open, a pedestrian could walk from one end of town to the other without missing a word or joke of the Amos & Andy show. Abe joined the crowd late in 1927 and bought a radio. He obtained the services of a moonlighting electrician to erect an antenna on the roof and run a ground wire to the earth. The electrician explained to Norman the function of the ground wire to prevent lightning strikes against the house. If an electrician could be so knowledgeable, Norman thought, perhaps he could someday become an electrician, or perhaps even an electrical engineer!

The following year, the Republican National Convention—the one that nominated Herbert Hoover for President—was held in Kansas City, Missouri. Abe's brother, Herman had his rabbinic pulpit in Kansas City. Herman was invited to give the convocation address at one of the Convention sessions to be broadcast on national radio. Abe rushed home early from the store to listen. Family and selected friends gathered around the radio centrally placed in the living room. "His voice is so clear," Abe exclaimed. "He sounds as if he is in the next room!"

Pottstown Junior High School occupied the old high school building at Walnut and Penn Streets. Norman's junior high class was the first under the new three-year junior high, three-year senior high school system. Until then, junior high school was two years and senior high, four years. Norman walked to school twice every day with his buddy Al Leblang. They attended the same section. Lunch break lasted an hour and a half. Each class had thirteen sections of 25 to 30 students each. Norman's section consisted of the most academically advanced students, that is, the upper seven percent. Each section went as a unit to each classroom throughout the school day. Norman and Al had little contact with the other Jews in their grade, Harry Pollack's sister Betty, Gerald "Peanuts" Princenthal, and Emmanuel Pollack.

Norman's musical talent was never appreciated by his music teachers. On the first day of school, the students formed a line in music class. Each sang the scales for the music teacher as she played a piano. When Norman's turn came, the teacher asked him to sing the scales, repeat them then repeat them again. The result was terrifying. "That was awful!" and other nasty comments, among the chuckles, emerged from the line of students. In desperation, the music teacher ordered Norman to sit in the last seat in the last row. "Don't sing!" she instructed. "Whatever you do, DON'T SING!"

Norman got even. Every morning in school assembly, for 'Onward Christian Soldiers,' he sang in his loudest voice.

During assembly the students also sang "You Take the High Road and I'll Take the Low Road" and other popular tunes. Mr. Sotter, the school principal, conducted bible readings from the New Testament on the Sanhedrin and the Pharisees and Sadducees.

At the time Norman had no idea what his discourses were about. Who ever listened to the principal, especially first thing in the morning? Afterwards, he realized that Sotter's lectures were laced with Christian anti-Semitism.

After school and on weekends, Norman spent more and more hours assisting his father at the shoe store. At first his duties consisted of breaking down shoeboxes and vacuuming and sweeping the floors. Nathan Pollock removed the flattened shoeboxes as junk. Whenever he stopped by the store, Pollack preached world socialism. Norman performed stock work, mostly moving shoes from one shelf location to another and restocking the shelves with shoes received from the shoe companies. Eventually, he began waiting on customers. If business was slow, and it often was, Norman did his homework on a table in the stock room. The store was open thirteen hours on Saturdays. His mother often came in to help for an hour or two. If Norman attended Shabbat services in preparation for his Bar Mitzvah, or later when he played on the Pottstown High School football team, he was in the store up to nine hours on Saturdays. At other times, he worked the full thirteen hours.

On those evenings when the store was open late, Abe and Yetta brought chicken sandwiches from the house for dinner. "If I have to work," Norman insisted, "I must go out for a milkshake." Since Abe did not pay his son a regular wage, he grudgingly conceded this point. For his evening meal, Norman made a beeline across High Street for the Texas Hot Weiner Stand. "Shorty" Lappis made the best hotdogs with the best sauce in the world! Norman sat at the counter and eagerly ordered. Shorty knew his customers well and began preparing Norman's order as he entered the swinging screen door. Norman asked for the identical meal every time. The hotdog straight from the grill was already placed in a bun when, with a sly smile and a wink, Shorty took the order. Norman watched ravenously as Shorty smothered the dog with sauce and onions. Norman paid ten cents for the hotdog and five cents for the Coke. He returned to the store reeking of hotdog and onions. He naively thought his father would believe he had dined on only a milkshake.

Not every day was a workday for the youngster. High Street stores were not open on Sundays. Even his parents could not always come with chores. Immediately after Sunday school Norman took off with his Jewish classmates. He frequently hiked with his pals to Ringing Rocks Park, a hilly three miles from town. The boys generally took the Keim Street route past quiet farmhouses—most families were still in church. Where Keim Street crossed Sprogel's Run, they built a fire and roasted hotdogs—"Peanuts" Princenthal's father was Pottstown's kosher butcher—and baked beans and potatoes. At the park a trolley trestle crossed a ravine. Norman did not have the nerve to cross the narrow trestle. The boys had heard that a trolley once came by as Sid Pollack was hiking across. He had to hang onto the side of the ties as the trolley car crossed above.

The friends also spent summer afternoons swimming in Manatawny Creek. Walnut Street ended at a grassy area by the stream. There, on especially hot sunny days the boys assembled. Other neighborhood groups occupied their own special swimming sites along the Manatawny. Freda and Ruth Rosenthal, Norman's second cousins, often met the boys at the favorite spot. Although the site was hardly secluded, there was plenty of shade and flat area to sit.

A large chestnut tree with a long limb overhung the stream. To swing out over the Manatawny, the youngsters used a thick rope tied to the limb. Gripping the stout rope, the next in line jumper balanced precariously on the leaning tree trunk. Then, each boy pushed off to swing as far as possible over the water. At the end of the arc, with a shout of "Geronimo" or an indecipherable yell, the boy let go of the rope and plunged into the cool water cannonball style. A big splash with spray reaching the creek bank accompanied by the deep "thump" of the plunge into the water meant the jump was especially successful. Calls of "that was a dozy" rang out from the shore.

Manatawny Creek at this point was about ten feet deep, or so the boys surmised. The depth had never been accurately measured. The creek bed consisted of a very soft muck that the boys tried to avoid. Except for the cow flops that drifted downstream in the coffee colored water, the swimming was not considered "too bad." On especially hot, humid afternoons, it was not uncommon for upwards of fifty kids to be swimming there. The line at the tree might reach a dozen or more.

The Manatawny was not the only option for swimming, although it was the cheapest. Sunnybrook Restaurant and Park opened its pool to public membership. It offered a very low junior membership price. Every member of Norman's Hebrew School class joined up. Since Norman already knew how to swim, he was in his glory! What a change from swimming at Sprogel's Run or Manatawny Creek. The water was actually clear, straight to the bottom of the pool!

A radio repairman, Mr. Schultz, came by almost every afternoon to swim. Since few people had radios and most radios were too new to yet require much repair, Schultz seemed to have plenty of free time. Schultz took a personal interest in Norman's aquatic skills. He taught the lad the finer points of diving—and from a diving board no less. "Hold out your arms straight," he called out. "Bend your knees. Keep your head down." Under his tutelage, Norman became a skilled diver.

When cooler weather arrived, the "south of the railroad tracks gang" to which Norman belonged hung out at the "new"— erected in 1913—YMCA building at King and Evans Streets. Norman thought the "Y" was off limits to Jewish boys until one of his buddies who belonged to the gang invited him to come along. He explained that community drives raised membership money for under-privileged boys. "You will be able to get in for free," he assured Norman who asked his parents for permission to join. A flustered Abe swiftly offered to pay the seven dollars for a year's Junior Membership. How could he do otherwise? What a stir it would have caused they realized if the son of a High Street businessman joined the YMCA as a charity case!

At the YMCA Norman was again in heaven. He excelled in diving and swimming. He played softball in the gym. The ball was much softer than softballs became in later years. Gloves were not needed. Very seldom did the boys have the strength to punch the mushy ball beyond the infield. That was not so bad since the gym was very small. To his knowledge, Norman concluded, he was the only Jewish kid in the YMCA program. In fact, he realized that he was the only kid in the program who lived north of High Street, certainly, the only boy from Chicken Hill. Yet no one said a word to him. Not one person mentioned that he did not belong. Nor did anyone make comments when Norman was absent during the Jewish holidays.

*   *   *

To Pottstown's Jewish youngsters, both boys and girls, the Hale Street *shul* on Chicken Hill and the Hebrew School served as the axis of their religious universe. They attended Shabbat services on Saturday mornings. The girls sat in the balcony with their grandmothers and aunts. The boys often also escorted fathers or grandfathers to Sunday *chevra* meetings. Norman spent many Saturday and Sunday mornings with friends both inside and outside *shul*.

Until they reached the age when attendance at services was not optional, the boys frolicked outside the *shul* while services went on. It was certainly more fun playing outside than praying inside. If his buddies and Norman could raise five cents, they bought a bag of broken pretzels from Hendrick's pretzel factory. Once the pretzels were consumed, the paper bag was stuffed with grass and used as a football on the lawn next to the synagogue. During services and while fathers participated in the animated *chevra* meetings, Norman and his pals played football. The rhythmic chanting of the *hazzen,* the piercing wails of some of the *daven*ers, and the boisterous debate at the *chevra* provided the acoustical backdrop for the games. The boys pretended they were performing before a thunderous crowd at a sold-out football stadium!

Football with a grass-filled paper bag was not the only form of entertainment. The *shul*'s outside stairway led to a second floor landing and the door to the women's balcony. From the wooden stairs the braver children jumped to the ground, perhaps six or even eight feet below. For crazy Paul Jacobson, those heights were not enough. He once leapt from the landing itself, a fall of at least ten feet. Instead of the ground, he hit the small cement patio and lacerated his knees and hands. A nice stain of blood was left on the cement.

Older kids, including Jake Leblang, played another game during services. They called it *"rebala."* The *rebala* sat facing a victim who was bent over frog-style with his *toches*, his rear end sticking out. Behind the victim stood a semi-circle of participants. With a nod the *rebala* gave permission for one of the spectators to deliver a *"pootch"* to the victim who kept eye contact with the *rebala*. Then the victim was required to identify who delivered the *pootch*. With their best acting faces the spectators each howled to give the false impression that their hand was in pain from administering the *pootch*. When correctly identified by the victim, the *pootcher* became the new victim.

Not all synagogue activities were fun and games. Norman began Hebrew study at age six and continued until his Bar Mitzvah. Hebrew School, or *chedar*, ran for two hours daily after school.

When Rabbi Maxwell Farber arrived in Pottstown in 1927, he expanded the *chedar* to include summer sessions as well. Because of insufficient space for classrooms, the *chedar* was not located at the *shul*. Instead it met in a house six blocks away on Chestnut Street. Norman's class included Harry Hoffman, Leon Prince, Sidney Erkis, Lawrence Cohen (no relation), and one of the Friedman brothers.

In due course, the Hebrew School was moved to the second floor of the Hartenstein Drug Store at 451 High Street. Adolph Printz owned the building. By this time Printz seemed to own half of High Street. Printz was also the Congregation president, a position he had already held for almost twenty years. Whether his position in the congregation hierarchy had anything to do with the selection of the Hartenstein building for the *chedar* was not a concern of the students.

While the new Hebrew School classrooms were superior in size to those in the Chestnut Street house, they were also noisier. Pottstown's Young Men's Hebrew Association, the YMHA, was located across the hall from the classrooms. The YMHA did not quite compare with the YMCA. There was no pool, no gymnasium for playing softball. Nor did the YMHA have barbells or even punching bags. What it did have was a self-playing piano on the right side of the auditorium. A card game was constantly in action. On one wall a plaque held the names of Pottstown's Jewish World War veterans, including Robert Markowitz. The name William Labor had a star next to it. The star signified he was killed in action. He was the son of the widow Mrs. Labor. The YMHA did not last very long. Hartenstein's second floor became, more appropriately, Bob Printz's Pool Parlor. The income must have been better. A craps table seemed always to be in operation. It caused many clients, mostly Pottstown's Jewish youth, to loose their shekels.

Except for learning Hebrew and reciting the prayers, Norman accomplished little in Hebrew School until he reached age twelve. That's when Rabbi Farber appeared on the scene. Before Rabbi Farber the *chedar* suffered from a rapid turnover of so-called Hebrew teachers and pseudo-rabbis. How they were selected for the all-important role of teaching Pottstown's Jewish youth about Judaism Norman never could fathom. From this string of teachers, Norman remembered almost nothing except some of their last names: Gordon, Schochet, Whitner, Bless, Shultsinger, Zubin, Cohen, etc.

One day Jake Raden marched into the classroom. His face was beet red; it was obvious he was enraged. Raden charged up to the instructor and discharged him right there on the spot. He accused the teacher of maltreating his daughter Lillian. The teacher did not protest his innocence or deny the allegation. But he did ask to finish the lesson period. Permission was flatly denied. That afternoon the students enjoyed an abbreviated class.

For good reason, the Hebrew School teacher that stood out most for unscrupulous behavior was Mr. Whitner. In class, the students referred to him as Rabbi. Like the other teachers he was not an ordained rabbi. Anything but! On the contrary, Whitner was a conniver, a wheeler-dealer, a *gonef* without honor or principle. The students knew it. The farce was obvious. From day one, Whitner seemed less interested in instruction than in deception. Somehow, the message did not sink in with adults. Whitner ruled the *chedar* as his own private monarchy.

His first summer in Pottstown, Whitner convinced parents to purchase baseball jerseys with the logo P H R S, for Pottstown Hebrew Religious School. While the boys certainly loved baseball, they saw little purpose in forming a Hebrew School team. There was even less reason for jerseys. In their world of sandlots, organized baseball in a formal league against other established teams was beyond comprehension. The boys never wore the jerseys for the purpose for which they were intended since a baseball team was never formed. Norman and the other boys suspected that Whitner received a nice kickback from the clothing supplier.

Another Whitner scheme appealed to the congregation's more religious parents. He proposed selling *tallit katan*, small *tallisim*, to be worn as an undershirt by the *chedar*'s male students. The *tzitzit*, fringes, at the four corners of the *tallis* would be exposed in proper Talmudic fashion. A center opening in the shirt permitted it to be easily slipped over the head. The wearing of *tallit katan* was not uncommon among boys from Orthodox families in East European *shtetls* and New York City neighborhoods. However, it was almost unheard of in small town America. Such blatant religious symbolism would have opened the door to ridicule and taunting from non-Jewish peers. The boys dreaded the thought. After Whitner sold the idea, and the *tallit katan*, to the parents, the novelty of wearing them quickly subsided. Imagine being tackled by the *tzitzit* during a game of football!

The most outrageous Whitner plot concerned the entire male Hebrew School enrollment. Under his auspicious he proposed that all the Hebrew School boys go to a camp for an entire week. The charge for the week was fifteen dollars. Yetta willingly paid the money for her son. She thought the camp would be both religious and educational. Perhaps she was happy to get Norman out of the house. Norman suspected trouble and did not ask to go. But once the trip was paid for, he had no choice. It turned out to be completely non-religious. But boy, even Norman had to acknowledge, was it educational!

Saturday evening after Shabbat, the boys were herded into the back of the Pollack junk truck. Phil Wolf rode shotgun with the driver. Whitner led in his car. Without Whitner's knowledge, Phil Hoffman, the father of two of the campers, Nathan and

Emmanuel, followed some distance behind the caravan in his vehicle. Alone among the parents, Hoffman understood what kind of person was leading the group. The caravan drove eastward across Pennsylvania and crossed the Delaware River into New Jersey. There, at the east end of the bridge, it became evident that Whitner had no idea where he was heading. The group was lost and the hour very late. Hoffman overtook Whitner. "Where are you heading?" he called out from his car. Whitner could not answer. Hoffman asked Whitner about the ultimate destination. Whitner again did not have a clue. No arrangements had been made. Hoffman then took charge. His car took the lead spot in the caravan.

Near Pleasantville, Hoffman sighted a convenience store that by some miracle was still open. Behind the store, large empty cabins surrounded a picnic area. A stream fifteen feet across flowed nearby. The storeowner could not believe his late night good fortune. Hoffman swiftly negotiated a price for renting the cabins for a week. He assigned Phil Wolf to be in charge as 'scoutmaster.' "Hootch" Printz would be his assistant. Norman was the second youngest member of the party, unsurpassed in age only by Emmanuel Berger, his second cousin. Hoffman who could not remain with the group past Sunday, left specific instructions how the boys were to behave and returned to Pottstown.

No imagination was lost in preparation of the meals. They consisted of baked beans, three times a day, cooked over an open fire. By the end of the week the convenience store was denuded of canned beans. In the evenings the boys held contests. Who could make the loudest noise passing wind? Norman never came close. Except for one hurried trip to Atlantic City, the boys never left camp. The other boys had received allowances from their parents. They used their allowances to buy candy at the convenience store. Yetta did not trust her son with the dollar allowance. Instead she had handed it to Whitner to "dole out" during the week. The "chaperone" was not always in attendance. When Whitner did appear, Norman asked him for five cents to buy an O Henry candy bar. Whitner looked away, his hand fiddled with some unseen object in his pants pocket. "The funds are unavailable," he said. "I needed the money to cover unanticipated 'expenses.'" Norman's mouth watered as he watched the other boys eat their candy.

To pass the time there was not much to do. One of the boys had a jack knife. For hours at a time, the boys used it to play "baseball". The game was played on a wooden picnic table. The entire group gathered around. The knife was opened with the long blade fully extended. The small blade was left half way out, perpendicular to the knife. The small blade was planted into the wood with the knife handle resting on the table. The large blade protruded like a cannon barrel. The person playing "baseball" placed his index finger under the handle and twirled the knife into the air. If the knife landed flat, as it usually did, that signified an out. If it landed as originally started, that is, on the small blade and the handle, it was a single. When the knife landed entirely on the small blade, it was a double. Sometimes the knife landed on the large blade, a home run. The game did not have triples.

When Whitner's shenanigans extended into the adult world, even Norman's mother could not ignore them. Each spring Whitner charged three local dairies, Levengood, Grow, and Swavely, to certify their milk as kosher for Passover. He must have viewed it as free money. By this time, however, Yetta had lost trust in him. During Passover week she took her own pails to the Swavely farm and asked the elder Swavely to milk the cow directly into her pails. When the Swavelys offered to pasteurize the milk, she naturally refused. As families became wise to his scheming, Whitner's days in Pottstown were numbered. He exited the community as surreptitiously and mysteriously as he had arrived.

Fortunately, during this drought in his formal Jewish education, Norman received plenty of informal support. Two uncles, Abe's brother Herman and Yetta's brother Sam, were now rabbis. Both sent books to their nephew. The books contributed to his love of reading. Norman relished books brought by the mailman from the Bloch Publishing Company, a major Jewish publishing house. The works inspired him, especially the writings of Israel Zangwill and the novelist Lion Feuchtwanger. Although the books were tough reading for a kid Norman's age, he did not complain. On the contrary, Norman unconsciously sensed they were the perfect exposure to Judaism and Zionism. They enhanced the boy's pride in being Jewish. Norman knew Sam grew up devouring Frank Merriwell adventures. He became a rabbi. "What would I become?" Norman wondered.

* * *

By the mid-1920s Pottstown's Jewish community exceeded one hundred families. It had severely outgrown the *shul* on Chicken Hill. In 1925 a new synagogue located at Warren and High Streets was dedicated. The *chedar* classrooms were located in the basement. A year and a half later, Rabbi Maxwell Farber was installed as Pottstown's first ordained Rabbi. The days of Whitner and the other *shmendrik*, inept Hebrew School teachers were over. Rabbi Farber brought order and organization to the school. A graduate of the Jewish Theological Seminary in New York, Farber knew his business. His arrival in town was fortunate for Norman who was already twelve. His Bar Mitzvah was rapidly approaching.

In one of his first acts Rabbi Farber organized a Boy Scout troop, Troop #13, for the boys twelve and older. The troop was the pride of the entire community. Even some non-Jewish boys from the neighborhood wanted in. Not only did the troop exceed all other local troops in the accumulation of merit badges, it was selected as the outstanding troop at the Washington's Birthday

Boy Scout Jamboree at Valley Forge! For a new Boy Scout troop, it was an amazing accomplishment.

Charlotte Street ran north out of Pottstown towards Pennsburg. Seven miles beyond town, a mile east of Gilbertsville, the road merged for 200 yards with East Philadelphia Avenue to cross Swamp Creek. An old stone bridge traversed the stream. A few years later, the State of Pennsylvania issued these roads state route numbers 663 and 73. After crossing Swamp Creek, the two thoroughfares again separated. Charlotte Street continued north past Hoffmansville to Pennsburg. Philadelphia Avenue curved east towards Zeiglerville, Schwenksville, and eventually Philadelphia. A service station was situated at the fork in the road. Behind the station, among the mature oak and maple trees stood a half a dozen rental cabins and picnic tables. A sign read "Welcome to Hickory Park." Swamp Creek widened at this point, perfect for swimming. Hickory Park was the destination for the troop's first overnight outing. Rabbi Farber chaperoned.

The boy scouts intended to hike to the park, spend the night, and hike back the next day. The scouts set out on Charlotte Street. They trudged up Ringing Rocks Hill, crossed Swamp Pike in New Hanover Township, and reached Hickory Park by mid-afternoon. It was a hot, muggy summer day. Sweat poured down the faces of the scouts as they lugged their packs. No matter. The tired boys were enthusiastic and proud for having made the march from Pottstown. As the troop reached the park, weary and hungry, the clouds thickened. A thunderstorm broke over Hickory Park and drenched the campground. The troop huddled within one of the cabins. But the scouts were unconcerned. The cabins were reserved for their use.

After the rain, the scouts erected a campfire and scouted for dry wood. The boys succeeded in starting a fire. They began grilling kosher hot dogs on long sticks whittled to sharp points. As the boys waited to eat, a car pulled up unexpectedly. Yetta emerged from the passenger side of the car. Norman smelled trouble. No good reason existed for his parents to show up at Hickory Park. Unfortunately, his nose did not fail him.

"Norman, we're here to take you home" his mother insisted. She pronounced her words deliberately and obstinately as if to preclude the expected dispute. The last thing Norman wanted was to return with them to Pottstown. His mother knew this. Teeth gritted, his father remained in the car. He sat silent and stern in the driver's seat. Evidently, the two had been arguing, perhaps until the car pulled up. He stared at the road ahead and impatiently squeezed the wheel. "Let's get this over with," his face shouted from behind its mask.

Norman began to object. But Rabbi Farber admonished him to listen to his parents. "You parents are here to take you home. You must go with them." While Farber's words pleased Yetta, his tone was more than slightly acerbic. She did not discern Farber's subtly launched sarcasm. The other scouts noticed. Farber could conceal his rage from Norman's mother. He could not hide his anger from his "boys" with this uncalled for interference in the Boy Scout outing.

Once again, Norman felt, his conniving mother sought to embarrass her son. If that was the case, her effort failed to have the desired effect. Norman remained close to his Boy Scout colleagues. They were his best friends and sympathized deeply with Norman and his unhappy home life. Most knew his parents. Norman's buddies probably understood Abe and Yetta better than Norman. Immediately after the Hickory Park campout, Norman's peers selected him to be the first troop leader for Pottstown's first Jewish Boy Scout Troop.

The following summer the scouts participated in a five-day encampment along Perkiomen Creek near Collegeville. They slept in pup tents and prepared meals over an open fire. Rabbi Farber insisted the boys spend up to two hours each afternoon reading. For Norman's elective reading, he selected *The Three Musketeers*. One afternoon while he read of Porthos, Athos, Aramis, and d'Artagnan and daydreamed of "one for all, and all for one," Norman heard a shout. Rabbi Farber hurriedly summoned the scouts to the bank of the stream. Two fellow scouts, Joe Raden and Peanuts Princenthal, were observed in a rowboat. With strictest seriousness Rabbi Farber had ordered the boys not to go onto the water without permission. Following their embarrassing public reprimand, the two guilty and now mortified boys would have preferred to have been under the boat rather than in it.

On another occasion, the scout troop went to Camp Delmont, near Green Lane, for the weekend. Although he was underage for the Boy Scouts Philip "Butch" Raden, younger brother of scouts Norman and Joe Raden, came along. Since Camp Delmont was strictly for boys, the scouts felt little reason for modesty. However, if by chance a female did appear, a contingency plan would go into effect. The lookout's warning would be "fire on the campus!" Unexpectedly, a member of the opposite sex did come by the encampment. Butch was the first to spot her. He gave the alert. "Fire on the lot!" Close enough. Within the troop Butch became known as "Fire on the Lot."

In the year prior to his Bar Mitzvah, Norman attended synagogue services regularly with his *chedar* classmates. Although still new to the community, Rabbi Farber swiftly developed a close bond with the Bar Mitzvah cohort. Norman especially was fond of the Rabbi. He absorbed everything Farber taught, carried out any errand Farber needed, and defended the Rabbi at the dinner table when Abe questioned some point about how the Rabbi led services.

In the new synagogue on Warren Street the women's balcony was eliminated. However, in deference to the orthodox views of some congregants, women and men sat on opposite sides of the center aisle. The Bar Mitzvah boys congregated together in the first row, on the men's side, just below the *bimah*.

At services one Saturday Norman was singing one of the Shabbat melodies. Corky Printz gave him a sharp elbow in the ribs. "We are in *shul*. You should not be clowning!" Corky did not know Norman was not fooling around. Norman would never behave silly in the presence of Rabbi Farber.

Norman then had a traumatic thought. His musical skills, non-existent at best, had not changed since in strident revenge against his music teacher he decided to sing "Onward Christian Soldiers" at the top of his lungs. His vocal talent, Norman feared, would not past Bar Mitzvah muster. The notes he attempted to sing had no relationship with those preceding or following. A chill descended over him. Norman grasped a reality he had repressed so long. He did not have the voice to lead his Bar Mitzvah ceremony. And he was just a few months short of turning thirteen!

Rabbi Farber attempted to remedy his student's shortcomings. With Norman beside him, Farber patiently demonstrated the *trup*, the musical notes for chanting the Torah and Haftorah readings. Every Bar Mitzvah boy was expected to perform both to the best of his ability. Norman practiced for hours. But even Rabbi Farber's instructional efforts were not enough. In desperation, Farber enlisted Abe to assume some of the burden.

"At this note, you raise your voice," his father instructed. Norman tried, but it was not correct. "No, not louder, raise your voice!" Abe stood higher on his toes to emphasize his message. With a stentorian voice that echoed throughout the house, Abe demonstrated the proper melody. "*Ba-RUCH AH-tah a-do-NAI . . .*" Norman tried again and again but could not master it. The musical notes floated in chaotic cacophony. In frustration Abe told Rabbi Farber that Norman was not making progress. Finally, Rabbi Farber came up with an alternative. He suggested Norman not sing his *mofter*, the final torah portion, or chant the Haftorah. "Norman, just read it."

Outwardly, Norman was disappointed. But inside, he felt a huge sense of relief. He took comfort that if Rabbi Farber said it was okay, there was little to worry about.

The day of his Bar Mitzvah arrived. Norman awoke in nervous anticipation. He dressed in his suit and carefully measured and knotted his necktie. The new shoes shined. He went to the kitchen. Abe came down the stairs. Norman noticed immediately that his father was wearing his business suit—not the usual one for *shul* but one of his store work suits. Nor was he carrying his *tallis* bag or his prayer book. Perhaps, Norman thought, his father had some errands to run before going to *shul*. Maybe his mother had forgotten to have his father's synagogue suit cleaned and pressed. His dour continence though was unlike his usual light-hearted manner when preparing to go to *shul*. Norman expected encouragement and assurance. Instead, he received silence. Abe did not speak to his son.

His mother came to the kitchen in her *shmalta*, her house dress. "Mother, why aren't you dressed to go to *shul?*" Norman asked.

Yetta tried to avoid her son's eyes. For a split second, Norman sensed his mother's confusion. She had not prepared a response to the obvious question. In a shameful, biting tone she spat out an excuse, "I cannot tolerate those people at *shul*." Her pretext about being angry with the congregation was obviously lame.

Both mother and son knew it. Then she added "who would take care of Russell?" now a toddler.

To Norman, his mother's excuses were perfectly believable. At one time or another Yetta was angry with half the world. She rarely appeared at *shul* for Shabbat services. When she did attend services, she found fault with something or someone. Afterwards, the family would hear no end to her criticism. If Yetta did not want to go somewhere, a team of mules could not budge her.

But, Norman wondered, what about his father? Wasn't he going to the synagogue? Abe did not respond to his son's query. He seemed not to have even heard, although, Norman was certain, he clearly did. Why was his father ignoring him? Norman knew better than to ask twice. Although his father was far better at controlling his emotions than his mother, when Abe was angry he was a tempest. Abe sat at the kitchen table and drank his coffee. Norman starred at his father. Going to *shul* for his father was as natural as getting dressed each morning. Why not today?

At 8:45, Norman walked alone out the door. Alone, trance-like, in a state of numbness, Norman walked down King Street to the synagogue. A minute after Norman departed Abe left the house to go to the store. Norman had already turned the corner and did not see his father turn the other way. During the two block trek to Warren Street, the Bar Mitzvah boy felt a pain enter his head. Such a rare headache would normally chase him back to the house. To lie down and place his pained head on a soft pillow seemed so desirable. He dreamt of a pillow in which he could hide his head and choke his scream.

But he could not turn back. His Bar Mitzvah cohorts expected him to lead the service. So did Rabbi Farber. How could he explain his absence from his own Bar Mitzvah to the rabbi? Norman thought with sorrow of the men who would be attending the service. They would be sorely disappointed at not getting the traditional schnapps with herring and *challah* always served at the Kiddush following a Bar Mitzvah.

After Norman rendered his *mofter* and *haftorah*, he received a warm and positive charge from Rabbi Farber. The Rabbi was genuinely pleased with Norman's performance even if he had not chanted. If Rabbi Farber was perplexed about the absence of family members, he did not show it. Norman returned to the front row. He mechanically shook hands with his friends in formal acknowledgment of their praise. He sat next to them.

From the second row, behind him, a congregant approached Norman and leaned over his shoulder. He whispered in Norman's ear "your grandmother wants you to sit next to her." Norman looked back. There on the women's side towards the middle was Deborah Rachael Epstein Cohen. The diminutive lady was hidden by taller women. In his embarrassed nervousness and reluctance to look at the congregation while on the *bimah*, Norman was unaware of her presence, that she was attending the service. In fact, Norman did not know that she was even in Pottstown!

At the time his grandmother lived in St. Paul, Minnesota, where her son Rabbi Herman had his pulpit. She visited Pottstown infrequently. Norman had never been to Minnesota. He barely remembered what his grandmother looked like. What he did recall was her almost Puritan comportment and strict religious beliefs. Her religious zealotry exceeded even her late husband's, Norman's grandfather. As far as Norman knew, no smile ever crossed her face. No lighthearted comment escaped her lips. She possessed a stern continence that surpassed even his mother's. His grandmother was not a warm person. She was pure stone.

Did she come to town to attend the Bar Mitzvah? Norman was not sure. His parents mentioned nothing to him about her presence. She obviously was not staying at the house. Despite

Yetta's care not to criticize her mother-in-law in Abe's presence, Norman was aware that his mother and grandmother disliked each other intensely. The antagonism was natural. The two were so similar.

Norman mechanically crossed to the women's side. He sat in the now vacated seat next to the elder Mrs. Cohen. His grandmother did not hug him, nor did she offer her hand.

The next words out of her mouth chilled Norman to the bone. With a stare that melted lead, she remarked, in Yiddish, that he was a "bad boy!" The word *nebekhdik* actually meant something more like 'pitiful.' And to refer to her grandson as a *yingl*, a boy, on his Bar Mitzvah day! Norman was beyond shock, too flabbergasted even to cry. The blood drained from his face. Norman felt he had just reached the nadir of his life.

That one sentence from his grandmother was the total extent of dialogue that Norman remembered ever having with her. She would be dead less than two years later. He presumed she knew English. But then, did it really matter if she didn't?

Norman weighed in his mind why she was so bitter. Perhaps because of her orthodox chauvinism, he thought, she viewed her grandson poorly for reading, and not chanting, his *mofter* and Haftorah. If so, Grandmother Cohen evidently did not realize, nor cared, that the three Bar Mitzvah boys who preceded Norman, Joe Raden, Peanuts Princenthal, and Max Lerner, had not performed near to Norman's standard. Nor had they received the high compliments given Norman by Rabbi Farber who lavishly praised Norman's efforts in Hebrew School and leadership in the Boy Scout troop. Fortunately, Rabbi Farber had not asked Norman to deliver a Bar Mitzvah speech, the one he had prepared. It was almost identical to that given by the older boys, thanking parents for bringing him to this point in life, etc. The Rabbi knew it would have been highly inappropriate, embarrassing, and, frankly, hypocritical. Congregants were well aware neither Abe nor Yetta were in attendance.

His grandfather Adolph was there. He had sat unobtrusively towards the rear of the sanctuary. Adolph's squabble with congregation leadership over payment of his building pledge for the new synagogue was still fresh. He did not want to spark a commotion during his grandson's Bar Mitzvah. During the service, he beamed proudly at his eldest grandson. He was aware of Norman's inability to chant. Nonetheless, he admired Norman's flawless Hebrew and appreciated a good performance on the *bimah*.

Although Norman felt too ashamed to sit with him, Adolph understood. He knew Norman's grandmother was in attendance and had already paid his respects. But he could neither rescue Norman from Grandmother Cohen, nor magically make his parents appear. At the Shabbat *Kiddush* afterwards Adolph stood by his grandson as Norman made the blessing on the wine. He provided the *Kiddush* schnapps that satisfied the men. Of course, it was not the same. Norman seemed on the verge of tears. "If I had delivered a Bar Mitzvah speech," Norman pondered, "imagined the snickering that would have followed."

These questions plagued Norman long after the events of that day receded into a distant point of empty darkness. Most sadly, on the day when under Jewish law Norman turned from boyhood to manhood, he was left contemplating what he could not comprehend. Nor even if he had possessed the insight, would he have been able to fathom the depth to which his mother's treatment of him could yet sink.

* * *

The day after his Bar Mitzvah, Norman was attending Sunday school. While he was there, Rabbi Farber went to the house.

The purpose of the mission was kept from him, but he learned about it nonetheless. While Norman and his classmates spoke of Jewish history and ethics in their synagogue classroom, in the front room of 77 Franklin Street the Rabbi held nothing back. He severely upbraided Abe and Yetta for not attending their son's Bar Mitzvah.

Thirteen

Sunerling

During his *sunerling*, teenage years, all of Norman's pals lived south of High Street. His two closest friends continued to be Max Lerner and Mush Estreicher. Teens from the south side of the railroad tracks were considered the "rough" crowd. Yetta called them "honkeys." With their comments about the extracurricular activities from the night before, Norman received a practical education—and it was not the Sunday school variety. The teenagers played baseball and football on a vacant lot between Pottstown Library and Citizen's Bank, just one block from Norman's house.

Following school one afternoon, Albert Leblang and Norman were "shopping" at Newblings 5 & 10 store. Al's father had a second-hand furniture store on High Street. It was a rare day; Norman actually had a nickel in his pocket. A sign on the candy counter above a display of white, unmarked paper bags read "two for five cents." Norman took two packages and gave the salesgirl his nickel. He handed one of the packages to Al. Norman opened his package and started to consume the candy even before the boys got out of the store. When they got outside, Al let out a suppressed laugh. "If there are two candy bars in each bag," he hooted, "then don't you think you are entitled to only one bag?"

Norman was mortified. The mistake tormented him. Was this theft, had he shoplifted? What could he do? He already spent his fortune in the store and opened both bags. For the rest of the day he suffered from a guilty conscience.

Abe's friend Jake Markowitz had a shoemaker's shop on Charlotte Street, not far from Wabin's shoemaker shop. He also operated a grocery store around the corner on Beech Street. One summer Jake traveled to Europe to visit relatives. He returned enthused with an idea. Armed with a new European formulation, Markowitz began preparing chocolate covered frozen bananas on a stick. On hot summer afternoons his frozen bananas at seven cents each sold out quickly. Al was related to Jake Markowitz and worked for him, on and off, behind the grocery counter. He learned the "Jake Markowitz secret" for the banana confection. Al's grandfather Zelman had his own grocery store on South Washington Street, just down the street from Prince's bakery. Al decided to go into business for himself. He used Zelman's premises for making frozen bananas, using the Jake Markowitz recipe. He sold them for a nickel. This perturbed Jake no end!

During Norman's thirteenth year, his father became very sick. Abe remained at home in bed. In the 1920s ill people did not go to a hospital. That was a place you went to die. Instead, doctors came to the patient. Doctor Porter called in Dr. Nicholson, Pottstown's first internist, for a consultation. His diagnosis was double pneumonia. The same illness had claimed the lives of Abe's father and long deceased brother. Visitors to the house recited the prayer for the sick. One of the men making the *minyan* downstairs repeated in a sad tone, "*Mit klaner kinder, mit klaner kinder,*" "with small children, with small children." Over time, Abe recovered. Years later during a routine annual physical examination, a specialist claimed that it could not possibly have been pneumonia. However, he was unable to determine what illness Abe had.

During his father's incapacitation, Norman spent every available hour in the store. He assisted Miss Bertie Beecher, the sales girl, in tidying up the store, putting shoes away, making bank deposits, etc. One evening on closing out the day's receipts, the store was a dollar short. When Norman reported this to his father on his sick bed, Abe became very angry. Despite his fever, Abe rose out of bed and severely scolded his son. "How could you make such a mistake?" he demanded to know. "But what did I do wrong?" Norman asked. In truth, Norman handled cash only infrequently. However, it was also extremely rare for his father to display anger. Norman naturally felt depressed over the incident.

Another occasion, Abe grilled his son about a check mailed to a manufacturer in payment for shoes. The check had not reached the company. Instead, it was cashed by John Kessler who was the head teller at the Security Trust Company. Abe interrogated Norman. "Did you mail the check? Did you forget to put it in the mailbox?" Norman often deposited the outgoing mail in a nearby mailbox. He could not account for every envelope or to whom they were sent. The check could have been taken from the desk at the rear of the store. The desk was close enough to the sales area for a customer to walk off with it.

"Why isn't Kessler responsible?" Norman asked. In check cashing, the common warning was "KNOW THE ENDORSER." Of course, Security Trust would not admit responsibility. And Kessler was never questioned. Norman, although absolutely correct to point his finger at the bank, was afraid to pursue the matter further. He sensed that his father had lost trust in him.

When not performing his regular duties, Norman sat in the rear of the store and listened to various conversations with customers, shoe salesmen, and his father's cronies. Although he formed his own opinions about what he heard, he never spoke out about what was being discussed. At times, it was hard to contain what he was thinking. He reflected on how he would have handled the sale or what style of shoes might be popular with young people.

Abe's brother-in-law Francis urged Abe to carry the well-known Friendly Five line in the Royal Shoe Store. It was a prudent suggestion. At the time Francis was a Friendly Five salesman. He knew the shoes well. Friendly Five was one of America's biggest brands. Instead, Abe went with an unadvertised and poorer selling brand of shoes, Beacon. The Beacon salesman was a baseball fan and a good conversationalist. When in town, he and Abe spoke interminably about baseball. Norman sensed instinctively that Beacon was not the right shoe line for the Royal Shoe Store. But he did not say a word. Soon after, Dutenhofers, a competitor shoe store to Royal, picked up the Friendly Five line.

Selling shoes became Norman's most important duty. He addressed customers as Madam or Sir. It was "No Mam" or "No Sir." He also trimmed the store's display windows, preparing them with "back to school" or Christmas themes. He dusted the shoes and added new shoe styles to the window as they came into the store. His father did not have the touch or patience to perform these tasks. Each summer his sisters and kid brother went with their mother for a week at the beach in Atlantic City or Wildwood, New Jersey. Then, the girls went to summer camp. Norman stayed at home and labored in the store, fifty or even sixty hours a week. He swam in the ocean the day the family was dropped off and the day they were picked up. He hated it. While the more privileged portion of the family romped in the surf, Norman felt that for him there was no swimming or playing with the 'honkies'!

During one of these summer periods, Abe received a somber Friday phone call from St. Paul. His mother passed away. The funeral would be Sunday. Yetta and the children returned from the beach that night by train. Surprisingly, Abe decided not to go to St. Paul. "It would be a violation of Shabbat to travel," he said. Norman did not accept his excuse. Instead, he suspected it was really a matter of finances. It cost a lot of money for his mother and siblings to spend a week in Atlantic City, then for the two girls to attend summer camp for at least four weeks.

The next June Abe and Yetta decided to forego the beach. Instead, the family would make a motor trip to Bloomington, Illinois, and St. Paul to visit Yetta's brother Ben and Abe's brother Herman. Norman stayed back. He had to take care of the store. Besides, the car did not have enough room for one more passenger. Norman became flunky of the store and master of the house.

"What can I do with an empty house?" Norman rhetorically asked himself. The answer was obvious: a daily party! Not yet fully interested in girls, Norman decided it would be just his buddies. Loud perhaps, but not raucous. One night the police called to ask that the noise be curtailed. Mrs. Miller next-door had complained. At least the shoe store did not have any dollar shortages during his parent's absence. Also in Norman's favor, his mother was still not on speaking terms with Mrs. Miller. Yetta never learned about the call to the Pottstown Police.

Two movie theatres operated in town, the Opera House on King Street and the Hippodrome on High Street. From his parents Norman never requested the fifteen cents for movie admission. His first visit to the movies occurred when Abe took his sisters and him to a movie house in Norristown. "It talks!" Lillian exclaimed. Norman had no comment. He had never even been to a silent movie. The girls, by now old movie hands, excitedly critiqued the performance. Norman admitted later that until then, he had not really missed attending movies until his friends began talking about Lon Chaney, the man of a thousand faces in 'The Phantom of the Opera.' They spoke of Chaney's facial expressions and debated how he had performed them for 'Phantom.' From Al Leblang's description, Norman tried, unsuccessfully, to imagine how Chaney actually appeared.

* * *

Two weeks after his fourteenth birthday, Norman entered high school. Early in tenth grade, he realized teachers routinely called on him for answers, although he had not raised his hand. It happened simultaneously in Joe Forest's history class, in Mr. Shoemaker's chemistry class, by the English Literature teacher, and by Mr. Martin, the 'Problems of Democracy' instructor. "Why," Norman questioned, "were they picking on me?" He always feared responding to questions in front of the class. He did not want the attention. Then it dawned on him. Algebra class!

One afternoon in algebra he was staring out the window at a girl's gym class conducted by Miss Hutt. While gawking at the girls, he was startled from his reverie when he heard his name being called by Miss Altenderfer. The teacher asked Norman to solve an algebraic equation she had written on the board. Walking to the chalkboard, Norman had enough time to study the formula. The only difference, he noticed, between this equation and what the class had already been taught was that this one contained squares, or powers. When he continued to give the proof, she stopped him and told him to return to his seat.

"How did you get that brainstorm?" a stunned Johnny Vasil whispered to Norman as he sat down. Norman did not understand. Vasil explained that Altenderfer wrote the equation but had not yet explained it. Norman assumed she must have related the episode to the other High School teachers.

No member of the Pottstown High School class of 1931 who took Mr. Shirer's biology class actually learned the definition of "osmosis." The students knew the textbook definition. "When a heavy liquid goes through a membrane, etc, etc." However, none was able to apply osmosis to an actual example or picture. Shirer had rushed through the topic with no time for questions. His answer: "Water going through a membrane that holds the sugar water as in an egg . . ." No one knew what he meant.

Norman played football his junior and senior years. His uncles suggested he try out for the team. This made it impossible for his mother to object. Members of the team played both offense and defense. Norman's position was right end. He did not catch passes. Football was strictly a running game. The ball was shaped like a balloon and difficult to throw. A second incomplete pass in a series caused a five yard penalty. The only other Jewish player on Pottstown High's team was Murray Kressen, a lineman. His family had a dry cleaning store on Charlotte Street. The only African-American was Dick Ricketts, the team's star fullback. He and Norman had been playmates since primary school. Pottstown did not field strong teams in either 1929 or 1930. Only in its two victories in 1930 did Pottstown even score.

Football games were played Saturday mornings against teams from Berwyn, Norristown, Phoenixville, and elsewhere in the area. The team did not need to eat meals on the road. Basketball games, however, were played at night and in towns a greater distance from Pottstown. Ricketts also played on Pottstown's varsity basketball team. Even in southeastern Pennsylvania, some restaurants would only serve "white" patrons. During most away games he could not eat with his colleagues. Coach "Mush" Bechtel gave him fifty cents to buy his meal. This was a rude awakening for Norman until one of the Pottstown High teachers, Norman Martin, entertained his class with a tasteless joke. "Draw me a picture of black people returning from a funeral on a dark night," Martin requested. The result Martin was looking for? A plain black sheet of paper!

During high school Norman did not have much of a social life. But one evening during his senior year, he enjoyed one of his rare dates. He met the girl in Reading the summer before. Being Saturday night he was allowed use of the family car. Norman came home late to find the entire family, younger sisters included, waiting for him! That was the end of both the car and the romance.

One rare morning when there were no classes, Norman and his friends decided to drive into Philadelphia. They wanted to see a burlesque show at the Trocedaro. The trip required high finance. In addition to the dollar for five gallons of gas, each person needed the admission price of thirty-five cents. After lending and borrowing was completed, the gang piled into a family Buick. There was plenty of time to make the show. However, the boys had to be back in Pottstown for afternoon classes. Assistant Principal Showalter would check the classes for laggards.

At the end of the parkway across from the Philadelphia Museum of Art, the boys passed a Duesenberg automobile agency. The Duesy was possibly the best, most expensive make of car available on the market. They were long, sleek, cat-like machines with lots of chrome, big whitewall tires, and plenty of horsepower. Someone made the suggestion, "Let's stop in!" A well-dressed salesman with highly polished black and white two-toned shoes approached the boys. "What can I do for you gentlemen?" he asked.

"We're interested in a car" one of Norman's buddies replied in perfect seriousness and surprisingly mature demeanor. One boy asked about the gas consumption, another asked about maximum speed, while a third kicked the tires. The salesman had endless patience—until the boys asked for a test drive.

The burlesque disappointed the boys. Hawkers sold large unbranded chocolate bars for twenty-five cents and a dirty picture with every purchase. Among the boys there was not an additional quarter to be shared. Without payment, the hawker refused to show them the pictures. Inside, the audience, for what it was, consisted mostly of unshaven old men in well worn suits who yelled "Take it off!" over and over again to the scantily costumed performers on stage. It was Norman's last visit to a burlesque house.

Of all of Pottstown's Jewish boys, Norman to his knowledge was the only one not to have a Bar Mitzvah party. Still, he received numerous cash gifts from family members. With the money Norman collected, he opened a savings account at the National Bank of Pottstown. Norman did not want to place his money at the Security Trust Company where Royal Shoes held its accounts. The memory of the improperly cashed check by Kessler, the head teller, was still raw. It would be his bank account, no strings attached. Savings accounts earned 3 percent interest. Since the average Bar Mitzvah cash gift was five dollars, the account began in the low two figures.

At the completion of his junior year, Norman took the train to Reading. He wanted to find employment on his own terms. Abe was reluctant to release his son for the summer from service in the shoe store. But given his own footloose past when he was the same age, Abe did not have much of a leg on which to stand. Anyway, the shoe business looked like it would be slower than normal that summer. In 1930 the economy was sinking. Pottstown's level of unemployment was rocketing upwards. Local factories were cutting back. A few had already closed down. For the first time, there was a soup kitchen in town. Citizens down on their luck lined up for food. Norman's mother believed her son would return promptly to Pottstown when he failed to find a job. "Let him go. He'll be back immediately." Abe consented to Norman's departure.

True enough, Norman was turned down at the first shoe store he visited. However, while on his way to a second store that had been recommended by the owner of the first, he noticed a new shoe store with a striped awning at 335 Penn Street. Painted on the window he read "Fogelman, First for Quality at Low Prices." He walked into he store and asked if the store needed a clerk. Hyman Fogelman interviewed the lad. He was impressed with Norman's knowledge of shoes. "How old are you sonny?" Fogelman inquired, raising one eye and peering closely into Norman's face. "I completed eleven years schooling," Norman replied truthfully. That answer satisfied the skeptical Fogelman who agreed to pay Norman $14.50 a week for six days plus one evening. The fifteen-year old enjoyed free room and board with his Uncle Francis and Aunt Ida in their apartment on Perkiomen Avenue. Francis recently had begun working as a clerk at Schwartz's Arch Health Shoe Shop at Penn and Tenth Streets.

Norman worked the entire summer at Fogelman's shoe store. The experience was highly beneficial for the shy teenager from Pottstown. The job required Norman to initiate conversations with strangers in an attempt to induce window lookers into the store for a sale. Success in making such sales boosted the boy's ego tremendously. Norman no longer was selling shoes to the small town Dutch farmers who shopped in Pottstown. He was now selling shoes to the big city Dutch farmers! Moreover, living with his uncle and aunt was a calm, pleasant experience in contrast to the volcanic upheavals that plagued 77 Franklin Street. In early September he informed Fogelman that he had to return to school. The owner was sorry to see him go but wished him well. Norman saved every cent he earned that summer. He deposited close to two hundred dollars into his National Bank account. A bank account in the three figures was considered a small fortune. Norman considered it a large one.

One afternoon during his senior year, Norman took his passbook to the bank to have the interest posted. Banks posted interest every three months on the anniversary of the date an account is opened. Norman presented his passbook, page open, to the teller. A blank, frozen expression crossed the teller's face. He did not even consult his records. The clerk looked at Norman with a sad air. He knew what was coming. He had already seen it too often during the last year since the October 1929 Stock Market crash.

"Your father already closed the account."

Norman was stunned. "You must be mistaken. My passbook has no withdrawal entries."

The teller looked down for a moment, then, shrugged his shoulders. His helpless look spoke the universal confession of clerks everywhere, "what can I do?"

The ground was shaking under Norman's feet as he marched back to the store. He had never felt so cheated, so violated. Abe was away somewhere. His mother was covering the store. Although Norman knew without a shred of doubt that she was the instigator, he focused his fury on his father. "I'll have Daddy arrested!" he shouted. Yetta let Norman have it as only her temper could. She did not deny that the money had been taken. But that did not stop her from unloading her own rage. It was a day Norman would never forget.

At about the same time, the Cohen family made its annual pledge of $250 to the Jewish Agency. That amount plus the money confiscated from Norman's savings account would have easily funded at least one year of college, perhaps two.

After the confrontation with his mother, Norman arrived home early one afternoon from school. He noticed a new girl's bicycle on the back porch. In astonishment he inquired as to the bike's owner. It belonged to his seven-year old sister Sylvia. "Why, Sylvia asked for it," Yetta told her son when he questioned her. Norman's reaction was not envy but shock. Once again, the young man failed to fathom what had happened. Oh, how he had wanted a bike, a sled, ice skates! Once, while shopping with his mother at Rabfogel's, a general store featuring house wares and hardware, Norman remembered being admonished by her for just admiring a blue and white bicycle.

The new bicycles for both sisters, Norman learned, were purchased from the Supplee Bittle Company, Philadelphia. He was not to have even seen the bikes! However, Sylvia neglected to remove hers from the porch before he had come home from school. Five-year old Russell was with their mother in Philadelphia when the bikes were purchased. He pleaded with his mother and cried for a bike but never received one.

Norman's brother was fortunate still to be around at age five. Two years earlier, tragedy struck the precocious child. Early one March Sunday morning while the family was still in bed, the three-year old Russell dressed himself in his Purim clown costume. Yetta sewed it for the approaching holiday. Occupying the same room as his older brother, Russell shook the sleeping Norman awake. "Norman, I'm on fire!" he cried. Russell had been playing with matches and the flimsy cloth of the costume burst into flames. Norman called out for help. Abe dashed into the room and father and brother quickly extinguished the flames. They rushed Russell to Pottstown Memorial Hospital.

Russell suffered burns over a third of his body. For weeks his life hung in the balance. However, Doctor Porter helped pull him through. Afterwards, Doc Porter refused to take Abe's money for saving Russell. However, he did accept a pair of fine French Shriner oxford shoes as "compensation." For years after Abe kept Porter in the best quality men's shoes. At Jefferson Hospital in Philadelphia, Russell later underwent numerous skin graft operations to repair his damaged body.

Incredibly, despite his near death experience, Russell remained fascinated with fire. Nearly two decades later, fire struck the James Hotel—the same building built by Adolph during his landlord years. From the heavy smoke emerged a figure wearing a fireproof suit. Two bottles of booze from the hotel bar were in his hands. "Who the hell would risk their life for a couple bottles of whiskey?" a witnessed exclaimed. When the suit was pulled off, it was Russell.

Now a senior approaching graduation, Norman was lost in a trance. His dream of attending college had been punctured by his mother's stern castigation. "Norman, you know we cannot afford to send you to college." Thanks to the draining of his account, he was penniless. To add to his misery, by now every one of his male acquaintances had applied for and received his driver's license, a routine rite of passage after a sixteenth birthday. Most boys began driving during their junior or even sophomore years. Norman's timid request for permission to obtain his license received a firm negative response from his mother. To Norman it seemed like a lifetime before Abe gave his son the money to apply for a learners permit.

Although he was under no illusions about what his parents would say, Norman felt entitled to $3.50 to have his photo taken for the Pottstown High School yearbook and to receive a copy. At the same time the senior class planned a three-day trip to Washington, D.C. By selling a certain quantity of tickets to the class play, Norman could pay the $7.00 cost for the trip, including the train fare. Classmates asked Norman to take a leading part in the play. However, he declined. His time would be more profitably spent, Norman felt, if he used all his spare hours to sell tickets. He made the trip to Washington with his classmates. But his picture did not appear in the yearbook. His parents did not give him the $3.50. Strangely, his name was missing from the senior class list. Nor did he receive a copy. However, in order to be listed on the "compliments of" page, the Royal Shoe Shop contributed the minimum donation. Had Abe not made any contribution to the yearbook, Yetta feared the oversight might lead to corrosive gossip within Pottstown's tight-knit gentile community.

The only money Norman specifically requested from his parents was for the yearbook photo and the yearbook itself. He asked AFTER they seized his money from the account in the National Bank. Norman knew each of his uncles possessed a Pottstown High yearbook with their photographs. He had read them in his grandfather's attic. But Norman's request was flatly denied. "The family cannot afford it," Yetta said.

Worse was to come. The Pottstown High School graduation ceremony, held in the school auditorium, overflowed with family members and friends. After the usual valedictorian and commencement addresses and other speeches of praise and cautionary wisdom, the seniors dutifully paraded up to the stage, received their diplomas, shook hands with Pottstown's school superintendent and the school principal, and filed back to their seats and families. Norman had no one to rejoin. No one from his family was in attendance. He walked home with his buddy Al Leblang, Al's mother, and Al's older sister Rae Swartz who had come from Camden, New Jersey, for the graduation. Being alone made for an awkward situation. For a long time, he regretted that he did not just sneak home that day by himself.

That night Yetta received an unusually long phone call. For a change she did all the listening. Norman quietly moved closer to the stairs to listen but there was little to hear. Abnormally subdued, her hand shaking, his mother replaced the phone apparatus. She sat still for a few minutes. He carefully tried to overhear the conversation between his parents. In an unusually low tone, his mother related to her husband what the call was about. Norman froze in place.

". . . Then, she said, that if necessary, 'I would have scrubbed floors to have my child's picture in the school yearbook!'"

His mother did not mention the caller's name. But Norman easily guessed. He assumed it was Al's mother, Mrs. Leblang, a widow with thirteen children.

Fourteen

The Depression

After the stock market crash in October 1929, the Royal Shoe Store felt the impact. Business slackened but after a few months gradually recovered. Although the stock market crash initially had a moderate effect on the store's fortunes, from the perspective of family finances, Wall Street's collapse was traumatic. Abe lost his shirt in the stock market. Unbeknownst to his wife, Abe had been placing money with a stockbroker in Philadelphia. He invested in supposedly "blue chip" companies such as Niagara Hudson and Southern Utilities. A telegram from the stockbroker addressed to Abraham Cohen arrived at the house. The stockbroker requested that Abe meet his margin call. The stock value had fallen by more than the purchase money Abe had put up.

Yetta read the telegram twice, then a third time. She was furious. Her scream pierced the walls of the house, frightening Russell to tears. When Abe arrived home that afternoon, his wife was in a terrible rage. She threw dishes and other kitchen items at him. The shouting could be heard next door at the Millers, across the street at the firehouse, down Franklin Street. Neighbors hardly noticed the scene. After Black Tuesday, October 29th, similar shouting matches were being repeated throughout the neighborhood, throughout Pottstown, everywhere in America.

The mounting economic depression caught up with Royal Shoes. By 1931 dramatic changes occurred in the community. Noticeably fewer cars were being driven up and down High Street. They moved slower as if stuck in mud. Drivers sought to save gas by keeping the clutch in longer than normal and coasting whenever possible. Safety, never really a priority, took a back seat to fuel economy. Pedestrians walked more slowly as if they too needed to save energy. Undoubtedly, many did since hunger now stalked Pottstown. There was little urgency to go anywhere. Unemployed men desperate for any job waited in line outside City Hall. Women and children knocked on doors asking for a bite to eat, a couple of pennies. Houses went unpainted. Broken windows went unrepaired; instead, they were boarded up. The sharp sound of Pottstown's once ubiquitous factory whistles became rare. Dozens of empty boxcars sat in the rail yard on the west side of town. They served as shelter for an increasing number of homeless. Flower gardens all but disappeared, replaced by vegetable gardens. Vacant lots became potato fields. The vibrant laughter and inanity of the 1920s was replaced by a shadowy somberness and feeling of worthlessness and hopelessness in the new decade.

The Depression approached its darkest times as Norman graduated Pottstown High. At the Royal Shoe Store, pitiably few customers purchased new shoes. Who had money to buy shoes? The store was all but dead. For all but the town's diminutive affluent class the new Sunday suit, the latest Easter dress, and back-to-school shoes became mournful memories. Even window shoppers with stoic but forlorn visages were reluctant to step inside the store. Men and women too frequently broke down in sobs at the sight of shoes once easily affordable, now as unobtainable as emeralds. Hardly anyone remarked about the shoes in the display window. Abe and Yetta did not know how to cope.

Yet, despite the impending abyss, opportunity literally came knocking. Early in the economic downturn, before the writing on the wall was obvious and well ahead of the Royal Shoe Store's slide towards its commercial nadir, a pair of men walked into the store. Norman was alone in the store with Miss Beecher. An hour earlier, Yetta had grabbed her husband to go to the cemetery. The graves of her mother Rose and grandmother Lena needed their periodic trimming. Chris "the Greek" who operated the Crystal Restaurant next door accompanied a well-dressed man.

"Is your father in, Norman?" Chris asked.

"He'll be back within the hour," Norman replied.

The stranger sat down in one of the customer chairs. "I want to speak with you dad and see if we can make a deal to buy this building." He showed Norman a thick wad of high denomination bills that he kept deeply buried in the inside pocket of his suit jacket. A wry smile crossed his face. "I want to make your father rich!" Chris and the stranger waited twenty minutes. Then they left the store.

When his parents returned, Norman informed them of the stranger and his offer. Abe rushed next door to the restaurant. He soon returned with a sad face. His shoulders sagged markedly. "Chris persuaded the guy not to buy the building, but instead, to invest the money with him!" Norman never had seen his father so tired. Not physically, although that was probably true enough. Instead, he observed weariness as if his father was lost, stuck in a maze with no exit. Norman noticed the same gloomy eyes on many men and women. He feared his father was about to give up.

Abe was demoralized. He already sensed that the store was not going to recover. Such a deal, he knew, could have made a big difference in their future. The family was beginning to live a hand-to-mouth existence. Only food was not economized. All other funds, including money that could have sent Norman to college, were spent on pre-paying the two mortgages: the store and the house on Franklin Street. The common expression around the house was "the faster we pay off the mortgages, the less interest we have to pay!"

After graduation, Norman intended to return to Reading to ask Fogelman for his old job. If that did not pan out, he would seek other opportunities. Perhaps he could take courses part-time at Albright College. To begin, he felt the best courses would be geometry and physics. His uncle and aunt would welcome him back at their apartment. Once again, he would try to save every nickel. This time, though, Norman would be more careful where he placed his earnings. Not only were bank failures distressingly common, Norman did not want his parents to know in which bank his account was located.

However, Norman committed a fatal error. The young man failed to make his complete intentions known to his parents. Norman admitted later it was a costly mistake. He did not tell his mother about his plan to go to Reading or take college classes. To mention Albright College to Yetta, he surmised, would cause an eruption. "How could you consider taking classes for fun?" she would say. "That is such *schvoiltook*, such an extravagant excess!"

Norman packed his clothing and a few books into an old suitcase for what he thought would be his departure for Reading. He carried the suitcase downstairs. Before he could seek out his mother to say good-bye, Yetta stepped forward. She placed herself in front of the door. Norman sensed immediately it was not to wish him luck. There was no "where are you going?" expression on her face. Instead, he again observed an intensity that came with knowing something he did not. His mother had made other plans.

"Norman, we found you a job." Her words caught Norman completely unprepared. "You are going to work for my cousin Aaron Weiss and the Triangle Shoe Company. It's all arranged. Aaron is on his way over. He'll take you to Wilkes-Barre."

Norman stood frozen in place. His mouth was open, but he was unable to croak any words. He stared at his mother a moment then looked down in surrender. Norman knew he could not look his mother in the eyes. Instead, his vision focused on a crawling insect on the worn rug. His mind shifted to the surreal. "I wish I could exchange places with that lucky creature," he thought. Norman made no protest. He sat down to wait for Weiss.

His first week in Wilkes-Barre, Norman lived with Weiss and his wife Tess. He labored in the Triangle Company stockroom, doing simple, mindless tasks. "Were they testing him?" he wondered. He decided no. It was simply where the work was. The Weiss's were gracious hosts. However, Norman felt uncomfortable staying in their home. He found lodging with a Jewish family named Fink, walking distance from Triangle. On Saturdays when the stockroom was closed, Norman worked in the local Triangle Shoe Store. He soon graduated to shoe sales and left the stockroom for good.

One day Weiss called Norman into his office. "Norman, I want you to go to our store in Pottsville," Weiss instructed. "There are unexplained inventory shortages there. Go investigate and fix the problem." Norman wanted to please Weiss who, so far, had been so kind to him. He repacked his suitcase.

The Depression

Before he reached Pottsville, Norman assumed that the "inventory shortages" were probably the result of sloppy book keeping. What other reason could it be? One Saturday evening, the store manager, an older woman named Helen, came to Norman. She had observed one of the sales clerks leaving the premises surreptitiously with a bulge under her overcoat. The bulge turned out to be a pair of shoes. Norman was shocked. To imagine that co-workers, people whom you actually knew, whom you trusted, might steal! To the young man, theft was an occupation committed by masked intruders in the night darkness. It was a harsh lesson.

A regular workweek in the early 1930s was sixty hours. But there was no maximum. To be ready for any potential customer who might appear, shoe stores remained open significantly more hours than that. Store hours usually ran from 8 a.m. to 6 p.m. One or two days each week, closing time was 9 p.m. There was no sitting, no coffee break. Employees had just a half hour for lunch. When not assisting customers, clerks still had plenty to do. The shoes on display required constant cleaning. The dusty heel seats of display shoes were cleaned with a cloth wetted in alcohol. In the back stockroom shoeboxes required constant reshuffling on the shelves. Customer purchase histories written on 3"x5" cards were alphabetized and filed. Window trims and some stock work was performed at night or on Sunday afternoons. Full time employees put in their regular hours and worked the extra chores without additional compensation.

Norman's salary was fifteen dollars a week. Without warning, it was reduced to $13.50. On Weiss's next visit to Pottsville, Norman raised the topic of his salary reduction. "Am I performing poorly in running the store, Mr. Weiss? You know that sales have actually increased and the inventory problems have vanished."

Weiss demurred. "You are doing a fine job, Norman." He put his hand on Norman's shoulder. "You are aware there is talk of enacting legislation establishing a minimum wage of $13.50. Since some of our employees are making less, we had to raise their salaries. To compensate, I had to reduce yours."

In the hope that his previous wage could be reinstated and perhaps increased, Norman agreed to take on additional responsibilities. In addition to Wilkes-Barre and Pottsville, Norman's tour of duty with Triangle Shoes took him to coal region shoe stores in Scranton and Pittston, to Lebanon and Reading, to Akron, Ohio, and elsewhere. His value to the company, Norman felt, was being proven. He deserved more pay. The best value for his time, and the only way to raise his income, he believed, was *selling* shoes. Norman made a deal with Weiss. He knew at many of its stores Triangle's women's shoe business was suffering. "Uncle Aaron, I'll work on strictly on a commission basis in the stores that sell women's shoes exclusively. No minimum pay."

Weiss was impressed with Norman's audacity. At the height of the Depression, it was a gutsy move that showed more *chutzpah* than sense. At least a salary of $13.50 a week was real money. Commissions were not. Commissions were based on the retail price of the shoes sold. No sales, no commissions. And in 1932 and 1933, as Weiss well knew, sales were tough. Choosing to focus on *women's* shoes was doubly plucky. Women's shoes were less expensive than men's shoes. On a $1.99 pair of ladies shoes, Norman's commission would be just ten cents. For a more expensive $2.99 pair, Norman would receive twenty-five cents. Men's oxfords usually went for about $4.99. Thus, by staking his commissions on the sales of *women's* shoes, Norman gambled he could make up the difference in volume. "Go ahead Norman. I really do hope you succeed and that I'll be paying you lots of commissions!"

Fortunately for Norman, the gamble paid off. By focusing on sales, his income improved. The following Mother's Day, Norman bought his mother a genuine leather handbag for $15. Yetta was extremely proud and grateful.

Norman knew there were two sides to the ledger. While augmenting income, he still needed to keep his own expenses down. Wherever he worked, the young man found a room near the store for which he paid $2.50 to $3.50 a week. Often, the room was on the top floor of a private house. Many were eager to rent rooms. Breakfast consisted of fresh orange juice, ten cents, and coffee and toast, five cents each, for a total of twenty cents. For lunch he purchased at a nearby grocery store a quarter pound of cold cuts and a five cent Coke. He took the items to his room. There he kept a loaf of sliced bread and a bottle of mustard. Dinner consisted of "Sloppy Joes"—ground beef, onion, green pepper, garlic powder and ketchup on a bun, just 35 cents. Norman kept a strict accounting on an unneeded Green Shoe Manufacturing Company order pad.

With the Great Depression in full force, Norman knew he was fortunate to have stable employment. Moreover, based on Norman's performance and easy demeanor, Aaron Weiss felt fortunate to have Norman in his employ. He perceived a great future for his cousin's son within Triangle Shoe, if greater opportunities had then existed within the company. Perhaps, Norman might be placed in charge of a region of stores. Circumstances, however, swiftly altered plans for both Triangle Shoes and Norman.

Bad luck struck Norman in the form of a freak automobile accident, one in which he was neither passenger nor pedestrian crossing a street. Norman was standing on a corner in Lebanon, Pennsylvania. A two car collision occurred in the intersection. One of the spinning cars jumped the curb onto the sidewalk. It knocked Norman over. He fell hard and hit his head on the sidewalk. He was taken to the hospital. His injuries were dressed.

"You can leave now son," the doctor said. Norman got off the table. He went for the door. He walked into a wall instead. The doctor changed his mind about releasing his patient.

The following day, a friend on his way to Philadelphia stopped in Pottstown to inform Norman's parents of the accident and his injury. They left at once for Lebanon. Abe asked that his son be given to them to be taken back to Pottstown. Norman's sixty mile ride from Lebanon in the back seat was terribly painful. The pillow felt as hard as steel. When Norman reached Pottstown, Dr. Reivenberg immediately sent him by ambulance to the hospital. X-rays showed that he suffered a double skull fracture. With the accident, Norman terminated his employment with Triangle Shoe Company.

His parents could not object. He had done what they arranged for him. In three and a half years with Triangle, Norman batted around from one forlorn Pennsylvania town to the next. He had lived an uninspired existence and endured one interminably long workday to the next. He observed in the gray industrial cities which once hummed with machinery and factory whistles, the shuttered gates of steel mills and die casting shops. Long queues of hungry, unemployed men in threadbare suits and crumpled hats sought jobs that no longer existed. Whenever a job vacancy sign was posted, hundreds, even thousands, lined up. Norman witnessed once proud men standing despondently in line at storefront soup kitchens run by the Salvation Army and church groups. In their dejected, miserable eyes, Norman detected not just resignation but outright defeat. From their point of view, Norman knew he should be gratified for the opportunity to work, even for the pittance provided by Triangle Shoe.

But Norman was not pleased. He was bitter. These were years he should have been in college. By this time, assuming a normal course load, he would have been looking forward to completing his senior year. As a college graduate, jobs would not be so scarce. He could have commanded a living wage and practiced a profession with a future. Instead, the last three years were, in his opinion, a total waste. As life moved forward, he knew the college dream could only recede unless he took action.

Following a long recuperation period, Norman began working for the A.S. Beck Shoe Store on Market Street in Philadelphia. This was a big city shoe store and a far cry from the two horse towns and eight chair stores that belonged to Triangle. Norman anticipated permanent employment in Philadelphia. He considered enrollment in evening courses at Drexel University, perhaps in science. The tuition at Drexel, however, was too steep for his budget. Norman next visited Temple University. The student guide who escorted him through campus recommended against taking science at Temple. Norman listened. Instead, he enrolled in a marketing class. It was a practical suggestion. "If I am working in retail," he reasoned, "such study would be beneficial." However, he was deeply disappointed. Although Norman earned a few credits, he perceived no advantage to a marketing degree if he were stuck selling shoes.

After the stint in Philadelphia, Norman returned to Reading. He worked for the Park Lane Shoe Store on Penn Avenue, a competitor store to Fogelman's. Norman spoke often with his old boss who mentored his former employee and provided an occasional lunch. If there was an opening, Fogelman assured him, he would hire Norman straight away. Norman lived at home. He commuted daily by train from Pottstown. The weekly ticket cost less than two dollars. His usual lunches consisted of a malted milk shake for fifteen cents and a peanut butter sandwich for an additional five cents.

One day Abe informed his son that he had rented a storeroom in Royersford, a sleepy hamlet eight miles east of Pottstown. He took Norman to see the shop. The front sales area was empty, lacking even one chair. Empty shelves heavily laden with dust made up the stock room. "This is the former Peterman Shoe Store," Abe told his son. "Peterman did a good business." All Norman could see were Royersford's empty streets and sparse customer base. Norman asked how much business did Peterman do—and when? His father did not know. But Abe needed his son's assistance. Norman agreed to give the store a go.

With scant inventory and minimal furniture, Norman reopened the shoe store. He kept careful note of the dollar amount of shoes being ordered and sold. Neither number was overly impressive. No matter how much effort Norman invested in promoting sales, customers were a rarity. Dixon's Drug Store was next door. Each day for lunch Norman went to Dixon's and ordered a grilled cheese sandwich and a coke from the lunch counter. Norman enjoyed the company of Joe Mills who had his barbershop two doors away. Between the shoe store and the barbershop was a taproom set back from the street. This allowed Mills clear observation of any customers seeking haircuts.

The first formal accounting of the store showed it had almost broken even. Somehow Norman had found customers where none seemed to exist. Abe was elated. "But Dad," Norman pointed out, "that's with *no* payroll." That took the wind out of Abe's sails. But he would not give up. Before Norman realized what had happened, his father obtained another "bargain" business, this time in nearby Phoenixville. It was the old Weber Shoe Store. To turn Weber's around, Norman instinctively knew, would take a Herculean effort. "What a mess," Norman bemoaned. Meanwhile, family fortunes continued to slide.

* * *

Yetta's cousin Sam Fuerman was the son of her Aunt Mindel and Mindel's first husband, Yitzhak. Fuerman operated a watch and jewelry store on High Street. He had also amassed significant real estate holdings in town. Fuerman had been one of three ushers at Abe and Yetta's wedding. He was Yetta's guiding light, the son of her favorite aunt, and a success in business—in contrast to her *nebbish* husband. For financial advice there was no one better to turn to, she believed.

With the launching of President Roosevelt's New Deal, there was hope that good times would return. By the mid 1930s the nation seemed to be slowly emerging from the worst depths of the Depression. Unlike many of its competitors, the Royal Shoe Store had somehow endured, although barely. But later in the 1930s, the economy hit another bump. Shoe sales declined, although not as precipitously as in 1930-31. Abe and Yetta feared a duplication of the hard times they barely survived. Their fear took on an edge of panic. Following the formidable effort to avoid fiasco with the former Peterman store in Royersford and the Weber store in Phoenixville, no one knew better than Norman the state of play with the family business. But Abe and Yetta could not bring themselves to confide their worries with their eldest son. Instead, Yetta insisted they turn to her savvy cousin, Sam Fuerman. At this auspicious moment, Fuerman agreed to assist. He paid a visit to his cousin at her home. "I recommend you and Abe file for bankruptcy!" Fuerman advised Yetta.

It was an audacious recommendation. Until that moment, the couple had not given any thought to such a move. There had never been a late payment on either the store or house mortgages. In fact, the family had paid down significantly the principal on both properties. Abe seemed shell-shocked when he heard the suggestion. But Sam's rationale appeared to be convincing. New bankruptcy laws protected the debtor. Creditors would not be able to touch the corporation, the Royal Shoe Store. Many small businesses, Fuerman emphasized, had already sought protection through bankruptcy and they were emerging stronger than ever. Moreover, there was no need for costly lawyers, he added. The entire process could be settled for court costs. Abe and Yetta agreed to do it. Until the deed was done, Norman did not know what his parents were planning.

Against all advice, including her father Adolph, her brothers, and the Security Trust Company which held the mortgages on the store and the house—even despite a personal visit by the esteemed Doctor Porter who begged them not to make such a mistake—Abe and Yetta turned over the keys of the two properties to the bank. The family vacated the Franklin Street house. A new location for the shoe store would have to be found. The local common court confirmed the bankruptcy.

After the fact, Abe approached Fuerman. Why had he recommended they declare bankruptcy? Abe asked. That the question had not been put to Fuerman earlier is an unfathomable mystery. Fuerman told his cousin's husband he did not find the question unreasonable. But his reply certainly was. "I wanted to get even with the bank!"

Morris Weitzencorn who owned the clothing store next door to Royal Shoes was the first to learn about the bankruptcy. Weitzencorn rushed across High Street to the Security Trust Company. He swiftly reached a deal with bank leadership. They were ecstatic to settle the matter. For the amount still owed on the two mortgages, Weitzencorn bought both the High Street building and the house at 77 Franklin Street. He gave the house to his brother Max who at *shul* commented to Abe that Morris had made a "good buy!" It was an understatement. In his attempt, however, to "get even" with the bank, Fuerman failed. By promptly disposing the properties to Weitzenkorn, the Security Trust Company did not loose a dime.

The Depression

Of course, the bankruptcy had other unforeseen consequences. Upon hearing of the bankruptcy, the Freeman Shoe Company salesman contacted Abe. "Are you going to continue to carry my line?" The salesman asked.

"Of course," Abe replied, "why do you ask?"

The salesman said he was confused. Ben Berger, Fuerman's brother-in-law, had just contacted him, he explained. Berger's own shoe store was a direct competitor to Royal Shoes. "Berger asked if he could obtain the exclusive local franchise for Freeman Shoes. He said you were going out of business." The news struck Abe like a blow to the belly. He had no intention of *closing* the Royal Shoe Store. The bank account had adequate money to keep operating. There were no outstanding invoices; all creditors had been paid in full after the bankruptcy. One company, the Mishawaka Rubber Company, had returned Abe's check because a 2% cash discount had been deducted. The check from Royal Shoe Store had arrived at the company one day past the discount due date.

Abe Cohen finally saw the light. He and Yetta had been duped. There had been no financial necessity for the bankruptcy decision. The store was solvent. Mortgage payments were made on time each month. The ignored warnings and pleadings had been on the mark. But the chips were already cashed in. Abe and Yetta Cohen had lost. In bitterness, Abe told Fuerman he would not repay a note the two had co-signed prior to the bankruptcy. That caused an acrimonious war between the two families that lasted the lifetimes of the participants.

From the comfortable Franklin Street house, Abe, Yetta and the children removed their belongings. They moved to the home of a widower named Greenstein. Greenstein had been married to the widow Mrs. Labor who herself had passed away. His house on Walnut Street, near Grant Street, was inelegantly close to

Adolph's residence. It was a reminder of how little distance the Cohen family had progressed. Of course, Yetta gave no consideration to moving her family back in with her father. Despite Adolph's advanced years, relations between the two remained strained. But the arrangement with Greenstein was awkward at best. Within a few months, the family moved again, this time to 521 Beech Street. One of the new neighbors was a veteran of the Spanish-American War, one of Teddy Roosevelt's "Rough Riders."

After years of observing Abe's business frustration, Yetta understood well that her husband was probably incapable of operating a store profitably. Her rationale and logic though took some strange twists. She confided as much to Norman after the move to Beech Street. "How fortunate we were that twenty years ago Joe Printz cheated your father out of that good property!" she commented. "He would never have been able to open and manage a business in such a good downtown location!" Norman was speechless.

If it was to remain in existence, Royal Shoes required a new location, preferably a *good downtown* location. Yetta asked her son to assist. She and Abe eyed an empty storeroom at 268 High Street. Although the storefront itself was very narrow, only 14 feet wide, and stockroom space was limited, it was as prime a commercial location as was available for rent. Abe had sought to strike a deal for an interminable period of time with the owner, Mrs. Laura Bahr. Understandably, Bahr was reluctant to rent the property to Abe. The bankruptcy severely tarnished his reputation in town. She considered him a poor prospective tenant.

Sensing her son's presence might swing the negotiations, Yetta told Norman to accompany his father to another interview with Bahr. Norman knew the opportunity might be his father's last chance to keep the business afloat. Sensing another fiasco in the making if he did not go along, Norman cautiously agreed. He accompanied his father to meet Bahr. Abe led the discussion. He introduced his son as the actual "operator" of the store. He provided only one positive reference, his brother-in-law Benjamin Markowitz. Ben had been a high school classmate of Mr. Bahr and was among his best friends. Bahr carefully eyed Norman as if to take his full measure. Finally, she consented to rent the property to Royal Shoes.

The store reopened. However, Norman refused to handle three stores, the one on High Street and the shops in Royersford and Phoenixville. Abe relented. The keys to the Royersford and Phoenixville stores were turned in. The inventory, negligible as it was, went to Francis' store in Honesdale, Pennsylvania, just in time to be washed away two years later in the Honesdale flood of 1941. Norman stayed in Pottstown operating the new Royal Corrective Shoes. The word "corrective" was inserted into the store name to differentiate it from the competition. One result of the bankruptcy and the loss of property assets was a measurable improvement in the business' overall liquidity condition.

* * *

The upheavals at home and with the store were not the only headaches faced by the Cohen family. Norman's brother Russell had become a tremendous challenge to his parents. If Norman was the dutiful son, Russell was the defiant one. His early teenage years augured an even more rebellious and difficult period.

One day Mr. Miller, the assistant principal at Pottstown Junior High School, called Yetta in for an interview. "I want to speak with you about your son." Yetta went to the school and sat down in his office. She waited for the shoe to drop. "You have to do something about that kid of yours," Miller insisted. "Get him to stop associating with those 'niggers!'" Yetta took the tirade stoically. Her face registered no shock. While she resented

Miller's implications about her son, she also knew there was little chance Miller's demand could be met. In frustration Yetta confided her worries to Doc Porter. "When will that boy ever settle down?" Doc Porter frowned. "When he is thirty years old," was the reply.

One Saturday Abe received a phone call at the shoe store from the Justice of the Peace in Chester County. "Is this Abraham Cohen? Do you have a fourteen year old named Russell and do you own a Buick?"

"What's he done now?" Abe asked.

"He's in custody for driving without a license."

Abe left the store on the busiest day of the week. He bummed a ride across the river. In a corner of the JP's chamber, he found his contrite son and his buddies. From the bench the Justice held the car keys in his left hand. His eyes fixed on Abe's. "Are you this boy's father?" he asked. Abe nodded; he did not allow his gaze to fall. He would not give the JP the pleasure of thinking he was submitting meekly to the power of the bench. "Yes, I am the father."

"Your son was the driver and he is going to be charged," the justice asserted.

Abe approached the justice. He grabbed his car keys and started for the door.

The Justice was stunned at Abe's audacity. His jaw dropped. He looked glassily at the departing Abe. As Abe approached the door to the chambers, the JP caught his senses. A moment more and Abe would have been out the door. He called out "you don't understand! You have to pay the fine! Thirty-five dollars!"

Abe swung back. "I'll not pay!" he shouted. He reached for the door handle. The heavy door swung open.

"Okay, pay twenty-five dollars!" the JP said.

Abe stopped midway through the door. Anger seething, he resolutely looked back at the justice. His voice reached out to the parking lot and half way across Chester County. "I'll not pay TWO CENTS. YOU CAN KEEP THE KID!" The door slammed behind him. A boom reverberated throughout the courtroom.

The JP knew he was licked. He discharged Russell and his friends, no fine. They quickly left the courtroom. Outside the JP's chamber, Russell caught up with his father. Abe seized his son's arm and half lifted him. They headed to the Buick. Russell's friends stood nearby and watched. "Can't we take my buddies back to town?" Russell asked.

"I'M NOT RUNNING A TAXI SERVICE!" Abe harshly retorted.

The episode in Chester County did not end Russell's joy rides. But he did become more careful not to use Abe's Buick. In cahoots with his teenage buddies, Russell *borrowed* a car from the parent of an acquaintance. The gang drove to a country inn known for its excellent food. With but nickels among them, the boys nevertheless ate to their heart's content. After the meal, one of the young men left the table and went outside. He retrieved the car from the parking lot. He pulled up to the front door, engine running. When the group heard the car pull up, they ran out and jumped in. Unfortunately for the boys, the driver was a bit nervous. He backed the car into a utility poll. Fortunately, from the boys' perspective, no charges were pressed. The owner of the car was family to one of the gang members. The inn agreed to receive payment the next day for the food consumed.

Luckily for Russell, his parents never heard about the incident.

* * *

Norman's return to Pottstown had a side benefit. He was able to take up in earnest his passion for horses. Norman's attachment to horses began with exposure at an early age to his grandfather's team. The young boy frequently observed Adolph or one of his sons hitch the peddling wagon. As a teenager he began riding horses. Adolph Wolf's sons had a "riding academy" on Cherry Street. When business was slow, they allowed the youngster to ride. When he was riding, he felt more comfortable, less afraid to open his mouth. Norman dreamt of owning his own horse. On his dependable friend, he envisaged long rides across the Pennsylvania countryside on trails first laid down by local Indian tribes. He fantasized being a pioneer in a deerskin coat, riding into uncharted territory with nothing but his wits and his Pennsylvania long rifle for protection. He visualized himself on a champion mount, winning derby day races by multiple lengths over the competition. The cheers of the crowd would ring down loudly as his sorrel stood passively in the winner's circle.

Now that he was back in Pottstown, as soon as he could afford one, the twenty-three year old made the decision to purchase a horse. His mother again objected to this "frivolous extravagance." She asked her brothers to discourage Norman from his plan. For once, Norman's uncles flat out refused to get involved. "What's wrong with Norman having his own horse?" Robbie asked. Since the family now depended on Norman's management of Royal Corrective Shoes, Yetta sensed her arguments were doomed to fail. Her protests lacked zeal. She let the matter rest.

Norman's first horse was a chestnut mare up in years and, by all appearances, physically run down. The purchase price was quite low. After being restored to good health, the horse proved to be quite swift. One Sunday morning, Norman was out with his riding buddy Marvin Herbine. They met some other riders, including a young man named Murphy whose family had a nearby farm. The young men spoke about horses. They debated which local horses were the fastest on flat tracks, which were the best jumpers, the best for long runs across pastures and on forest trails. Knowledgeable about horses and conservative about money, Herbine nonetheless voiced a challenge. "Norman's horse is faster than your best runner." It was a dare impossible to pass up. Murphy and his friends looked at each other and smirked. "You're ON!" Murphy snapped.

Known from races at county fairs as fleet a foot, Murphy's horse was certainly no plodder. On the other hand, Norman had never raced. He did not know how well his horse could keep pace head-to-head with another. Although nervous, Norman trusted his partner's judgment. The two pooled their money, about five dollars, and placed the bet on a mile run down a dirt road. At the word "go" Norman and Murphy tore down the lane. For the first half mile, the two raced side by side. Then, Norman's horse edged forward gaining almost a yard each second. Norman on his horse won the race by over ten lengths. He had hardly even urged the horse to run.

On the ride back to town, Herbine and Norman spoke about the race. "Norm, you should enter your horse at the Berks County Reading Fair," Herbine suggested. "In distance, no one can outrace you." Norman concurred. "But we'll need to get in racing shape. We'll go to Jake Wolf at the 'riding academy' to prepare for competition."

Neither Jake Wolf nor Norman knew the first thing about "how to prepare." As part of the training, they took the horse to the Spring City racetrack where other running horses were stabled. This was a real racetrack. The smell of horse sweat and saddle soap permeated the paddock. The moment the horse entered the track it became excited and tugged firmly at the bit. Norman figured it best to let the horse do what it wanted. He let it have its head. The two, horse and rider, flew around the track.

Norman looked down and saw the top of the inside railing whirling by. It was unbelievably fast. By-standers stopped what they were doing to witness the speed. Talk ceased. Cigars were put down. After Norman tired, he turned the horse over to Jake who rode some more. To get a horse in shape to run, Norman and Jake believed, it had to run a lot.

When the two young men had finished and the horse panting heavily, another owner, a man named Lynch, came over to speak with them. "What in blazes were you two doing to that horse?" he hollered. "That's not how you train a horse to run in a flat race!" Norman and Jake looked contrite. They had not even considered whether their method of preparation was the correct one. Lynch let his fury pass. It was evident the two men in front of him knew nothing about training horses and desperately needed advice.

"To get a horse ready, breeze through a lap, run hard the second lap, and cool down the third." He now had their full attention. "That," he said, "is a full day's workout. Give the horse a good rubdown afterwards. Don't let it eat too much for at least an hour." Lynch took a liking to the naïve youngsters. Norman's horse, he observed, was surprisingly fast. He explained the theory of how best to run a race. "It's all in the preparation. My own horse is running in the steeplechase at the Berks County Fair. You should come by with your mare. See if it can show anything." Norman and Jake shook his hand. "We'll be there."

The track at the Reading Fair Grounds opened a few days prior to the fair. Norman brought his horse to the track. He went to the registration office. A craggy faced clerk looked from his tally sheet. Cigarette ash that had missed the overloaded ashtray covered the desk. Immediately, he read "greenhorn" in Norman's baby-face mug. "Another chump," he remarked under his breath. "What do you want?" he caustically shot back. "I want to race my horse," Norman said.

"Has it raced before?"

"Yes," Norman said truthfully. He was thinking of the race with Murphy down the country lane.

The clerk sensed this would be an easy mark. "This sucker wants to throw away his money," he thought, "who am I to stand in his way." He starred at Norman. "What's its name? Aren't you registered with the Thoroughbred Association?"

Norman never considered the possibility that a racehorse required papers. Instantly, Norman came up with a name. "It's 'Full of Run,'" he said. "Do you have any staff?" asked the clerk. Personnel associated with the racing horses automatically received free passes to the fair grounds. Norman listed the names of the *associated* personnel: Norman Cohen, owner; Jake Wolf, trainer; Eggie Moyer, Assistant Trainer; Al Printz, Assistant Trainer. The clerk reluctantly wrote down the names. When Norman tried to add a groom and assistant grooms, the clerk drew the line. "The fair operator don't allow so many *assistants*. With only one horse entered, no more personnel are entitled to passes."

On race day, Norman and his "race team" gathered under the grandstand where betting was taking place. Old men huddled around a small table. There, Sam Lipkin's brother was taking bets. Cash was being counted and passed in a flick of an eye. Although betting was illegal in Pennsylvania, everyone knew what was going on; it was a sort of a hush-hush. Sam was a shady character, neither mobster nor Boy Scout. His industrious wife had a dress shop in Pottstown. When asked what the line was on their horse, the young men were quoted three-to-one on Full of Run.

"Three-to-one! That's ridiculous!" Jake said. Lipkin replied that he did not know the horse and could not do better. Out of loyalty to the horse, they bet on Full of Run. A jockey was hired for five dollars.

The race started from a rope that was dropped. The riders took the horses up to the rope. As the rope was being dropped, Full of Run's jockey pulled tightly on the reins. He turned the horse's head around in a complete circle. Full of Run crossed the rope a full ten lengths behind the pack. The horse vainly attempted to close the gap. At the end of the race, it had caught up to the middle of the pack, just three lengths behind the leaders. The races were fixed. Norman was angry. If left to run in an honest race, he knew his horse could have won.

Before the steeplechase, Norman and his friends were quoted seven-to-one on Lynch's horse. They put the rest of their money on the horse, which won. Norman took Full of Run to the stable and returned to watch Lynch's horse run its second race. The odds now dropped to three-to-one. The horse won again, leaving the team financially well ahead for the day. But it was the end of Norman's racing career.

* * *

By the end of the 1930s storm shadows covered much of the world's surface. War in Europe began September 1, 1939. Japan threatened in the Pacific. Although the United States was not yet a belligerent, involvement in war against the Axis Powers seemed only to be a matter of time. Passed by Congress in September 1940, the Selective Training and Service Act created America's first peacetime conscription. Norman knew he would be among the first to be called. Sure enough, a few months later, the draft notice came in the mail. Norman began preparing for induction into the army that would soon follow.

Six years earlier, Congress passed the Gold Reserve Act. The Act took the United States off the gold standard and effectively banned U.S. citizens from ownership of gold coins for currency usage. Instead, the country's only legal tender would be in the form of central bank notes. Following years of spending less than he earned during his tenure with Triangle Shoes and afterwards, Norman again managed to accumulate some savings. With the promulgation of the Gold Reserve Act, customers frequently bought shoes with their souvenir gold pieces. Norman drained his savings account to purchase the $2.50 and $5.00 gold coins. By 1941 he had accumulated a nice coin collection.

With his pending induction Norman knew he could not take his coins with him. He pondered what to do. After much contemplation, he decided to entrust his collection with his parents. He provided detailed instructions on its safekeeping. As long as they followed his guidance, what could his parents possibly do with his collection?

Despite the bad blood from the bankruptcy, Abe spoke frequently with Sam Fuerman. He found it difficult to hold a grudge with Yetta's *mishpoohah*. The two men met at *shul* regularly. They were Jews after all and Jews had to put aside differences, he felt. After services one day, Abe casually mentioned his son's gold coin collection.

Fuerman looked askance at Yetta's husband. "Abe, holding such a collection could cause you 'serious trouble.' The law forbids the hoarding of gold, and that's what you're doing. Jewelers know all about this. As a favor, I can 'get rid of it' for you. Perhaps, I can get close to face value for you."

Amazingly, Abe agreed. Once again, Fuerman swindled Abe. Worse, he swindled Norman. When he discovered his father's action, Norman was crestfallen. Why had his father not listened to him? He hated to think of the profit Fuerman made from the transaction! Norman knew well that private coin collections such as his had been exempt from the federal ban.

Fifteen

The Army

On induction day, May 13, 1941, Norman departed the house for the final time and walked downtown. From Pottstown City Hall a dozen inductees marched in a short parade to the Reading Railroad Station. Businessmen came out of their stores to shake hands with the draftees, housewives stood on front porches, kids on bicycles stopped in the street. All waved to the young men who were nervously waving back. "God bless you," they yelled, "be safe! We'll see you back soon!" Young boys went up to the inductees. "Are you really going to fire guns?" some asked. Family members and friends cheered the inductees on. Most walked with them to the station. At the train, there were farewell hugs.

But no family escorted Norman to the train. Except for the many businessmen he knew and occasional friend, he did not spy a familiar face. His mother had not left the house. It was just supposed to be one-year duty, she said. "What is the big deal?"

Norman promised he would be back when he had weekend leave. That was enough for her. No big deal. Norman's absences from home during his exile with Triangle Shoe had been longer. Norman felt it was his high school graduation all over again. If his father had come out to Hanover Street say farewell, Norman had not seen him.

For basic training, Norman was stationed at Pine Camp, New York. Chilly in summer and downright frigid in winter, Pine Camp not only resembled an immense construction zone in 1941, it was an immense construction zone. Hundreds of buildings were being assembled including mess halls, hospitals, warehouses, officer's billets, and enlisted men's barracks. Located in heavily forested Jefferson County not far from the icy shores of Lake Ontario, Pine Camp was home to the newly activated Fourth Armored Division, Norman's first unit. Rifles, tanks, artillery pieces were in desperately short supply and basic training was conducted with whatever was available. It was a time of calisthenics, long hikes, bayonet practice with straw dummies, and mind-numbing sentry duty with broom handles for rifles. For many young men away from home, Fort Drum provided three square meals each day for the first time.

Following basic training, Norman kept his promise to return home to Pottstown every available weekend. From Pine Camp, Norman shared driving with Whitey Rhoads who lived near Pottstown and drove back frequently to see his elderly parents. At noon on Saturday, immediately after barracks duty was complete, the two men departed camp for the ten-hour drive to Pottstown. The return trip to Pine Camp began no later than 7 p.m. on Sunday in order to arrive in camp early Monday morning before reveille. During his visits home, the few hours he had in town, Norman tended to shoe store business. He trimmed the windows, checked the books, and ordered shoes. In his pressed military uniform, he occasionally attended shoe shows in Philadelphia and New York. Even after Pearl Harbor and the U.S. entry into the war, although uniformed soldiers were no longer a novelty, the presence of the young soldier among the middle aged salesmen never failed to attract attention.

With the war, procurement of shoes from factories immediately became difficult. War production came first, consumer goods last. Raw material inputs used in shoe manufacturing, including leather and rubber, were doled out to factories in very limited quantities. Numerous shoe manufacturers already shifted production to army and marine boots, webbing and holsters for side arms, lambskin leather aviator helmets, and bomber jackets. Shoes manufactured for the home front were tightly rationed at both the wholesale and retail ends. To control the supply of vital raw materials, limit speculation, and counter war profiteering, the War Production Board instituted price controls. The newly created Office of Price Administration's War Price and Rationing Board issued ration books to the public with coupons for shoes. But few shoes were available to civilians. Retailers had customers, but little merchandise to sell. Since prices were rigidly set, profit margins remained narrow.

At the start of rationing, all retail stores were required to turn over a physical inventory to the Office of Price Administration (OPA). On that basis, each store's own ration of shoes was officially determined. Stores received only a percentage of normal pre-war stock levels. Abe theorized that "the war will be over soon and we'll be stuck with all this inventory of poorly made shoes!" He decided that low quality "war pairage" would be unsellable as customers sought higher pre-war quality footwear. From where during the war shoes would miraculously appear, whether better made or not, Abe never seriously considered. Intentionally, and quite bizarrely, he provided OPA with a lowball figure for the Royal Shoe Store's current inventory. As a result, the Royal Shoe Store faced chronic shortages of wholesale ration coupons to provide to the shoe manufacturers. Abe was now stuck with pitifully few shoes to sell with little prospect for more.

Recognizing he needed help, Abe turned to his son for assistance. "Norman, see if you can get us more inventory." Norman agreed to try. He pleaded with shoe companies for more "pairage" for Royal Shoes. His uniform helped greatly. Yet, when Norman succeeded in ratcheting loose one or two hundred extra pairs, Abe again became critical. He thought his son excessively reckless in his shoe purchasing. But once again, Norman knew his father had it wrong. For a retailer to turn down merchandise during World War II was astounding. It was like refusing to make money. Despite his father's disparagement, Norman persisted in his search for more shoes.

Before the war, Abe occasionally asked Norman to travel to "upstate" shoe factories—upstate being nearby Berks, Lancaster, and Schuylkill Counties—to purchase "close outs" or "FDs" at reduced prices. Norman's Uncle Mike from Norristown sometimes accompanied him. One of their regular stops had been the Curtis-Stephens-Embry factory in Reading. The company sold high quality calfskin infants white high top shoes at $0.60 wholesale. In the store the retail price was $0.95. With shoes now hard to obtain, Norman suggested to his father that the two of them meet with Embry to see if any shoes were available. Abe demurred. He was too embarrassed to go. Apparently, his brother-in-law had offended Embry by offering money under the table to get shoes. Embry had kicked Mike out of the factory.

Before the war, the Royal Shoe Store's principal children's line had been Edwards Shoes. In an attempt to get more shoes, Norman went to meet the salesman for Edwards Shoes, Mr. Payden. "Why is our allotment of your shoes so low?" Norman asked. Payden chuckled then shook his head. "Your father himself asked that the allotment be reduced! I already reallocated the quota to another dealer." No amount of pleading by Norman could reinstate the original allotment for Royal Shoe Store.

The Army

While home on a weekend pass one Sunday, Norman decided to telephone the Health Spot salesman, Mr. O'Rurick. Norman knew O'Rurick before the war but had not seen him since joining the service. O'Rurick was glad to hear Norman's voice. He asked many questions about the army and inquired how Norman was handling army life. Finally, Norman got to the purpose of his call. "How many pairs of Health Spot children's shoes can I order?" Norman asked the salesman. "Order as many as you wish and I'll submit the request," O'Rurick replied. Norman ordered as if he were buying shoes for an entire chain of stores. When Abe found out what Norman had agreed to, he was enraged. "How could you do this? We'll be stuck with these shoes!" Incensed, he ran out of the house, slamming the door, and did not return to see his son off for Pine Camp. During the long ride back to New York Norman suffered his father's censure in self-absorbed silence. Perhaps, he wondered, he had been too ardent in ordering so many shoes.

When the Health Spot shoes began arriving in Pottstown, his mother described the impact as if "*manna* was falling from heaven!" For the rest of the war years, the Royal Shoe Store enjoyed Pottstown's best children's shoe business. For the first time the store also developed a reputation for superior quality. Abe never admitted to his son the good fortune provided by the unlimited supply of Health Spot shoes. He never expressed appreciation nor commended his son for his initiative. Yet, Norman's one phone call put Abe and Yetta on what she later described as "Easy Street." By the end of the war, due to the prosperity endowed by the Health Spot shoes, Abe and Yetta Cohen were, for the first time in their lives, financially independent.

* * *

Norman's initial army assignment at Pine Camp was to Headquarters Battery, 66th Field Artillery (FA) of the 4th Armored

Division. His bunkmate was a short, scrappy Italian from Baltimore, Tony Ariko. The new conscripts were welcomed by a pre-war cadre of regular army non-commissioned officers, mostly Southerners, uniformly ill-educated, with an anti-Yankee chip on their shoulders. Not a few were blisteringly racist and flagrantly anti-Semitic. As privates, the new soldiers received just $21 a month, out of which was taken insurance and laundry money. Married men received an extra stipend. Being only a high school graduate, Norman was on the lowest rung of the education ladder among the conscripts, although his education level was well above the majority of the non-commissioned officers. Over half the fellows in the battery were college graduates, including at least ten lawyers. One of Norman's fellow conscripts was a Harvard Law School classmate of the son of his mother's cousin, Morris Weiss.

Norman's distaste for the army came early. For his first assignment after basic training he drove a jeep carrying officers to the firing range point of observation, a command center. A field telephone provided direct communication with the battery, an old field artillery piece leftover from the First World War. The officers directed their commands to the battery to provide proper settings and adjust fire on the designated target, a pile of junk. Norman had nothing to do but satisfy his curiosity and observe. The command was given: "Fire!" A puff of smoke showed where the shell landed. Then the fire was adjusted to "bracket" the target, to hit its opposite side. The command rang out, up or down, right or left, in unit measurements of degrees of arc. "Fire!"

The battery commander, John Hector, had been a star football player at a university in California. The young handsome lieutenant stood tall and erect, chin stuck far out. He appeared to have arrived for his current role direct from the casting studio in Hollywood. Hector delivered his orders with the assurance of the truly clueless. "No John," Norman reflected while he watched Hector perform, "that shot was OVER the target. You should adjust DOWN, not up." Of course, Norman kept his thoughts to himself. The officer had no idea what he was doing. Norman fretted. "If we ever go to war, is HE going to lead us?" (After the war, Norman read an article by syndicated columnist Drew Pearson about a Colonel John Hector who was indicted for employing conscripts for personal use at his home on an army base in Louisiana.)

The new soldiers performed many duties essential to the national defense, for example, policing the grounds for cigarette butts. The non-commissioned officers stood over the trainees like mother hens. They shouted "asses up, heads down!" while prodding with a baton or stick those who failed to adhere properly to their orders. The barracks were scrubbed and rescrubbed, then washed again. On bitterly frigid nights—locals described the winter of 1941-42 as the coldest in memory with temperatures at Pine Camp routinely descending under 30 below zero—the shivering conscripts walked guard duty. They carried rifles without ammunition. Norman felt that grown men were being coached to perform menial tasks capable of being done by a twelve year old. That was the point, of course, which Norman did not yet appreciate. The conscripts had to learn how to follow orders instinctively, no matter how ridiculous they might appear to be.

With the Japanese attack on Pearl Harbor on December 7, 1941, all thought of a short "one year" military obligation to Uncle Sam dissipated like fog burnt away by a bright morning sun. Most of Norman's friends applied immediately for Officer Candidate School (OCS). The first cadre of draftees, inducted like Norman earlier in the year, had over half a year experience. They were far ahead in mastery of military skills than the young men now volunteering in recruiting centers across the country. And besides, lieutenant's pay was damn better that that of a private or corporal. Norman paused before applying for OCS.

He waited until the division received orders to participate in Tennessee Maneuvers. By then, he had his sergeant's chevrons.

For the OCS application Norman was required to take an I.Q. test. The test was so easy Norman thought it was meant to measure whether the test taker was fit to remain in the service. Which weighs more, one question asked, a ton of bricks or a ton of feathers? Following the test, the battalion's lone warrant officer, its top enlisted man who was in charge of personnel, called Norman into his small office. Norman appeared. "Would his I.Q. test score qualify him for OCS?" he asked. The warrant officer harrumphed and grumbled something unintelligible. He looked down again at the document in front of him. Without looking up, he chortled. "Your score was 176."

Norman had no idea what that number meant. "Is that score good enough for OCS?"

"Is it . . ." the warrant officer caught himself. He could not finish the sentence. In fact, he seemed to have a hard time keeping his composure. He weighed whether the buck sergeant standing in front of him was teasing or ridiculing a superior. The warrant officer's face turned beet red, the veins in his neck hardened. He looked steely at Norman. Nothing in Norman's deportment suggested malice, he observed. If anything, the young man's expression was anything but malicious. He decided the sergeant was not trying to humiliate him. He really was clueless. Finally, he spoke ". . . it was the highest score in the unit."

Norman was baffled. He had no idea what unit the warrant officer meant. "Do you mean the platoon, the battalion, the regiment?" Norman realized he touched a raw nerve. He escaped from the warrant officer's presence as soon as he could without an answer. He checked with other OCS candidates. Most had scored in the 130s and were satisfied with the grade. Norman was too embarrassed to mention his score.

The Army

Norman was called to appear before the Officer Candidate School Board. When he entered and stood at attention, he faced the largest accumulation of brass he had ever seen. He answered all their questions, was excused, saluted, did an about face, and moved towards the door. A general stopped him. "Sergeant, is it better to be too early or too late?" the general asked.

"It is better to be too early, Sir." The question struck Norman as odd. After all the other technical responses, why question his judgment in such a blatantly condescending way. He inquired of the other OCS candidates whether they too had received such judgment questions. None had. Norman could not help but wonder. Did his lack of a college education prompt some lingering doubt among his interrogators?

Norman departed Pine Camp for Tennessee Maneuvers. He knew he could no longer attend to the needs of the Royal Shoe Store on weekends. His father would just have to do without him.

One weekend, Norman planned to spend some leave with his buddy Tony Ariko. They agreed to meet at the YMCA in Nashville. Norman needed directions to the "Y". He spied a dignified gentleman with a well-trimmed beard, dressed in a white suit—a later generation might identify such a man with Colonel Sanders of Kentucky Fried Chicken fame. "Sir, excuse me, could you direct me to the YMCA?" It was war, Norman was in uniform, the question, he thought, was routine. "Damn you Yankees," the man retorted. "Why don't you go back north from where you came!" He spit a chew of tobacco which just missed Norman's shoes. Norman was stunned at the vehemence of the old man's loathing. He had never thought of himself as a Yankee. Moreover, his uniform was brown, not blue. He figured his accent gave him away.

While on maneuvers, Norman suffered an injury. As the only non-commissioned officer on a half-track, Norman stood next to the driver. It was the best position to direct the vehicle crew. An airplane flew by. Without looking ahead the machine gunner, a hillbilly from somewhere deep in Appalachia, quickly swung the .50 caliber machine gun towards the plane. With its arc, the gun barrel's trajectory caught Norman dead in its sights. To push the machine gun away from his face, Norman instinctively threw his hand in front of his body. The barrel sizzling hot from previous firing caught Norman across the palm of his left hand. It could have been worse, much worse.

Norman was taken to the Evacuation Hospital in Murfreesboro. Later, he was transferred to Station Hospital, Camp Forrest, Tennessee, where he would spend almost a month. To his family, Norman described the injury as a "stupid accident." Although the injury itself was relatively small, it was serious.

On his first pass from the hospital, Norman returned to his outfit in the field. The first person he met was the battalion warrant officer for personnel, the same one who delivered the news to Norman regarding his I.Q. score. "Cohen, where in hell have you been? I was looking all over for you." Norman showed his injured hand and explained his stay in the hospital. "Well hell's bells Cohen, you're still being carried on the Daily Report as ON DUTY!" The warrant officer told Norman that his OCS orders had come through. "You're to leave tomorrow morning for Ft. Knox OCS." These were the orders for which he had been waiting.

Norman carried his orders to the hospital. He knew there would be a problem. The only official "by-the-book" way for his discharge from the hospital was to be assigned to FULL DUTY status. With his hand thickly bandaged and his arm in a sling, that the hospital would release him was about as likely as a ten-inch snow during a Tennessee summer afternoon! The night duty officer was a young green lieutenant. Norman used all the power of persuasion at his command to convince the reluctant Lieutenant Sherman to let him go. The lieutenant began to waver. "I promise Sir," Norman assured the lieutenant, "that by the time I get to Fort Knox, I'll turn myself in at the first sick call." The lieutenant relented. By the time Norman reached Fort Knox, Kentucky, his arm was out of the sling and the bandage was removed from his hand.

During the first week of OCS, the class attended motors class. The officer candidates had to perform a task that required both hands. Since Norman was unable to use his left hand, the instructor sent him to the colonel in charge of personnel. The colonel covered his face with his hands and shook his head, "What am I to do with you?" He may have been talking to himself, but Norman answered anyway. "Sir, may I suggest that I be given a fifteen day furlough." The colonel gave in without another word.

Norman spent the first week of his furlough in Bloomington, Illinois, with his Uncle Ben and Aunt Brick. Norman and his uncle spent every available moment together, mostly horseback riding. It was a hobby both loved. They spoke of the army, of college, of Ben's medical practice, of horses. Uncle and nephew bonded. At the dinner table, Ben remarked "Norman, you are not the person I thought you were. Your mother gave me a completely different impression of you." Twelve years earlier, Norman learned, his uncle made an offer his sister Yetta. "I told your mother, 'Let Norman come here to Bloomington to live with us. He could attend the local university.' Did she ever tell you this?"

Norman recalled vaguely something his mother once told him. It occurred before the money was emptied from his bank account, before his mother said the family could not afford to send him to college. Yetta told Norman he could live with Uncle Ben in

Illinois. At the time Norman remembered being perplexed by her offer. Not that he had anything against his uncle or aunt, his uncle's medical practice, or Bloomington, Illinois. But why would his mother make such a suggestion? There were perfectly satisfactory colleges nearby, Norman thought. Albright and Ursinus College were close to home. Moreover, his mother had not yet told him that he could NOT go to college. There was only one motive, Norman now reasoned. His mother somehow anticipated that by living with Uncle Ben, a medical doctor, he would have become interested in pursuing a medical degree.

Norman traveled from Bloomington to St Paul, Minnesota. He spent Thanksgiving week with his uncle, Rabbi Herman Cohen, his father's younger brother. Norman talked at length with his uncle. They had not seen each other in many years. The two discussed subjects neither had ever brought up with the other. Herman recollected a shy boy who rarely spoke. Now he observed a confident young man who possessed exceptional common sense and sensitivity. Finally, in earnest concern for his eldest nephew, Herman paused to ask a serious question. An issue evidently was praying on his mind. He looked straight at his nephew. "Norman, why didn't you graduate high school?"

Norman was staggered by the question. He paused to compose himself. "Of course, I graduated. There was never any doubt of my graduating." Herman's face showed bewilderment. "I was the youngest student in the class of 1931. I was just 16! I was the best math student in the senior class." Herman reeled in disbelief. "Do you want to see my high school diploma?" Norman asked.

Herman sank deeper into the sofa. He was a shorter, softer man than his brother Abe. Now, Herman looked even smaller. His hands fell to his side. "I don't understand," his uncle said. "Your mother left me with the impression that you hadn't. That is why you could not go to college, she said. I don't understand. I don't understand." His words trailed off. It was Herman's turn to show bewilderment. He then remembered the books he sent the adolescent Norman. They had been classic Jewish histories and philosophy texts challenging even for experts in the field. That Norman read such difficult books yet could not graduate high school was illogical, he realized. "I . . . . I had no idea," he murmured.

Norman returned to Fort Knox. He immediately transferred to Fort Sill, Oklahoma. Fort Sill was concurrently the home of the United States Army Field Artillery School and Artillery Officer Candidate School (OCS). As an officer candidate Norman was billeted with five other fellow candidates in a Quonset hut. The OCS students were assigned their living quarters alphabetically by last name. In his hut Norman was the only officer candidate not to have attended that year's Reserve Officer Training Corps (ROTC) program. In fact, he realized he was the only officer candidate in the group never to have gone to college. Yet, he could discern no difference in ability or knowledge with his colleagues.

For the only time in his military career, Norman was teamed with an African-American colleague, Estes Cole, the only one in the entire OCS class. Cole, Norman realized, had to possess immense personal courage and integrity to put up with the not-so-subtle prejudice directed by so many in the school. Another roommate, Henry Cobb, from Birmingham, Alabama, displayed blatant bigotry. Each ignored the other. Norman could not comprehend Cobb's deliberate disdain. "Cobb, what the hell is wrong with you? Why are you so bigoted?"

"You Northerners don't understand niggers," Cobb retorted. The venom in his voice spit bullets. "That's the way these people are. That's the way things are down here. I don't have to like 'em, and I don't!"

Norman understood well. There was no talking with Cobb. The army contained too many Cobbs and too few Coles. How could Norman depict to this bigot his growing up on Chicken Hill? Could he tell of life on the streets with his African-American playmates? How could he illustrate the racist stupidity of his high school teacher, Norman Martin? Could he describe the hidebound treatment of star halfback Dick Ricketts during Pottstown High School's away games? Would Cobb care about the "No Jews Allowed" sign at the park in Royersford? No, Norman decided. If Cobb had known, he wouldn't have cared one bit. Cobb's attitude was too deeply ingrained, too narrow-minded.

Upon graduation from OCS, Norman was commissioned a Second Lieutenant. It was two years to the day after his induction. He was assigned as a Field Artillery Survey Officer to the 28th Division, the Pennsylvania National Guard's own Keystone Division. He reported for duty at Fort Bragg, North Carolina. The unit was preparing for embarkation, most likely for England according to the scuttlebutt. Norman was prepared. There was just one more item to take care of before getting his orders to ship out. Norman was told he must qualify on the firing range with the Colt .45 sidearm. "But I qualified as a sergeant," Norman pointed out. "That may be lieutenant, but it's not on your record."

The standard U.S. Army issue sidearm during the war was the Caliber .45, Colt M1911, a slide injected, single action, semiautomatic pistol. The Colt .45 is a powerful weapon with outstanding stopping power. All field grade officers had to be qualified with the .45.

Norman went to the firing range and signed in. He was issued a weapon and assigned a target lane. Being right-handed, Norman held and fired the pistol with his right hand. He had no difficulty scoring on the target. His injured left hand, the scar across his palm still raw, was not strong enough to pull back on the slide action. After expending his eight rounds, a full clip, Norman shifted the weapon to his left hand to reload. He pulled back the action with his uninjured right hand to chamber the first round. Then, after chambering the round, he shifted the .45 back and took aim.

"CEASE FIRE, CEASE FIRE!" The shrill call came down the line. Firing came to a halt. Norman placed his weapon on the gun tray. The call came down the line, Norman's number was called. He pulled out of the line and walked up the stairs to the observation office. He reported to the range commanding officer.

"What the hell was that, Lieutenant?" the colonel asked. Norman showed him his scarred left hand. "There's no way you can qualify like that!" the colonel retorted. "What would you do in combat? Will the war wait for you while you shift your weapon back and forth? I'm washing you out!" Norman was reassigned straight away to Tilton General Hospital for reclassification to "Limited Service."

Every junior officer from Headquarters Battery, 28th Division, all of Norman's closest friends, men with whom he had attended OCS, were casualties. The 28th participated in exceptionally bloody fighting, first in the Hurtgen Forest, then during the Battle of the Bulge. It was a raw, rainy morning when Norman viewed the posting from the "Field Artillery Journal" of the Division's casualties. The list was posted on the information board outside the S-1 office (Personnel). The names jumped off the pages and tore straight into Norman's heart. The rain concealed his tears as he found the names Captain FA, Jim Bennett, Lieutenant Larry Flem, and First Lieutenant FA, Stan Rzokna. They had been his closest buddies. Other acquaintances cried out from the long list. There was one strange name, First

Lieutenant FA Earl Flynn. Norman presumed Flynn had been the replacement for First Lieutenant Norman Cohen.

Norman's thoughts returned to the day he last saw his friends. Bennett mentioned he was going to Philadelphia on three-day leave to get married. "Is it a good idea to get married when you have one foot in the boat, Jim?" Norman questioned his buddy. "If I don't get married now," Bennett replied, "she won't be waiting." Norman thought how unfair that sounded. Their last conversation in the barracks centered on dates of rank and who was next in line for promotion. Norman saw that Bennett was one of the few to have quickly made captain. He felt proud for his friend. From that day, Norman was unable to complete the Mourners *Kaddish* without thinking of Bennett. His buddy would never serve on a corporate Board of Directors—his father was Vice President of the Pennsylvania Railroad. Stan, the New Yorker, would not return to his flower stand in Grand Central Station.

As a result of the hand injury Norman never left the United States. He never fired a weapon in anger.

On a weekend visit home during the final spring of the war, Norman took a drive with his father into Chester County. Although his grandfather died a few years previously, Norman felt Chester County belonged to Adolph Markowitz. The peddler had known every farmhouse within a dozen miles. He knew where scrap metal and bundles of paper could be obtained, all the country roads and their condition in sloppy weather. Adolph had been familiar with cornfields where a few ears might be filched and Amish farmers with whom he could communicate in a combination of German and Yiddish, which friendly farmers allowed evening shelter in their barns and unfriendly ones who ranted against Jewish peddlers. "Yeah," Norman reminisced, "Chester County still belonged to Grandpop."

The Army

Norman remembered other casual drives through Chester County. In the years immediately preceding the war when his uncles visited Pottstown, Norman went "peddling" with them. He served as their chauffeur and loved it. Uncle Mike possessed a new Buick with the latest technology: an automatic transmission, power steering, power brakes, and even dual windshield wipers. While Norman drove, his uncles reminisced. They chatted about the Chester County trails and paths where years earlier they drove the junk wagon. They laughed and laughed with outrageous accounts of incidents and people, each one more hilarious that the previous. Norman never entered the discussion.

On one trip, Norman reflected, one of the Markowitz boys mentioned that at the spot the car was passing, a dead body was once found. "Ah, a dead body has no value," another retorted, in jest no doubt to get a rise out of the others. "Everything is relative." All eyes in the car turned to the driver. Conversation ceased. Norman was on the spot. He had spoken. Now he needed to get out of it. "Everything is relative," Norman repeated. "To a shoe man, a body is of no value except for the sale of a pair of shoes for the burial. To a junk man, possibly 30 cents for the bones." His uncles kept silent and listened. "To a doctor, there is greater value . . . but to a Rabbi! A Rabbi can bleed and bleed it!"

"Is THAT Norman Cohen? Was that ABE COHEN's son talking?" The brothers were all chattering at once. In those few moments, Norman received more encouragement to speak that he had received in twenty years.

Before that instant, Norman never even thought of entering such a conversation, especially with his college-educated uncles. Once, he remembered, Sam remarked to his son, now a budding lawyer, that he should be ashamed for taking fees from union crooks. He called it "dirty money." "Dad," his son reasoned, "you don't ask your congregants from where they get their money, do you? Why should I?"

Norman bit his tongue. He had wanted to say that if Sam had recited the issue to HIS father, Adolph Markowitz would have chastised him severely.

"You really are a *fertzel Reb*!" Adolph would have said. "Certainly not a Rashi, Akiba, or Maimonides!" Adolph, he believed, would have instructed his son what he should have told his lawyer grandson. Sam's response should have been "Son, you are saving their *tocheses* from the slammer. I am saving their souls which I consider more important!"

Norman and his father drove past a small Chester County farmhouse that seemed in good shape. A "For Sale" sign in the front yard caught Norman's eye. Norman stopped the car. A man who was not the owner was trimming some bushes. He said the house was vacant and could be purchased through a realtor. Norman met the realtor the following day. The asking price was $1,700. The stone house sat on three and a half acres of land. The property included a cold house and a running stream. The property looked attractive to Norman. The war was almost over. Gas rationing would undoubtedly end. Norman sensed that real estate outside of town would appreciate in value. "Dad, I want to buy that property across the river." He handed a signed blank check to his father. "The price is fine. Go ahead and put a deposit on it or buy it outright."

On his next visit home, Norman asked his father about a settlement date for the house in Chester County. Abe confessed had not used the check. "I didn't want to tie you down with real estate," his father said. The "For Sale" sign had been taken away.

* * *

The Army

On March 23, 1946, Norman received his discharge from the army. He had entered the army almost five years earlier. He was thirty-two years old. His accumulated savings from the army were not insignificant. Tony Ariko, his buddy since basic training, suggested they go into the "five and ten" business together in Baltimore. Norman knew Ariko was a smart operator and would be successful in any endeavor. The offer was tempting. Norman also considered beginning a new life in Alaska. He had heard stories about the wild North Country. Prices and wages were high. There would be many opportunities to make money. And, of course, it was far from Pottstown. Even further afield was Palestine. The Jews and Arabs there were engaged in a bitter conflict for control of the land. The *Yishuv*, the Jewish settlement in Palestine, desperately needed men with military experience. Norman weighed whether he should go. His family, after all, were committed Zionists.

Despite his better judgment, Norman agreed to go back to Pottstown, at least for a short while. Yetta asked her son to run the store. Abe did not object. Norman knew they had made enough money during the war to retire. If his father wanted to, he could sell or even liquidate the shoe store. In any case, in its current location the Royal Shoe Store would remain a small business with a limited future. But his mother still made the family decisions and she wanted to keep the store. His father felt he was capable of keeping the business going—with Norman's help. "Some day the store will be yours," Abe told his son. Frankly, his father's assurance was not much of an inducement, Norman acknowledged.

Norman debated. He was eligible for education tuition funding under the GI Bill. It was a great deal for which his heart yearned. Companions from the army had already begun enrolling in universities across the country. He was single. He had no debts. There was money in the bank. Now was the time to do what he always wanted.

But the pressure from home was too much. His sisters and kid brother had already left home. Lillian and Sylvia were earning their medical degrees. Russell had broken with the family in dramatic fashion. After a stint in the merchant marine, and not yet 20, he married his pregnant girlfriend, a *shiksa*, a non-Jewish woman. To top things off, they were married in a church! Russell did not tell his parents. The burden fell on Norman. He pondered. How could he find a way to break the news and get them to accept their new pregnant daughter-in-law? Norman met the couple in Washington, D.C. He obtained a promise from the girl that she would convert. But the stress was terrible. Before arriving in Pottstown, he bought a pack of cigarettes at a gas stop in West Chester. Norman had not smoked a cigarette during his five years in the army. He would not kick the nicotine habit until six years later.

Ultimately, Norman figured his presence would be helpful to his parents. He stipulated, however, that his assistance would only be for a "limited time." Norman still desired to make a life for himself elsewhere. But perhaps, as his parents said, he could help them get "back on their feet" before moving on. The contradiction escaped him. If his parents had made enough money to retire, why did they need his assistance to get back on their feet?

Abe put his son on the payroll. The small shoe store, Abe said, could afford only a tiny salary. Norman's wage from his father was minimal. As an unemployed veteran he was entitled to $20 a week for a year (the 52-20 club). But Norman did not claim the entitlement, even though it was about the same as the salary he was getting from his father. It was a pitifully low salary for the late 1940s. It was hardly more than he earned at Triangle during the worst depths of the Depression. Norman knew what the store receipts were and what it could take in under his guidance. He asked for more money. Abe demurred. The Depression years, the bankruptcy fiasco, and the uncertainty of the war years

The Army

made him exceedingly cautious with store finances. If Norman lived at home, why would he require more? Yetta agreed with her husband. "Norman, you won't have any expenses here at home," she argued.

To resolve the debate over Norman's funds, Uncle Mike was brought in to arbitrate. Mike listened to both sides. He strongly supported Norman. Yet Abe and Yetta still could not fathom why their son needed more than "movie money." Abe repeated his position. "Norman, the business will soon be yours, and you will be getting all the profits." But their son was adamant. He still felt the weight of all the years of toil, of lost opportunities. If life repeated itself, like a phonograph tone arm automatically going back to the beginning of the record, at least he could make a living wage. A deal was struck. As store income rose, so would Norman's pay.

Within weeks of his decision, Norman realized his father's business acumen improved not at all in the intervening years since he last labored full time in the store. Abe remained old fashioned in his view of style, set in his ways on how to operate the store, and exceedingly insensitive to the store's stock inventory. He had done nothing to improve the dilapidated appearance of the store. The worn out chairs desperately required reupholstering, or better yet, replacement. The original fixtures Abe bought a quarter century earlier showed their age. The store looked old, or at least old-fashioned. If Norman were to remain, he would have to make changes.

First, Norman sought to upgrade the Royal Shoe Store's shoe lines. He attended shoe shows and met with dozens of salesmen. He sought the right type of shoes for the post-war customer, hungry for fashion. These people would have money to spend. Norman called on a shoe jobber in Philadelphia who was recommended to him. The jobber presented him samples of an unusual new style of shoe for young people. Norman was excited.

It was exactly what he had been seeking. He ordered a dozen pair, hardly an outlandish quantity. When the shoes arrived in the store, Abe threw a tantrum. "How could you have bought such a shoe?" his father argued. "They will fall off peoples' feet and we'll be stuck with them!" Penny loafers became an instant hit and stayed in style for half a century.

On another occasion, Norman stopped by the Kreider show room during a shoe show. Returning GIs were getting married and having families. Children's shoes, he believed, would be a vital part of the store's future. He inquired about obtaining their Growing Girls line of shoes. "As long as I control the line, I will NEVER, NEVER sell to the Royal Shoe Store!" the salesman barked. Norman was astonished. He asked why. "I once visited Royal to solicit an account," the salesman explained. "The owner cared little about my line, hardly even looked at it. Instead, he showed me all the junky shoes he was carrying. Then, he tried to explain how his shoes were superior to mine! What audacity!"

Norman comprehended a harsh reality. Under his father's control, the Royal Shoe Store drifted dangerously onto the shoals of commercial inconsequence. With mediocre shoe brands, styles more appropriate for pre-war depression than post-war prosperity, an unattractive storefront with small display windows, and growing competition, the Royal Shoe Store risked disappearing. Even though it had somehow survived both the Depression and the War, the business could collapse just at the moment, Norman felt, when the potential for business growth in Pottstown was the most promising since the 1920s! Although Norman remained torn between staying and leaving after the promised interval, he was determined to save the store first and thus assure his parents a secure future.

One morning after returning from his morning coffee at Peoples Drug Store, Norman met Johnny O'Brian, a salesman with the Green Shoe Manufacturing Company. O'Brian arrived at the store while Norman was out. He wanted to present a new line of children's shoes which the company called Stride Rite. For once, Abe did not intervene. He learned his lesson. Abe asked O'Brian to wait for his son. The children's line was just what the store required. Norman sealed the deal with O'Brian. As the nation's baby boom launched a massive demographic tilt towards children, Stride Rite became Royal Shoe's bedrock brand. The sustainability of the store was secured.

As O'Brian got to know Norman better, he realized his friend was unhappy. O'Brian observed that Norman was living in a rut. O'Brian also discerned that Norman was exceedingly capable and would no doubt succeed with his own business. The two men sat down one afternoon for a serious talk. "Why don't you leave Pottstown? Run your own life?" O'Brian asked. "I believe you can succeed anywhere." Norman listened. "Harrisburg is growing fast," O'Brian noted. "It's a great city. A shoe store there would do well."

Norman struck at O'Brian's baited hook. The decision came swiftly. He told his parents his mind was made up. He was leaving Pottstown for good. They half-heartedly tried to talk him out of it. But their son seemed determined. Moreover, with Norman's help Royal Shoes was already showing a comfortable profit. Abe also felt he could run the store without his son for a few more years. At 65 he was still physically trim. With a dependable sales clerk to assist, he believed he still had a good five years, maybe more, running Royal Shoe Store. Yetta lost interest in battling for her son's presence. She knew the family's worst days were behind them. Money was sufficient for whatever plans they made. She looked forward to a real retirement, perhaps even the purchase of a small bungalow or cottage on the Jersey shore. And Yetta and Abe knew well that Harrisburg was just two hours away up the Ben Franklin Highway. Their son would be close, no matter what.

With his accumulated savings, Norman opened a small shoe store in Harrisburg. The year was 1951. He was thirty-six years old, a bachelor, and for the first time, in control of his own destiny. He owned his own business, made all the decisions. He began dating and eventually met the woman who would become his wife. For its first six months, the store showed a $1,500 loss, the amount Norman spent on advertising. Over the next six months, the store broke even. For the third six months, the store showed a profit of $1,500. To turn a profit so quickly after opening was considered quite notable. Local businessmen were impressed with Norman's abilities. His store seemed destined for success. A shopping center was under construction in nearby Camp Hill. Norman considered placing a second shoe store there. Despite the frustrations of two decades, Norman was optimistic about his future.

One slow weekday afternoon when no customers were in the store, the phone rang. It was his father. His news caught Norman off guard. Abe told his son he received an option to rent the building at 248 High Street, a few steps away from the current Royal Shoe Store at 268 High Street. The proposed store property was a perfect combination of location, size, and appearance. The display windows were three times larger than the current store, as was the stock room. Moreover, Abe indicated the new landlord would be friendlier than the miserable one at the present store building. There would also be the possibility of purchasing the building outright. With High Street booming, such a property almost guaranteed lots of customers. It was the chance of a lifetime, he argued. "But to do this, you need to come back and take over." Norman paused. "I'm ready to step aside," Abe confessed. "If you want it, the store is yours."

Norman was torn. On one hand, he was now his own man. He undoubtedly possessed the ability to run a successful business. The possibility of eventually owning a chain of shoe stores appealed to him. And with marriage, he and his bride could start anew in Harrisburg, an exciting town that promised growth well into the future. But Pottstown's industrial base also looked healthy. The blue-collar families that made up much of Pottstown's customer base would need shoes. Norman knew the property his father had his eye on was outstanding. On all of High Street there was none better.

Sixteen

Redemption

Like a moth drawn to a flame, Norman made the decision to return to Pottstown. The choice, he suspected, would be definitive. Once settled back in his hometown, departing again would be difficult and complicated. He was now married. Children would be on the way. He was approaching forty. He did not want to uproot again. Moreover, he knew that without interference from his father he could make the new store successful.

With a mortgage from the Security Trust Company, signed by the bank's timeless president, Doc Porter, Norman purchased the vacant store at 248 High Street. He relocated Royal Shoes from its existing location, just up the block. He walked out of his father's worn down store, leaving his parents to lock up for the last time.

At that moment when he observed his parents, Norman was heartbroken. He realized, as if for the first time, how difficult *their* lives had been. He looked at his parents and now saw an elderly couple. "How they had aged," he thought. "How frail they seem." His mother's hair was streaked with gray. The lines on her face had deepened dramatically. She wore glasses, thick ones. Most noticeably, she smiled and even laughed. Norman wondered whether he was watching a different woman than the mother he knew. When had Yetta Cohen ever laughed? When did she even smile?

Norman looked at his father. Abe still retained his trim. However, his ramrod posture showed noticeable signs of bending. His strong shoulders were now rounded. His work suit hung more loosely than before. It appeared to be a size too large. His full head of gray hair had thinned. "What boney fingers he seemed to possess," Norman thought. They were nothing like the youthful, long-fingered hands that could pitch a fastball through a brick wall.

When Royal Shoes opened its doors at its new 248 High Street address, Norman placed his father on the payroll. He intended to provide his parents a regular income in their retirement. There was no formal agreement or understanding, written or oral, between Norman and his father. Each payday he deposited into their account the money for his parents. Abe occasionally took the bus into town and stopped by the store. But unless he saw a customer who was not being helped, he did not set foot in the store to work. Norman noticed that his father still liked to chat with the salesmen who visited the Royal Shoe Store with clockwork regularity. The shoe companies knew that Royal did a good business. Abe enjoyed gossiping with the men, some of whom he had known for almost four decades. As time progressed, however, Abe's appearances in the store became infrequent. Eventually, he stopped coming altogether.

When his father did walk into town, Norman took his father to lunch, and on evenings when the store was open, to dinner. Occasionally, they went to the Shuler House Hotel. The Shuler House arguably served the best food in downtown Pottstown. Usually, the pair went to the Crystal Restaurant, next door to the Royal Shoe Store's former location. The food did not vary much but it emerged quickly from the kitchen. The Crystal served a tasty chicken potpie. Pottstown's businessmen who were also synagogue members usually congregated at a long table in the rear, on the left side beyond the lunch counter. From the Betty Lee Shoppe there was Howie Kostiner. Norman's best friend Harold Wolf and Harry Pollock from the Levitz store were regulars. Wolf had a china & glass shop on High Street. From the New York Store one of the Hoffman brothers usually appeared. The men gossiped about the doings in town, recent changes on High Street, which properties were up for sale and which had been sold, the new high school, and nascent competition from a new commercial innovation, a shopping mall. A mall had just opened in King of Prussia, halfway to Philadelphia. The Crystal's peripatetic owner Chris the Greek stopped by the table to say hello.

Through the 1950s and 1960s, business flourished at Royal Shoes. Customers came from miles away to be fitted. When a millenary shop vacated the store next door, Norman grabbed the property. He knocked out the intervening wall and joined the two stores together. This greatly expanded the floor space for customers. Meanwhile Abe and Yetta seemed happy with retirement. More so, it appeared, since previous financial worries were now a fast receding memory.

* * *

One morning in March 1972 Abe called his son on the telephone. He was now a widower, eighty-five years old. Yetta had passed away the summer before. The last few months before her death were quite a struggle. Alzheimer's reduced the once energetic women to an almost vegetative state. Abe's own health was better. His memory seemed as sharp as ever. Baseball statistics still flowed as easily as the *maariv* prayers he continued to conduct at the synagogue. Abe was especially impressed with the outfielder with the Braves, Hank Aaron who was closing in on Babe Ruth's hallowed home run record. "I expect that boy to break 714 next season," Abe offered earlier that week.

"Norman, I have a pain in my shoulder," Abe said. As Norman took his father to the hospital, Abe grabbed his wrist. He took an item from his inside jacket pocket and handed it to his son. It was a bank passbook. "Here, take this. Hold on to it," Abe said. Norman laughed. "We're going to see the doctor. Why do you want me to hold your bank passbook?" Abe insisted. "Just take it, okay."

Norman thought nothing more about it. He placed the passbook in his pocket.

A few days later Abe passed away. The end came quickly, and, it appeared, painlessly. A month later, Norman turned the passbook over to the estate lawyer. "Your parents wanted *you* to have the account," the lawyer explained. Norman was stunned. He assumed the bank account would be placed into their estate and divided up among the siblings. Norman looked more carefully at the bank passbook. Cash deposits had been made biweekly into the account for years. He realized his parents never used the money he provided them from the store payroll. Instead they had left the deposited funds in the bank account, untouched. "I do not understand," Norman said.

The lawyer said "it's true. Your parents left all the money in the account to you."

Epilogue

"The one decision that I made in my life that to this day I consider foolish was my last return to Pottstown." The year is 1997. Norman completed his story. He is eighty-two. His health is poor. His mother passed away when she was a year younger than he is now. Abe died at eighty-five. His last uncle, Francis, has been deceased over fifteen years.

From the hill at Pottstown's north end, the town's entire tableau lay bare. Has it already been a full century since his grandfather looked out on Pottstown from the new *shul* on Chicken Hill? Seventy-five years since he and his friends played football behind the *shul*, using a grass-stuffed pretzel bag as a football? Sixty-five years since he labored for Aaron Weiss and Triangle Shoe Company? Fifty-five years since his injury during Tennessee Maneuvers, that, oddly, saved his life? Forty-five years since he moved the Royal Shoe Store to its present High Street location?

Norman sighs. He is tired. The full measure of his age is apparent in his sunken cheeks, his reddened eyes. Despite the electric shaver, he cannot seem to eliminate the stubble on his chin. His hair, still thick, much thicker than his father's, possesses only a tinge of its original brown color. The skin on his hands has become paper-thin. But there was one more task Norman feels he must do. In fact, he has already done it. He has registered to take courses at the local community college. Classes begin the next week. He has already purchased the books.

* * *

Church steeples still dominate Hanover Street. The trees of the Brookside Country Club hide the current Mercy & Truth Synagogue from view. Post-war middle class neighborhoods replaced the pastures and cornfields. Passenger trains no longer run; the last service to Philadelphia ended decades earlier. The era of Pottstown's peddlers is long forgotten. Norman is relieved that he remembers them. "Do you know the story about the Harmonyville blacksmith?"

"Yes Dad. I know. But go ahead. I'd like to hear it again."

To the southeast past the vacated factories, the twin cooling towers of the Limerick Nuclear Power Plant loom ominously like medieval castles over the valley. Each tower silently spews billowing white steam clouds. Sadly, hardly any local factories utilize the electricity produced from its two 1,200 megawatt light water reactor units. Since the 1960s, most of Pottstown's manufacturers closed for good. Mayer Pollock Steel Corporation, founded in 1888, still operates. Markowitz & Son did not survive the death of its founder. It disappeared, along with Printz's Bakery, Adam Wolf's peddling business, and most of Pottstown's Jewish-run retail stores. The Schuler House Hotel, the Crystal Restaurant, the Security Trust Company, and yes, the Royal Shoe Store, are gone. The children of the merchants moved on. Hardly any remain in Pottstown.

"... At the time, I did not understand my parents. All I knew is that we were poor. I had to work. It was my destiny, I thought." The bitterness is still there. His eyes already red squinted as he thought back at what might have been. He sighed. "Why did Mother treat me the way she did?" He is speaking to himself. "So she was angry with Grandpop. Did she have to take her anger out on me?"

His question was followed by a long silence. "Daddy never stood up for me. Instead, he used me. He never asked anything of my sisters or Russell. Only me. Only me did he force to work in the store."

"But he needed you. You were right. He was a lousy businessman."

"I'll never know if I did the right thing."

"What do you mean? Coming back to Pottstown the last time?"

Norman did not answer. Whatever was on his mind was undoubtedly complicated. After a minute, he already was thinking of something else. Norman let out a long sigh. Then, he fell silent.

The silence was broken by the long shriek of a train whistle. An occasional freight train bearing coal from Pottsville still passed through town. Echoing off the hills of Chester County where his grandfather and uncles drove their peddling wagon, the whistle filled the entire valley. Then, it faded away.

Edwards Brothers, Inc.
Thorofare, NJ USA
June 29, 2011